THE GUV'NORS

This book is dedicated to all
Metropolitan Police CID Officers -
this is what it was like.

And to Ann –
'Til the stars fade from above.

THE GUV'NORS

Ten of Scotland Yard's Greatest Detectives

Dick Kirby

First published in Great Britain in 2010 by
Wharncliffe True Crime
An imprint of
Pen & Sword Books Ltd
47 Church Street
Barnsley
South Yorkshire
S70 2AS

ISBN 978 1 84563 135 2

A CIP catalogue record for this book is
available from the British Library

Typeset by Acredula

Printed and bound in England
By CPI UK

Pen & Sword Books Ltd incorporates the Imprints of Pen & Sword Aviation,
Pen & Sword Family History, Pen & Sword Maritime, Pen & Sword Military,
Wharncliffe Local History, Pen & Sword Select, Pen & Sword Military Classics,
Leo Cooper, Remember When, Seaforth Publishing and Frontline Publishing

For a complete list of Pen & Sword titles please contact
PEN & SWORD BOOKS LIMITED
47 Church Street, Barnsley, South Yorkshire, S70 2AS, England
E-mail: enquiries@pen-and-sword.co.uk
Website: www.pen-and-sword.co.uk

Contents

Foreword

The great multitude of people who love detectives and detective stories will be enthralled by Dick Kirby's identification of some of the greatest detectives who ever served at Scotland Yard.

He has selected his subjects with obvious care and after much research and the result is an account of some of the very best detectives ever to grace The Yard.

I have said many times, and publicly, that the reputation Scotland Yard enjoys internationally was never established by its employment of new policing methods or the introduction of imaginative road management schemes. It was forged by the hard work, dedication, and incredible successes of the Criminal Investigation Department and by the devotion and commitment of its officers.

The ten described are outstanding examples of the kind of men who laid down the principles and working practices for the various departments and by their own dedication and qualities of leadership ensured their success.

These were men who founded great organisations, made important and far reaching decisions and led individuals, groups and finally extensive squads of men and women to breathtaking accomplishments.

One of the contributors, who was a very senior officer himself, describing one of the subjects suggests, "He was just one of three officers I knew whose men would follow him blindly."

I am satisfied that this ability applies to everyone of those portrayed in these pages. It was one of those attributes which made up each of their characters. It was accepted by men of that calibre as being a basic requisite and whilst they may have been aware of this quality it was gained without effort and came to them as naturally as breathing or saying "Good Morning".

Each of them was successful in differing ways but without exception they all achieved the required result when the odds were against them and a result was demanded. When a particular crime resulted in screaming headlines and extensive publicity, these detectives used their extensive experience, powers of leadership and natural abilities to achieve the necessary result. They were heroes at a time when heroes were needed. Each has an incredible and distinctive record which will never be challenged.

It may come as a surprise to learn that some of these great detectives were totally unlike their counterparts portrayed today in books or on television. It should be remembered that times were different when they were young policemen. It may have been fortuitous to settle some matters with their fists in those days or to disrupt the expectations of a trainload of pickpockets by warning them off the turf. That was the way the law was expected to be enforced in those days.

I enjoyed the good fortune of knowing many of them and working with some. I still feel shivers up and down my spine when I read their history and recall those times I met them and what an impression they made upon me as a young budding detective. Great men they were, inspiring men who could lead you to believe it was easy to perform miracles – and you were the man to do it. Grateful men. Full of praise for a job well done. Concerned for individuals and interested in their ambition and progress. Inspiring men who gave you the courage to believe you may be able to follow their example at some time in your future. Exceptional men who were modest in their accomplishments.

One thing is for sure, their like will never be seen again. The opposition to the personality culture which sought to play down the achievements of officers who began to distinguish themselves, the abolition of the career detective and the change in police procedures with regard to the investigation of major crimes have taken care of that.

I thoroughly enjoyed reading this book and I am sure anyone who wonders who the Big Five were, how the Flying Squad began or how some of those famous grisly murders were successfully investigated will find it equally interesting.

Incidentally, Dick Kirby is right about the term Guv'nor. I always saw it as a term that acknowledged achievement and a term of affection and respect. I left the Met 40 years ago and still get the occasional letter, e-mail or phone call, or I meet some of my ex colleagues – usually at funerals these days. When they use the soubriquet I still get a warm feeling of pride and satisfaction.

Leonard 'Nipper' Read Q.P.M

Acknowledgements

First and foremost, my thanks go to Steve Earl from the Metropolitan Police Museum, who has worked so hard on my behalf that if it were not for him it is fair to say that this book would never have been written. Running him a close second was the late Maggie Bird from the Metropolitan Police Records Management Branch, who was enormously helpful. My thanks to the Metropolitan Police Museum for providing some of the photographs; every effort has been made to contact copyright holders. The author and the publishers apologise for any inadvertent omissions. Chris Forester, the editor of *The Peeler* and other periodicals has been a tower of strength over the years. From the Metropolitan Police Library came the odd person who could not be bothered to assist; however, Mary Clucas, Ellie Haynes and Suzanna Parry were not amongst them, so my thanks to them for their kindness and assistance. I was overwhelmed by the response from the former CID officers who contacted me; the fact that they did was because Bob Fenton QGM, the honorary secretary of the Ex-CID Officers' Association orchestrated it, and I am most grateful to him for doing so. Robin Gillis and Ken Stone, formerly of the Metropolitan Police Museum and Archives Section have both been exceedingly kind and helpful, as has Alan Moss. My son-in-law, Steve Cowper helped enormously with the computer side as did my other son-in-law, Rich Jerreat; my thanks to them both.

Over the years, a number of people either assisted me considerably with my research or wrote or spoke to me with some wonderful stories about the men who appear in this book. In alphabetical order, they are: Philip Atkins, Brian Baister QPM, MA, the late Bill Best QPM, Trevor Binnington, Peter Binstead, the late Ernie Bond OBE, QPM, Kenny Bowerman GM, Doug Bowles, the late Terry Brown GM, Tony Bruce, Ron Chapman, Paul De Langhe, Chris Dodkin MBE, Anne Douglas, Kenneth Edney, Peter Elston, Steve Engel, Donald Fabian, Joyce Fabian, Michael Fabian, Paul Fabian, the late Ron Goodall, Martin Gosling MBE, Mick Gray, Rudi Gross, Joy Guest, the late Bob Higgins, Mike Hoare MBE, Rosemary Holman, Graham Howard, John Jones, the late Charles Kirby, Mark Kirby, the late Fred Lambert, Roger Lane, John Legge, Peter Legge, John Lewis, John Loader, Billy Milne, Julie Milstead, the late Terry O'Connell QPM, Gerry O'Donoghue, Hugh Parker, Geoff Parratt, Arthur Phillips, the late George Price, David Pritchard, Leonard 'Nipper' Read QPM, Bob Robinson, George Sharp, Laurie Sherwood QPM, LLB, John Simmonds, Daphne Skillern QPM, Arthur Stevens, John Swain QPM, Michael Taylor QPM, the late Lou van Dyke, John Walsh, John 'Dick' West, Peter Westacott and John Woodhouse.

Finally, my thanks to my wife Ann for her love and support during over forty years of marriage, as well as my unbounded admiration for her in her courageous fight against cancer.

Any faults or imperfections in the book are mine alone.

Dick Kirby

Prologue

In the constabularies, the comparable expression may be 'Boss' or 'Gaffer' - in the Metropolitan Police, however, 'Guv'nor' is the highest accolade that can be bestowed on an officer of the rank of inspector or above. It is not a right – it has to be earned. During over a quarter century of police work, I met only one senior officer who disliked the title, thinking it disrespectful. Because many thought him to be mentally ill, addressing him as 'Sir' caused nobody any distress. But many senior officers that I knew thirsted to be referred to as 'Guv'nor'; they were to be sorely disappointed and had to be content with 'Sir' for the rest of their service.

The application of 'Guv'nor' might well become sadly redundant with the system in recent years of the Metropolitan Police appointing 'Trophy Officers' – who have been chosen not because of their ability, because they possess little of that, but because of their ethnic background or their sexuality, be it straight or gay, male or female, to show what a caring concern the Police Service is.

This, coupled with the ludicrous 'Tenure' system of the 1990s, where officers were swapped in and out of specialist departments in the expectation that they would become Jacks or Jills of all trades (and in the event proved beyond doubt that they were masters and mistresses of none), plus officers who upon promotion applied for posts in departments in which they had no expertise whatsoever, spelled the death-knell for career detectives. What is particularly infuriating is that this type of middle management 'pretend policing' denigrates and undermines the efforts of the thousands of young men and women who make up the rank and file of the Metropolitan Police. They are keen, dedicated and their courage, to paraphrase Belloc 'makes one gasp and stretch one's eyes.' They deserve better than this – a lot better – and up to the latter part of the last century, they would have got it. The leadership that is now so badly needed in the Criminal Investigation Department would have been found in any of the senior detectives who served at New Scotland Yard and whose stories are told in this book.

I have told the stories of ten detectives, and if some readers criticize my choice, thinking that the stories of other notables from the golden days of criminal investigation should have been told, I sympathize with them; I simply ran out of space. Another time, perhaps.

Some of these unique detectives were rough diamonds; some were gruff whilst others possessed great charm. Few were perfect; all had their flaws to a greater or lesser degree. But their common denominator was that all spent their careers in the CID and knew detective work inside out. They knew how to investigate crime, and were able to get hold of a clue by the scuff of its neck and shake it until every single fragment of information was disclosed. The same technique was often applied to their prisoners. The old-time guv'nors were courageous and had the total respect of their men, because they would never ask them to do what they could not or would not do themselves.

As you read through this book, it is possible that you will choose your own favourite detective, be it Fred Wensley who acted with great courage at the siege of Sidney Street, formed the Flying Squad and became chief constable of the CID, or Bert Wickstead, that rough, tough, bull-in-a-chinashop gangbuster who instilled such fear in hardened criminals that when one of them heard that it was Wickstead who was going to interview him, had to be physically carried, sobbing, up the stairs to Wickstead's office. Take your pick. Contained in these pages is a miscellany of talent, with more than a century's-worth of dedicated thief-catchers. But what is incontestable is that these men were in charge of their staff, they knew precisely what they were doing, and they worked just as hard, if not harder than their subordinates who, in return, gave their bosses total loyalty; well, why not?

After all, they were 'The Guv'nors'.

CHAPTER 1

Fred Wensley – The Greatest of Them All

Mention the name of Horatio Nelson to an entrant into the Royal Navy and one would get (or at least, the examining board would anticipate receiving), instant recognition. Similarly, casually uttering the name of Guy Gibson VC, DSO, DFC to an applicant for the Royal Air Force would hopefully invoke the same familiarity.

It is a pity that the Metropolitan Police fail to give similar recognition to their detective heroes of days gone by. Consequently, the present-day youngsters in the CID can hardly be blamed for shaking their heads in bewilderment at the name of Fred Wensley. Nevertheless, it is unfortunate that that name should mean so little to them, because arguably, Wensley was the greatest detective of all time.

*

Frederick Porter Wensley was born on 28 March 1865 in Taunton, Somerset. He came from yeoman stock and after leaving school, he worked as a gardener. But ever since boyhood, he had nurtured the desire to be a detective; as to why, it is not clear. Certainly, none of his family were police officers; indeed, he did not even know a single police officer, but as 1887 drew to a close, Wensley travelled to London in order to join the Metropolitan Police. On a wet January morning the following year, he was one of forty-eight shivering applicants who were sworn in as police constables. Allocated warrant number 73224, Wensley was posted to Lambeth as Police Constable 60'L' and almost immediately jumped into the deep end of policing. Attempting to stop a drunken fight, he was thrown through the plate glass window of a public house. Bloodied but unbowed, Wensley next tackled a gang of hooligans who had challenged his authority. He was badly injured, as was the off-duty police officer who came to his assistance. A few of the gang were arrested and received sentences of between four and six months' imprisonment; Wensley spent a considerable ninety-four days off sick. On his next confrontation, he used his truncheon for the first and only time during his career. He was called to a public house where a man who had bountifully dispensed drinks to the clientele, refused to pay. As Wensley approached, he noticed that the man was carrying a cane; it was not as innocuous as it first appeared, since it concealed a sword-stick. Having unsheathed the weapon, the man lunged at him and Wensley slipped underneath the blade, drew his truncheon and 'sticked' him. "You'll be on report for this", lugubriously muttered a colleague, of the type who can be relied upon to make such remarks, but he was wrong. After attempting to attack the magistrate who later dealt with his case, the swordsman was sent to a lunatic asylum.

During his first year of service, the series of what became known as the 'Jack the Ripper' murders commenced across the river in Whitechapel, and Wensley was one of several hundred officers drafted in to patrol those mean streets of 'H' Division. He was appalled at the filth and squalor. At that time, the population of the area had swollen to enormous proportions as a result of the almost non-existent rules governing the torrent of immigrants from Russia, Lithuania and Latvia and would continue to grow, until the introduction of the Aliens Act, 1906. In consequence, the East End of London had become a huge melting pot of violent crime, courtesy of the home-grown criminals and their equally dangerous and unscrupulous immigrant cousins. Wensley, patrolling the grim Whitechapel streets, with strips of bicycle tyres nailed to the soles of his boots to provide a measure of silence, should the Ripper appear, could hardly wait to return to the green pastures of Lambeth.

Had he known that two-and-a-half years later, he would return to the East End, there to remain for the next twenty-five years of his service, he would have viewed the prospect with considerable dismay. And yet, in time, Wensley grew to love Whitechapel and the surrounding areas, and when through promotion he was given the opportunity of leaving the area, he strongly resisted it.

Back on 'L' Division, Wensley struck lucky when he overheard snatches of conversation between two girls and consequently arrested them. It transpired that they had broken into a girls' home in Hackney and stolen the occupants' money and the following day both were sentenced to three months' hard labour. Wensley received a commendation from the magistrate and this was endorsed with an additional commendation from the commissioner and a monetary award of 5s 0d (25 pence), well worth having when one considers that at that time Wensley's weekly wage was 24s 0d (£1.20). It was the first of many; Wensley's commendations spiralled into the hundreds and set a record which has never been broken.

*

In his autobiography, *Detective Days*, Wensley stated that early in 1891 he and several other officers were transferred into 'E' Division, following the dismissal of 39 police officers out of 130 men from Bow Street police station, who had staged an abortive strike over conditions and pay; and he was not there very long before being transferred to Whitechapel, on 'H' Division.

In fact, his posting to 'E' Division did not last very long at all; *Police Orders* dated 23 February 1891 records that PC 97'E' Wensley was to be fined three days' pay (11s 9d) and transferred to another division. The next day, he was; as PC 402 'H', at a wage of 27s 0d per week. What Wensley had done to incur this punishment is not known. *Police Orders* does not reveal it and Wensley certainly never did. Perhaps the transfer resulted from his youthful impetuosity which precluded him from keeping his mouth shut when it would have been prudent to do so; as will be seen, Wensley did not believe in suffering in silence what he perceived to be injustice.

Although he initially resented his punishment posting, Wensley threw himself into the maelstrom of violence and villainy that was Whitechapel - certainly, there was enough for him to do. One of the most prevalent crimes was robbery with violence, and inebriated sailors, flush with large amounts of money after a long voyage, were considered easy marks. On one such occasion, Wensley arrested

Francis Victor Mygren from the description of a victim who had been robbed five days previously. Mygren blamed his accomplice, Thomas Richford and vice versa; at the Old Bailey, Richford received eighteen months' hard labour and Mygren, three.

Wensley was tireless in his efforts to identify and arrest criminals; going off duty, he changed from his uniform into plain clothes and went out, met informants, kept observations and carried out arrests. This was how he happened to be on the scene a few months later, when an iron merchant was robbed of his watch-chain. Wensley was patrolling his beat when the victim pointed out his assailants to him but the two robbers escaped. Furious at being cheated of his prey, Wensley went home, changed out of his uniform into plain clothes and five hours later, arrested William Schennick and James Hammerman. The value of the watch-chain was tuppence (1p) but robbery was viewed very seriously in 1893. At the Old Bailey, Schennick was sentenced to five years' penal servitude and Hammerman to seven years' penal servitude, and Wensley was again commended. It seems almost impossible that he found time to court and marry Laura Elizabeth, but the wedding took place at the Parish Church, Hadlow, Kent on 3 August 1893 and the small dark-haired, hazel-eyed girl who came from Eastbourne, Sussex and was four years his junior, became his wife; their marriage lasted for almost fifty years.

He had less luck with his desire to become a detective; although he was commended and rewarded time and again for catching thieves, he had fallen out of favour with Tom Divall, his divisional detective inspector upon whom entry into the CID depended. Wensley would later have cause to dislike him even more; following Divall's retirement, he became a member of the racetrack police and was heard to compliment the gang leader Billy Kimber, the head of the Brummagem Boys, on being, "one of the best". Wensley had almost eight years' service under his belt as a uniformed constable, when his superintendent demanded to know why he had not applied to become a CID officer. Wensley told him; and the superintendent who was probably a freemason – Wensley certainly was – told him to put his application in. Within days, a police officer named Payne was pensioned off and on 4 October 1895, Wensley took his place as a permanent patrol – the rank would later become detective constable – in the CID.

*

Wensley was now thirty years of age. At five feet nine-and-a-half inches, he was not excessively tall, but he was powerfully built. His Roman nose gave him a hawkish look, his blue eyes were deeply penetrating and as he rubbed the bowl of his pipe, he would murmur, "Y'know, the truth is all that matters. The single object is to get at the truth." He had his work cut out.

At the time of Wensley's appointment to the CID, fingerprint evidence for use in the courts was still ten years away. Identification of criminals relied upon their photograph being in the Rogues' Gallery at the Yard, with the added confirmation of a prison warder who had seen them during their incarceration. Mechanised transport had appeared at the Yard just two years previously; two 10hp Wolseleys had been acquired for the use of the commissioner and the receiver only. Therefore, the detectives relied upon buses, trams, bicycles and shoe-leather to get around. And as for the gathering of forensic evidence - … well, it was almost thirty years in the future that the eminent pathologist, Sir Bernard Spilsbury would castigate Chief Inspector Percy Savage for picking up the rotting, putrefying flesh of a murder victim in his bare hands, with Savage rather gormlessly replying that nobody had seen fit to issue rubber gloves to the murder bag. It took another ten years after that to form the Forensic Science Laboratory.

The Jewish community knew Wensley well, and their nickname for him was 'Vensal' or 'Mr. Vensley', Many of them provided information for him. Information, surveillance and pure detective ability were what Wensley and his associates had to rely on, to catch criminals – there was nothing else. Providentially, Wensley possessed all three attributes in abundance.

With the streets full of the most desperate criminals, Wensley knew that the slightest indication of laxness in dealing with them would be disastrous; not that this only applied to the violent characters. On one occasion, he spotted a man stealing a woman's purse. Immediately, he grabbed hold of the suspect's wrist and arrested him, ensuring that the purse was put safely in his own pocket. The suspect impudently accused Wensley of being the thief; the victim and several bystanders had seen Wensley pocket the purse and an ugly scene followed. Only with the greatest difficulty did Wensley get both suspect and victim to the police station but Wensley's troubles did not end there – the man repeated the allegation, as he did at the police court and called witnesses to inform the court that he was a man of good character. The man was committed for trial at the North London Sessions but Wensley was now very worried, indeed. He was certain that the man had previous convictions but this was before the days of fingerprint identification, so how could he prove it? Eventually, after days spent looking through the Rogues' Gallery at Scotland Yard, he identified his prisoner as a convicted thief. But in addition, his criminal record revealed that more than once, the prisoner had previously played the same trick that he had played on Wensley, which had resulted in acquittals and police officers being criticised for giving untrue evidence. He confronted the man in court, who admitted both his previous convictions and the offence, and in giving the Judge the man's criminal convictions, Wensley also informed him of what the prisoner had done to him, as well as other officers in the past. The thief was sentenced to eighteen months' hard labour. The prosecuting counsel decided that Wensley's remarks had been vindictive and criticised him, but of course it was not the barrister who had been slandered and whose job and liberty had been put on the line. Wensley turned on the barrister and told him what he thought of him. The Judge intervened and asked what had caused the confrontation: upon being told, he sided with Wensley, saying that the court had every right to know the full circumstances of the case.

Six months after joining the CID, Wensley's reputation was enhanced after he arrested a murderer, whilst he was off duty. William Seaman, who had served a total of twenty-eight years' penal servitude made a highly detailed confession but at his trial at the Central Criminal Court, he denied everything and when his statement was read out in court, he told Wensley, "The whole of your evidence is a fabrication. Either I'm a madman to make such a statement or you're a rogue. You've been sworn on the Bible, but they ought to have sworn you on a pack of cards." It did him no good; he was later hanged with two other murderers, an occasion which marked the last triple execution to take place in London. On the same day that sentence of death was pronounced on Seaman, Wensley was again commended at the Old Bailey. He had witnessed an enameller being robbed of his watch-chain by three men; Wensley dashed forwards and chased the men, catching Thomas Marshall single-handedly in a dark passageway. He handed Marshall over to a patrolling constable before searching for the robber's two accomplices, but without success; Marshall was sentenced to three years' penal servitude.

More violent thieves were caught by Wensley: when he arrested Michael Callaghan and Charles Hutchins for robbing a ship's fireman of £2, they were sentenced at the Old Bailey to hard labour. Callaghan to twelve months, Hutchins to fifteen. Surveillance was also an important part of detectives' duties; the unfortunately named Shena Suck and her accomplice, Rose Greenbaum were followed by Wensley and other officers right across London, on trams and omnibuses as they visited one shop after another without making purchases, over a period of four hours. They were stopped in possession of two sealskin capes which Suck dropped, saying "Not mine". And they weren't, although later at the Old Bailey, both women stated that the capes were indeed their property, alleging that the police had destroyed their receipts. It probably contributed to Suck being sentenced to fifteen months' hard labour and Greenbaum, to nine. "I hope you will act fair and not put me away," said Robert Crundle plaintively, after Wensley arrested him in a pub for stealing a hundredweight of tea, four days previously. Wensley didn't, but a judge at the Old Bailey did: three years' penal servitude.

Three years went by and Wensley complained that he had not been promoted to sergeant but to be fair, very few officers were with only that length of service in the rank. His detective inspector was unsympathetic; he had not trained Wensley to be transferred on promotion after teaching him everything he knew, he said. So

Wensley complained to his superintendent – a different one from his predecessor, who had championed Wensley's cause – who sided with the detective inspector; whereupon Wensley stated that he would appeal to Scotland Yard. The superintendent was aghast. "It's a daring thing to do," he retorted and in normal circumstances, he would have been quite right. But Wensley was friendly with Sir Melville Macnaughten CB, who was then chief constable of the CID, who promoted Wensley to the rank of detective sergeant and allowed him to remain on 'H' Division, one man over strength. It was a wise choice, for Wensley was about to enhance his already considerable reputation.

In 1901, Mr. Cox, a seventy-one-year-old jeweller was attacked, tied up and gagged at his premises by three men, who relieved him of his entire stock. After being tied up for fourteen hours, he was extremely lucky to have survived the ordeal. Wensley heard that one of Cox's employees had provided the information to the gang and, at the same time, information was received concerning the spending habits of a gang of criminals. One gang member was seen with his son in Clapham Park Road, south London; as the son waited outside a house in that thoroughfare, so the father entered the premises. As he left, a short time later, the two were stopped some distance away and after it was discovered that the son was in possession of housebreaking implements, both were arrested. Meanwhile, the house which the suspect had just left was raided and the occupant, obviously in a state of shock, immediately (and erroneously) named and blamed Cox's venal employee for implicating him. "It looks bad for me, as I have a lot of the stuff," he said, adding virtuously, "It was not me who gagged Mr. Cox."

The rest of the gang was then rounded up. Wensley sent a telegram to Cox's employee, asking for a meeting and specifying a date and time – this, he signed in the name of one of the arrested robbers. He, too was arrested but because he could only be charged with conspiracy, the maximum sentence he could receive, much to the annoyance of the Trial Judge, Mr. Justice Jelf, was one of two years' imprisonment. The robbers fared less well; they were sentenced to penal servitude – one to twelve years, the other two to ten years, each.

Apart from displaying some clever detective work, this case was a landmark in criminal investigation. At a time when it was almost impossible to pursue a criminal who lived on one division and committed offences on another, without the express permission of the neighbouring division's superintendent – it was not always given – Wensley broke the mould. Here was a case where an offence had been committed on one division, the persons responsible located in a second division and arrested in yet a third.

Wensley utilized this strategy on his next case where offences had not even been committed on his division – but that was where the perpetrators lived. A series of burglaries had been carried out in the wealthy suburbs by this gang; on the few occasions when they had been challenged by patrolling police constables, the officers had been attacked by the gang, who escaped. No clues were left by them at the scene of the burglaries, no description of them was available and nobody had a clue as to their identities.

But Wensley's attention was drawn to a group of men he saw in Shadwell. Some of them he had seen before but that all of them he realized had a considerable amount of free time on their hands and plenty of money to squander. He employed his surveillance skills to discover where they lived and as the days grew into weeks, and the weeks into months, Wensley, in a variety of disguises managed to track each of the gang. Their main meeting place was a house in Albert Street, Shadwell and the visitors to that premises were followed home and identified. A frequent visitor, Bertha Weiner, who, like the rest of the gang was a German immigrant, had visited the house with her brother Ludwig and his two sons, who referred to themselves as auctioneers. Although Bertha lived a mile away, she nevertheless paid the rent for the house in Albert Street. Now, Wensley used his considerable talents to obtain information as to precisely what the gang was up to, from a top-class informer. The leader of the gang was Bertha Weiner, he discovered. She financed the operations, the gang who resided in Albert Street went out in groups of four or five and the stolen goods were disposed of through Bertha's brother and nephews.

The arrests were carried out, simultaneously, with tremendous results. The eight men who were arrested at Albert Street were so shocked that two of them hurriedly dressed in items stolen in two of the burglaries. Bertha Weiner and her lover were arrested at her address in Ship Alley and the officers arrived at Ludwig Weiner's house, just in time to stop a pantechnican driving off, which was found to contain an enormous amount of stolen property. At the police station, the eight burglars excitedly discussed their predicament in German; foreseeing such a possibility, Wensley had thoughtfully ensured that an officer who spoke fluent German was in the vicinity. Their overheard conversations quickly linked them to a total of thirty-six burglaries and at the Old Bailey eleven of the men were each sentenced to five years' penal servitude. One of the Weiner nephews was fortunate to receive just twelve months' imprisonment, but the heftiest sentence was reserved for Bertha Weiner, who had orchestrated the whole business: seven years' penal servitude. A riot broke out in the dock as the prisoners tried unsuccessfully to attack Wensley, whilst roundly cursing him. Fortunately, the native of Somerset was unable to understand a word they said.

At this time a protection gang had been terrorizing the East End; anybody who failed to pay up or crossed them in any way stood the risk of being shot, stabbed or having their premises burned down. A bookmaker, Myer Edgar, who refused to pay and who had enlisted the services of a bodyguard, was attacked in a billiard hall by four members of the gang wielding a cue, a knife and a chopper, who knocked him unconscious. The absent bodyguard was found in a near-by pub by the gang who attacked him too; fortunately, the licensee called the police. Two of the gang were arrested, but not without a struggle. Police Constable 243'H' Major Jones arrested John Bonn for riotous conduct, who replied, "Let go of me, I will have your fucking life, you bastard," and punched the officer on the jaw. James Brooks grabbed hold of PC Jones' collar, saying, "Come on Jack, have a fucking go for it," and he too was arrested. At Leman Street police station, the very arrogant Harry Sharper, the third member of the gang, brazenly told Wensley, "I am come here to see that they get fair play" and was promptly charged, together with his associates, with wounding with intent. The fourth member of the gang, James Edwards was spotted a couple of days later in a hansom cab, by Wensley. Edwards told the cab-man to whip up the horse and as the hansom cab thundered off along the Whitechapel Road, so it was chased on foot by Wensley who grabbed the horse by the head, forcing it to stop. Edwards was probably fortunate to be sentenced to four years' penal servitude at the Old Bailey; his companions each received five years.

The following year, Wensley focused on gang warfare between two rival groups of Russian immigrants, 'The Bessarabians' and 'The Odessians'. Two of the Bessarabians, Max Moses (who boxed professionally under the ring name of Kid McCoy) and Barnett Brozishewski, he already knew. He had arrested them, plus a third gang member, for robbery with violence on a visiting Russian police officer, who was disinclined to give evidence against them. But shortly after they were discharged, there was a pitched battle between the gangs in the York Minster pub, in Philpot Street. One man was stabbed to death and Brozishewski was arrested at the scene; within a few days, Wensley had arrested Moses and a fellow Bessarabian, Samuel Oreman. This time, the evidence was rather more compelling; Brozishewski was recommended for mercy and received six months' hard labour. Not so the others – Oreman received five years' penal servitude and Moses, ten.

Wensley was not averse to undercover work; when a couple of con-men – one Russian, (David Weinstone) the other Rumanian (Rosen Soulman) – tried a 'gold-brick' swindle on an East End businessman, under the guise of importing gold from Siberian gold mines, he introduced Wensley to them as a participator in the scheme. By 1903 standards, Wensley set the stage well, renting a smart, furnished house in Camberwell: when the fraudsters were arrested in possession of ninety pounds of brass filings, instead of the promised gold, weighing the same amount, both men were decidedly unhappy that the man whom they had tried to defraud out of £2,285 was the same man who charged them. They were even less pleased with the sentences they received at the Old Bailey: twelve months' hard labour for Weinstone, and eighteen months' hard labour for Soulman.

The years passed quickly for Wensley and as he was promoted to detective sergeant (first class) he continued to make massive inroads into the crime of the area. On 7 December 1905, Inspector Godley was promoted and transferred to 'K' Division and Wensley took his place, having been promoted to detective inspector (second class) - still, he was retained on 'H' Division. By now, the initial revulsion and resentment he had felt had disappeared and he loved the neighbourhood. He was completely on top of his job and he was supported by a very able team of detectives. These included Detective Sergeants Jack 'Jew Boy' Stevens, who, upon retirement, drew his pension until the ripe old age of ninety-one: William Brogden, later to be reduced in rank to constable, after putting a bet on with a bookmaker on behalf of another, but who nevertheless was commended on 135 occasions: and Harry Dessent, a brilliant detective, whose health precluded any further advancement in rank.

A Royal Commission was set up by the Home Secretary, Herbert Gladstone in 1908 to deal with allegations of police misconduct. This was seen as a heaven-sent opportunity by a thoroughly dangerous, vindictive and manipulative criminal named Arthur Harding, to allege that Wensley had committed perjury.

Born Arthur Tresadern in 1886 in 'The Nichol', one of the most deprived areas of Bethnal Green, Harding was the product of a wastrel father and a drunken mother, and his first prison sentence was at the age of fifteen when he received twelve months' hard labour for stealing. Shortly after his release, Harding was sentenced to twenty months' imprisonment for street robbery, and he later taught himself the rudiments of law, so that during a twenty-year period, he defended himself and was able to secure his acquittal on twenty-seven occasions.

Wensley had had dealings with Harding and featured in one of his many court appearances, hence the allegation of perjury. But nothing Harding said could be relied upon without the most stringent verification and the commissioner dismissed this allegation. It is interesting to note that years later, when he was ninety-one years of age, Harding admitted that giving evidence to the commission was the worst thing he ever did, because it put the police against him. No doubt the police collectively loathed Harding long before that, and *vice versa*, but as we shall see, it was not too long before the two antagonists met again.

In the meantime, Wensley was summoned from his bed during the early hours of 16 March 1909 after two seamen had been lured into an address by two prostitutes, Ellen Stevens and Emily Allen and then attacked by the girls' pimps, two brothers named Mark and Morris Reubens. One of the seamen had been murdered and robbed and the other seriously wounded. The body of the murdered man had been dumped some distance away and was found by a patrolling police officer. Wensley followed a trail of both the victim's blood and silver threepenny pieces back to 3 Rupert Street, where he found a bloody handprint on the front door, made by the murdered man as he had tried to steady himself. He arrested the brothers. Morris Reubens – a classic whiner – entreated, "Mr. Wensley, do what you can for us. We never meant to murder the man and you don't want to see a couple of young fellows like us, topped." Not that Wensley relied upon that admission for a successful prosecution. With a fine sense of the theatrical, he had the door removed, since fingerprints were now accepted by the courts, and produced it as an exhibit at the Old Bailey. No evidence was offered against the prostitutes who gave evidence against their former employers and Mr. Justice Jelf pronounced sentence of death on both brothers, who were hanged on 20 May 1909. The judge also commended all of the detectives for "their excellent conduct throughout the case" and in a macabre touch, Wensley later received a drinking glass upon the base of which the effigies of two men, hanging from a gallows, had been engraved. The inscription read, 'The Brothers Reubens. The last drop.'

On 16 December 1910, three City of London police officers were shot dead and two more were wounded by a gang of Latvian criminals. By 2 January 1911, Wensley and his men had traced the murderers to a second-floor flat at 100 Sidney Street. The following day, what became known as the siege of Sidney Street began. The

Latvians opened fire and Ben Leeson, one of Wensley's detective sergeants, was shot in the chest and carried into a nearby house. The only way to get him to hospital was across a roof. Wensley supervised his evacuation and remained on the roof until the stretcher party was clear, while was pinned down by a hail of bullets. The houses nearby were evacuated, five hundred police officers cordoned off the streets and marksmen from the Scots Guards were summonsed. Winston Churchill, then Home Secretary in the Liberal government and never one to miss out on some well-timed publicity, turned up and directed operations. This became the subject of a newsreel which was shown at the local theatres, where it rather backfired after the mainly Conservative cockney audience booed Churchill and added cries of, "Shoot 'im!"

Two of the gang members were killed and others were rounded up and arrested; Ben Leeson gradually recovered and later retired.

But for Wensley, there was no respite; he was requested by the divisional detective inspector of 'W' Division, Alfred Ward, to assist in a murder that he was investigating, that of an East End receiver of stolen property named Leon Beron whose body had been found by Clapham Common. Five days after the siege at Sidney Street had ended, Wensley had identified and arrested the murderer. Steinie Morrison was a hardened criminal who had served prison sentences totalling twelve years. His latest sentence had been one of five years' penal servitude for housebreaking and he had proved to be a recalcitrant prisoner in Dartmoor. He had attacked a fellow inmate, then a warder and for this had received twenty strokes of the cat o'nine tails, followed by three months in chains on a diet of bread and water. He had only been released from this sentence six weeks prior to Beron's death. Wensley arrested him in a café, saying, "Stein, I want you." Later, Morrison said, "You have accused me of murder. I want to make a statement." Wensley replied that he had made no such accusation and this was relied upon in court as a classic slip-up. At the Old Bailey, Morrison stated that Wensley had said to him, "Stein, I want you for murder," and this was, of course denied by Wensley and the other officers present, all of whom were subjected to the most hostile cross-examination. The waters became a little muddied after a police constable at Leman Street police station named George Greaves volunteered to give evidence for the defence, saying that he had heard the arresting officers tell Morrison he had been detained for murder. The unwise PC Greaves was somewhat discredited after it was revealed that he was currently suspended for making untruthful statements about his senior officers and that Wensley had had occasion to reprimand him for writing wild letters. Morrison was convicted and sentenced to hang but was reprieved, sentenced to penal servitude for life and died in prison, ten years later. Greaves discovered the inadvisability of making rash statements after he was transferred to Ruislip, probably the furthest posting away from home that it was possible to receive.

On 16 March 1911, Wensley was promoted to divisional detective inspector (still, naturally on 'H' Division) and four months later was awarded £25 by the Lord Mayor and the aldermen of the City of London for his part in the Sidney Street siege. Now, it was time for a further confrontation with his old adversary, Arthur Harding.

Considerable trouble had arisen between Harding and one Isaac Bogard, otherwise known as 'Darky the Coon'. Described both as a Jew and 'a man of colour', Bogard, who affected an American accent and wore a sombrero and other clothing reminiscent of a cowboy, was a vicious pimp. One of Harding's associates, Tommy Taylor, had attempted to recruit some of Bogard's prostitutes in a take-over bid; Bogard, not unnaturally, beat him up. On the evening of 10 September 1911, Harding and his gang, bent on revenge, cornered Bogard in The Bluecoat Boy, a pub in Bishopsgate. Bogard calmly tried to defuse the situation by offering them all a drink, which the gang accepted but they then set about him, slashing his face with broken bottles. This was one of several attacks. Later, shots were fired at Bogard and a stallholder from Walthamstow market and both men were attacked; they were greatly outnumbered by their opponents who were armed with knives and revolvers. Curiously, it was Bogard and the stallholder whom the police arrested for disorderly behaviour, although on the way to the police station, a determined attack was made by Harding's gang, to try to get at the two prisoners. The following day, the Magistrate at Old Street Police

Court bound the two men over to be of good behaviour but by now, Harding and a huge mob had blockaded the court, waiting for their opponents to appear. When they did so, they were pursued into Shoreditch High Street, where Wensley saw Harding put a revolver in his pocket and he and his men eventually arrested the gang. At the Old Bailey in December 1911, Mr. Justice Avory handed down sentences totaling almost twenty years' imprisonment to the seven accused gang members, who had been convicted of rioting, assault, shooting with intent and causing grievous bodily harm. Harding, who at that time was twenty-five years of age, had been convicted on fourteen previous occasions and he received twenty-one months' hard labour, to be followed with three years' penal servitude. Following their conviction, the press described the matter as an 'East End Vendetta'. The gang adopted the name, to become known as 'The Vendettas'. A name which few of them could understand or spell must have been a great comfort to Harding in his Dartmoor cell.

In 1912 Wensley was promoted to detective chief inspector and it would have been normal for him to have been posted to Scotland Yard. However, Alfred Ward, whose murder case Wensley had assisted, was also promoted, and it was he who went to the Yard; Wensley stayed where he was, which suited him down to the ground.

A year after his promotion, a fire broke out at a building in the Commercial Road which contained sixteen lodgers, two of whom were burnt to death. The tobacconist, Morris Loufer who owned the premises immediately came under suspicion after it was discovered that he was fully dressed at the time the fire was reported, at one o'clock in the morning. Wensley set to work and discovered that the tobacconist was in dire financial straits; his creditors were pressing him for payment, every penny he possessed had been used to pay the premium on the insurance for his stock and he had recently invested in an inordinately large supply of wax tapers and matches. When one of the surviving lodgers told Wensley that the tobacconist had mentioned that the only thing which could save him was a fire, Wensley arrested him and saw him sentenced to ten years' penal servitude for manslaughter and recommended for deportation.

Wensley might have been forgiven for believing that he would remain on his beloved 'H' Division for the rest of his service. However, when Alfred Ward was killed during a Zeppelin attack in 1916, Wensley took his place at the Yard. He was a natural choice since he had solved every murder that he had investigated. (This was in contrast to Percy Savage, the putrefying flesh handler, who actually boasted that he had probably had more acquittals in murder cases than any other officer; these acquittals included two separate murders where Savage actually witnessed the offence!) During Wensley's time on the Murder Squad, the first steps were taken to improve the detectives' lot, steps which would ultimately result in the formation of the Flying Squad.

Although the Assistant Commissioner (Crime), Basil Home Thompson, had had a varied and interesting life – soldier, writer, barrister, colonial officer and governor of a number of prisons – he was no police officer, so when he wanted to discover if detectives could become more streamlined and if they could become more flexible and adaptable, he took the sensible course of action and asked a real detective. Wensley replied that it would be quite feasible to recruit a roving body of detectives; in fact, he thought it was high time.

Wensley had long before broken through the barriers of the divisional boundaries, so jealously guarded by their near feudal superintendents. Now he formed a skeleton plan of appointing senior officers of experience, each of whom would supervise and co-ordinate the activities of detectives drawn from different divisions while remaining in constant touch with each other. This roving band of strictly supervised detectives would be able to move rapidly and operate in any division where there was an epidemic of crime - either independently or in conjunction with their divisional colleagues. But for the time being, this plan would have to be put on hold. There was a war on; offences under the Defence of the Realm Act and the Military Service Act had to be investigated - and the murders were never ending.

In November 1917 Wensley was sent by his detective superintendent, John McCarthy to assist in the investigation of the murder of a Madame Emilienne Gerard, whose dismembered body had been discovered, wrapped in a parcel in Regent Square, Bloomsbury. Written on the wrapping paper were the words 'Blodie Belgium', and suspicion fell on a butcher named Louis Voisin who lived at 101 Charlotte Street. During the interview, Wensley asked Voisin if he would write the words, 'Bloody Belgium' for him and Voisin obliged; five times. Each time, he wrote 'Blodie Belgium', the last of which bore a very strong resemblance to the writing on the parcel. At his appeal, Voisin vainly stated that this course of action by Wensley had amounted to entrapment. It was, however, not the only damning piece of evidence which would ultimately send him to the gallows. Discovered in his trouser pocket was a key which fitted the cellar door of 101 Charlotte Street; there were found the unfortunate Madame Gerard's head and hands, immersed in a cask of sawdust. Helpfully, the trial Judge, Lord Darling, passed the death sentence in French.

Slowly, the war came to an end. Crime, already high, had burst through the ceiling and was out of control. Men who had fought resolutely through the carnage of the French and Belgian trenches arrived home, seeking what Lloyd George had promised as "A land fit for heroes ..." They were to be bitterly disappointed. When the truth of the matter sank in – that the standard of housing was as poor as it was scarce and that employment was in an even worse state – many of these men, who had defended their country so bravely, turned to crime. Their number was swollen by young men who had known little discipline in the home, due to the absence of their fathers during the war and by many of the work-shy, thieving and thoroughly dangerous immigrants.

Offices were broken into and their safes cut open. Jewellers were forced to put up grilles on their windows to protect their wares from the smash and grab gangs. Gang warfare at the racetracks and on the streets flared to epidemic proportions. Cashiers of both sexes were assaulted and robbed and motorists were held up and relieved of their valuables: firearms were used more and more during masked burglaries, bank hold-ups and for the shooting of police officers.

It was clear that extraordinary measures would have to be taken. The commissioner of police certainly thought so, and in a memorandum dated 22 October 1919, he adopted Wensley's plan, splitting the Metropolitan Police District into four areas for the appointment of detective superintendents on special duty. One of them was the newly-promoted Wensley, who summoned a dozen detectives to his office. These men – sergeants and constables – were the cream of the Metropolitan Police. Drawn from all over London, they were proven thief-takers, with first-rate sources of information and an acute knowledge of the underworld.

Wensley invited the men to sit down and then in clear, concise terms he gave them their directions. They would work anywhere in London that they were needed, he told them. The criminals responsible for the outbreak of crime had to be identified, arrested and convicted. "The success or not, of this mobile patrol scheme will depend on you," said Wensley. "But in twelve months time, the commissioner must report to the home secretary. He will decide whether this experiment should either continue or be disbanded."

The twelve detectives filed out of Wensley's office, rather excited at being part of this ground-breaking scheme but also somewhat bemused as to the 'mobility' aspect of it. At that time, only the commissioner, the receiver and the four assistant commissioners were provided with motor cars. Within weeks, their curiosity was satisfied. Two horse-drawn wagons were put at their disposal, which had been hired from the Great Western Railway Company. As they trundled out of the Yard and into Whitehall, the wagons were filled with detectives, hidden from view in the back. Slots had been cut in the sides, into which were fitted boards, bearing the names and addresses of businesses, suitable for the locations that the officers were about to patrol. As the officers peered through the spyholes which had been cut in the sides of the covered wagons, whilst the horse ambled along, the thieves and tearaways were amazed at being grabbed out of thin air, just as they were in the act of stealing a car or picking a pocket. Not only were wagons used, but the officers also patrolled on foot and used public transport in their hugely successful efforts to catch criminals. The experiment was a resounding success, and the mobile patrol was made permanent.

They then progressed to motor vehicles; the first were two Crossley Tenders, formerly the property of the Royal Flying Corps. These heavy, ungainly 26hp vehicles had no front brakes and it was only when the engines were specially modified that anything approaching 40mph could be achieved – normally their speed was far less. The Tenders had aerials fitted to their roofs, which consisted of five parallel wires, mounted on adjustable arms which could be raised and lowered from inside the van and this, not unnaturally gave rise to their nickname of 'Bedsteads.'

On their first patrol, under the command of Divisional Detective Inspector Walter Hambrook, the officers in the tenders arrested a dangerous gang of shopbreakers who, a few nights previously had nearly killed an off-duty police officer who had tried to arrest them as they were breaking into a shop. Following a terrific fight, the shopbreakers were hauled into Gerald Row police station, and following their imprisonment at the Old Bailey, the officers were showered with commendations from the Magistrate at Westminster Police Court, the Trial Judge Sir Henry Dickens and the commissioner, who also made monetary awards to all of the officers.

There were two more plaudits to come. Four days after the arrests, on 22 September 1920, the crime correspondent for the *Daily Mail*, Mr. G.T. Crook wrote:

Flying Squads of picked detectives with motor transport at their disposal were based at police headquarters, ready to go anywhere at any time... The result of these live operations have been remarkably successful … scores of the most daring and dangerous criminals in London have been caught. They have been picked up by the flying squads at all hours of the day and night, some while actually engaged in a burglarious enterprise, while others have been stopped with housebreaking implements in their possession.

The name stuck. And although it would take another year before the term 'Flying Squad' would be adopted by the hierarchy at the Yard, it was nevertheless the Squad that the commissioner was referring to when, in his annual report to Parliament for 1920, he wrote:

Some excellent work has been done by a small centralised body of detective officers, working under the direction of the Superintendents of areas, in following up and arresting or dispersing gangs of criminals who are engaged in shop and warehouse breakings in different parts of the district.

*

During the early hours of 4 October 1922, a married couple, Percy and Edith Jessie Thompson were returning from the theatre to their Ilford home when Mr. Thompson was attacked by a man wielding a knife. He later died of his injuries. The investigation was overseen by Wensley, (who had taken control of Central Branch on 30 November 1921) and it was discovered that Mrs. Thompson had a lover, a young ship's writer named Frederick Edward Francis Bywaters who was due to return to sea the following day. Speed was of the essence – Wensley needed to stop Bywaters before he could set off and also to recover any incriminating evidence. The Flying Squad were used to travel to Bywaters' mother's house in Upper Norwood and all the usual places that he was likely to visit were staked out. Bywaters was arrested, and also recovered were a number of incriminating letters which had been sent to him by Edith Thompson, in which she admitted putting broken glass in her husband's food, and enclosed newspaper cuttings which dealt with three cases where people had been poisoned. At the pair's five-day trial, the jury disbelieved Mrs Thompson's counsel's assertion that she was a 'fanciful dreamer', and on 11 December 1922, after deliberating for two hours and eleven minutes, found both Thompson and Bywaters guilty. They were sentenced to death. Bywaters, a good looking young man with flashing eyes which had attracted Thompson to him in the first place, snapped, "I say the verdict of the jury is wrong. Edith Thompson is not guilty. I am no murderer, I am not an assassin!" Thompson cried, "I am not guilty; oh God, I am not guilty!" Their appeal, heard ten days later before the Lord Chief Justice of England, was dismissed and despite a heavily subscribed petition for her reprieve, Edith

Thompson was hanged, as was Frederick Bywaters on 9 January 1923; he at Pentonville, she at Holloway.

Later the same year, Wensley was involved in a case which to all intents and purposes was a suicide, by means of gas poisoning. A young woman had been found at her address in Tottenham, lying on a couch with a gas pipe nearby. She had been discovered by her boyfriend, who appeared distraught and the inquest into her death had been opened and adjourned. Digging into the background of the young man, whose name was Shepherd, Wensley discovered that he had previously attempted to strangle the young woman; not only that, but the previous year, he had given himself up for the murder of another young woman, in Reading. Doubt had been cast on the validity of his confession and he had been discharged. That Shepherd was mentally unbalanced was not in dispute; Wensley felt that he had induced and helped the young woman to die. "I'm not having this," he grimly told a colleague. "I'm going to see this fellow."

So he did; to ask the all important question – "Who turned the gas off?" It could not have been the victim and Shepherd was duly convicted of murder; when his appeal failed, he laughed in the faces of the Judges but he was reprieved a few days before his intended execution. Serving his sentence at Parkhurst Prison, he attacked the daughter of a warder and, not before time, was certified insane and served out the rest of his days at Broadmoor.

The same year, Wensley investigated the activities of three men – Joseph Engelstein, James Stolerman and Julius Brust – who, it was said, could arrange burglaries and fires at premises for a fee, in order to defraud the insurance companies. Stolerman's insurance company had previously paid out a claim, following a fire at his premises, but they were unhappy about the circumstances and informed him that when his policy expired in June 1923, they would not renew it. One month prior to the expiration of the policy, there was a tremendous explosion at Stolerman Brothers Ltd., in Columbia Road, Hackney. Three men were seen running from the blazing premises and the descriptions of two of them fitted Engelstein and Brust.

A zinc-lined box was found at the factory. It had been filled with petrol and a slow burning fuse had been attached, so that by the time the petrol ignited, the three men would have established compelling alibis far from the scene. But to make sure that the flames spread rapidly, they had sprinkled more petrol around the vicinity. When the match was struck, the flame ignited the petrol vapour; hence Stolerman's and Engelstein's impressive burns to their hands. Their explanation as to how they had received these injuries was found to be bogus; it led them to the Old Bailey where they received sentences of penal servitude – Engelstein, six years, Stolerman five years and Brust four years.

In 1924 Wensley was appointed chief constable of the CID and he took a healthy interest in his brainchild, the Flying Squad. Quite apart from the Crossley Tenders being cumbersome, they were now getting very well known amongst the London criminals, and following the successful test of a Lea Francis 14hp tourer, which had a top speed in excess of 70 mph, a fleet of these and some vans were purchased by the head of the engineering department at the Yard, a certain Major T.H. Vitty. It was the sight of these vehicles parked at the Yard which roused the Commissioner, Brigadier-General Sir William Horwood GBE, KCB, DSO to a fury. He lost no time in contacting Major Vitty, angrily pointing out that there could be no doubt in criminals' minds that the vehicles belonged to the police, since all of the tourers and vans were the same colour and had consecutive number plates.

Major Vitty, who until then had thought he had done quite well, suggested by way of report that the identities of the vans could be disguised by putting transfers bearing manufacturers names on the sides, and that the colours of the Lea Francis tourers could be changed to blue or crimson. The papers were passed to Wensley, who dealt with the matter in the characteristically straightforward manner of the consummate professional.

The vehicles should be painted in colours common to their make, said Wensley, bringing a touch of common sense to the proceedings, and the registration numbers of both the cars and vans should not, of course, be consecutive. The new vans should be utilised in exactly the way the plain vans had been in the Squad's formative years – slots to be cut in the sides and boards with different names and businesses to suit the location should be inserted. "Personally," wrote Wensley laconically, putting the finishing touches to his minute, dated 8 November 1927, "I never knew it to fail."

Also in 1927, Wensley supervised the investigation into a nationwide blackmail plot, involving the use of bogus police officers which had successfully (and lucratively) been operating for three-and-a-half years. Within weeks, the gang was rounded up and at the Old Bailey the ringleader was sentenced to penal servitude for life; the other five gang members received fifteen, twelve, ten, ten and eight years' penal servitude respectively.

As the 1920s came to a close, the Squad vehicles were constantly being updated, many of them being fitted with Marconi radio sets. The *Daily Mail* of 20 October 1928 described the Flying Squad as being, "Scotland Yard's quick striking arm": and in the same newspaper, two days later revealed, "More secrets of the Flying Squad - Mystery cars with pocket wireless – Scotland Yard's 'Q' Ships". Squad arrests for 1929 totaled 515: J. Ord Hume had composed *The Flying Squad quick march*, for both military and brass band and when the *Daily Mail* informed its readers that, "the Flying Squad of Scotland Yard is to be strengthened," four months later, on 6 August 1929, it was. The squad was completely reorganised under a detective superintendent of C1 Branch and its manpower was increased to forty. The author, Edgar Wallace, had added a play to his already successful book, *Flying Squad* and the hero of an Alfred Hitchcock film was a Flying Squad detective. Walter Hambrook who had led the Squad on their initial, bloody expedition nine years previously, was plucked out of his posting at Albany Street police station and promoted to detective chief inspector; he now headed the Flying Squad. After ten short years, the name of a small, dedicated section of the Metropolitan Police was on everybody's lips. The Flying Squad – thanks to Wensley - was crowned with success.

The following entry appeared in *Police Orders*, dated Wednesday, July 31, 1929:

The commissioner has much pleasure in notifying the appointment of Mr. John H. Ashley (superintendent C.I.

Department) to chief constable, *vice* Mr. Frederick P. Wensley, O.B.E., retiring on pension; to date from 1st. August. Mr. Wensley joined the Metropolitan Police on 16th. January 1888, and was appointed to the Criminal Investigation Department on 3rd. October 1895. He became chief constable in December, 1924.

His ability and devotion to the work of his Department has been a notable feature in its history. The secretary of state has expressed his appreciation of Mr. Wensley's long and exceptionally distinguished service, and with this expression, the commissioner wishes to be heartily associated."

It was a fitting tribute and an extraordinary one. Nothing like it had been seen before and it has never been repeated since.

*

With over forty years of police service under his belt, Wensley left Scotland Yard for the last time. He had been showered with commendations and awards. As the first King's Police Medal had been struck in 1909, so it had been awarded to Wensley. He had been appointed MBE in 1920; later, he was advanced to OBE. Wensley published his memoirs and these were serialised in the *Sunday Express.* There was an offer from the mayor of New York for Wensley to act as a consultant in the fight against the gangsters of the prohibition era, but Wensley stated that he would only accept the job if he was given complete autonomy in operations against the gangs and the offer was withdrawn.

So with a pension of £600 per year, he returned home to Laura and his house at 76 Powys Lane, Palmers Green, which overlooked Broomfield Park. Wensley had never really recovered from the death of his two sons, Frederick Martin and William Harold, both of whom died during the First World War and his remaining years were spent quietly, tending his beautiful garden and amassing a large collection of exquisite Goss china, which he displayed in large cabinets. He corresponded with his old contemporaries and proved to be a genial host to them, as well as being a loving husband and father. Laura died on 25 February 1943 and after twenty years of retirement, Wensley, too, died on 4 December 1949, at the grand age of eighty-four.

The following year, his daughter presented a copy of his memoirs to the Broomfield Museum. It is now kept in Enfield's local history library at Palmers Green.

This, then was the founding father of the Flying Squad. More than anybody else, it was Wensley who put the CID on a firm footing in the Metropolitan Police. A strict disciplinarian, he was nevertheless worshipped by his men. Detective Chief Superintendent Jack Capstick – 'Charley Artful' – who spent many of his thirty-two years' service on the Flying Squad and the Murder Squad said, "As a detective, he was one of the finest, if not the finest, in the Metropolitan Police." Peter Beveridge, later to head the Flying Squad, fondly remembered Wensley lecturing to him and his classmates at Peel House. "No one," said Deputy Commander William Rawlings OBE, MC, "knew as much about the East End as he did." Other detectives were put into proper perspective. Detective Superintendent John Gosling, in praising Divisional Detective Inspector William Salisbury as being, "the greatest of them all" added, "after Wensley". And when in 1923 Wensley appointed the legendary Ted Greeno to the CID, Greeno's brother jokingly asked, "Are you going to become another Nick Carter?" "No," replied Greeno. "Another Fred Wensley, if I can!"

"Because he solved so many famous crimes by finding clues a lesser man might overlook," said Lilian Wyles BEM, the twenty-third policewoman of the Metropolitan Police, "Frederick Wensley will always remain Scotland Yard's greatest detective." Nor were these accolades restricted to police officers. The famous barristers, Sir Edward Marshall Hall KC and Sir Richard Muir KC both admired Wensley and called him the greatest detective of all time.

Taking all the facts into account, it seems pretty certain that he was.

CHAPTER 2

'Nutty' Sharpe

When Fred Sharpe joined the Metropolitan Police in 1911, academic qualifications were not the highest consideration for an applicant, which in his case was just as well. As a detective chief inspector, a commendation report he penned for a subordinate was splattered with Americanisms – "he was among crafty men who were anxious to see how he received the 'dope' which they tried to foist on him." In his memoirs, *Sharpe of the Flying Squad*, written a few years later, the expressions, 'Hooey' and 'a real son of a gun' were used. If this was the best hc could do at that time of his life, then as a probationary police constable, when commissioner's commendations were awarded for 'keeping a neat notebook', young Sharpe's reports must have been truly terrible.

It was as well, then, that Sharpe had other attributes. He knew criminals, especially pickpockets, as few other officers did. He was a natural leader of men and he served for twelve years on the Flying Squad, ending up as its chief. Fred Sharpe – he was always known, as 'Nutty' – was also as hard as nails and he was utterly fearless, sometimes to the point of rashness.

*

Frederick Dew Sharpe was born on Christmas Eve, 1889 at 34 Windsor Road, Penarth, South Wales: when he was just eight months old, his parents moved to the Forest of Dean, a coal-mining area, situated on the border between England and Wales. They took The Crown public house at Drybrook, several miles east of Monmouth and when young Sharpe left school, at the age of fifteen, he became a miner. His physical hardness was developed by spending almost six years hacking away at the coal face; his aggression stemmed from his captaincy of the Drybrook Hornets' rugby team. At five feet ten-and-a-half inches tall, his body as hard as a lump of rock, Sharpe was one of forty-eight candidates who paraded at the Metropolitan Police training school at Renfrew Road, Kennington on the morning of 20 February 1911. Perhaps the clerk was hard of hearing, or perhaps it was Sharpe's accent which prompted him to enter the candidate's former trade or calling as 'farmer' instead of 'miner', but it was something that was never corrected.

He was allocated warrant number 99837, given a suit of blue and 8s 0d (40p) per week wages. After his initial six weeks' training, Sharpe was posted to Whitechapel as Police Constable 430'H'. His weekly wage had now improved to 25s 0d (£1.25p) per week and he moved into lodgings, next to the Salvation Army in the Whitechapel Road. At this time, married men who lived inside a six-mile radius of Charing Cross received rent allowance of 2s 6d (12p) per week; those rash enough to live further afield received a niggardly allowance of just 1s 6d (8p) per week.

A constable's working conditions could be dreadful. Violent crime (which included garrotting) was endemic and even though Wensley was now the divisional detective inspector, many incidents, murders included, were simply not recorded as such, reported or investigated. Street robberies were so common in those days that it was unsurprising that Sharpe's first arrest was for just that; he saw three men who had just robbed a man running towards him. Their arrest resulted in Sharpe receiving a commendation from the Trial Judge; it would be the first of many.

One year after Sharpe joined the force, the successful and popular dock strike commenced. The police were greatly resented for being used as strike-breakers rather than peacekeepers, and Sharpe had his hands full dealing with the fighting and arsons, arising out of it.

He became a winter patrol (a uniform officer who, aspiring to join the CID, patrolled in plain clothes), notched up some impressive arrests and on 16 April 1914, was appointed permanent patrol – this would later be reclassified as 'detective constable' – and was posted to 'J' Division's Victoria Park. Some four months later, The Great War broke out and much of Sharpe's time was taken up dealing with aliens and army deserters. But not all. His ingenuity and fearlessness was being noted. On one occasion, Sharpe saw 'Birmingham Maggie' and her two male accomplices take a drunken sailor into a back street. Noiselessly following them, he witnessed the trio relieving the sailor of his wallet. Sharpe then lay down in the gutter, feigning drunkenness. "Here's another one," said one of Maggie's accomplices, pointing to Sharpe's inert form, and as they went to rob him, both Maggie and one of her associates were mightily surprised when the 'drunk', displaying remarkable sobriety, came awake and grabbed both of them. In sentencing Maggie to four months' imprisonment and her helper to six, the Magistrate, Mr. Clarke Hall also commended Sharpe for his prompt action, as did the commissioner.

When four young thieves who had stolen a valuable parcel of glacé kid gloves were followed by Sharpe to their lodgings and then tried to escape, Sharpe stuck his head out of the window and called to a woman passer-by. Knowing that to tell her the real reason for wanting police assistance would be rewarded with a contemptuous shrug, he shouted instead, "Run for the police – there's a man in here who's just hanged himself!" Sharpe managed, without too much difficulty, to keep the thieves contained until assistance did arrive.

A warehouse in Mare Street, Hackney, was suffering a series of thefts. Any conventional type of observation to detect the thieves was impossible; but Sharpe bored eyeholes in the side of a packing case, had himself nailed up in it and delivered to the premises.

He was promoted to third class detective sergeant, (a rank soon to become defunct) on 8 March 1920 and three months later, to second class detective sergeant. With his reputation as a thief-taker growing daily, it came as no surprise at all when Wensley – who had been keeping an eye on Sharpe's career – summoned him to the Yard in 1922, to invite him to join the Flying Squad. Technically, because he was still on the strength of 'J' Division, he was 'on loan' – but now, he was in his element.

*

Divisional Detective Inspector Charles Cooper was in charge of the Squad which then numbered approximately twenty-five officers. At this time, the only mode of transport for the Flying Squad was the two Crossley Tenders, which often followed criminals out to the suburbs, in order to catch them in the act of breaking into suburban properties. At other times, the tenders would be parked up in central London and whilst one or two officers kept observation in the back, the rest played bridge: the driver would politely decline the overtures of prostitutes who requested that they be given a lift. When the tenders were not being utilised, the Squadmen worked in pairs, using buses, trams, the Underground or just plain old-fashioned shoe leather. Their most frequent prey were the gangs of pickpockets, of whom the most troublesome was the Titanic mob. This gang would often work the Underground system, relieving their victims of wallets and purses, on the platforms or the lifts. When confronted, they resorted to violence and not only to their victims; on separate occasions Detective Sergeant Tongue and Detective Inspector Kirchner were both seriously assaulted when they tried to arrest them. Sharpe was therefore in illustrious company; on one occasion he was alone when he arrested one such pickpocket on the Underground and managed to get his struggling prisoner into the lift at Earls Court Tube Station. Five of the pickpocket's associates also crowded into the lift and attacked Sharpe so severely that he was rendered unconscious, they then escaped with his prisoner. It took a year for Sharpe to identify and trace the six men – but he arrested every one of them.

There was a multiplicity of talent on the Flying Squad for Sharpe to work with; two such officers were Detective Constable Frank 'Squibs' Dance – a master of disguise – and Detective Sergeant Dan Gooch, who would be awarded a staggering 109 commissioner's commendations and go on to become one of Sharpe's predecessors as head of the Flying Squad. Both were present when Sharpe spotted nine pickpockets by Shoreditch Church, an incident which probably became Sharpe's most talked-about case. The men were followed to a bus stop by the Bethnal Green Road and soon they were seen jostling the people in the bus queue. Two buses which stopped for passengers then departed and still the pushing continued; obviously, the gang was busily at work. As a third bus arrived, the pickpockets, together with other members of the queue, got on board the bus, eight of them going on the upper deck, the other downstairs. As the bus pulled away, so Sharpe slipped out of the Squad car, jumped on board and quietly told the conductor to tell the driver to take the bus straight to Bethnal Green police station. This he did; and just as they arrived, the uniform late-turn was being marched out of the station, to their respective beats. Sharpe utilised them to form a guard of honour, to conduct the nine stunned pickpockets into the charge room. At Old Street police court the following day, Mr. Ivan Snell, the Magistrate gave Sharpe a tremendous commendation and committed the prisoners to the London Sessions to be sentenced for being 'Incorrigible Rogues'. The following week, Sharpe arrested a lone pickpocket who was brought, once again, before Mr. Snell. The Magistrate gave Sharpe a wintry smile. "Rather small fry for you, Sharpe?"

The pickpockets infested the racetracks all over the country and as the Squadmen closed in on them, the air would ring with the pickpockets' cries of, "Heads up! It's the Squad!" On one auspicious occasion, former Detective Superintendent Fred Narborough recalled that as Sharpe led the Squad to the Silver Ring at Epsom, tic-tac men flailed their arms about as Nutty's famous bowler bobbed along through the crowd. It signaled the first race of the day — pickpockets falling over themselves to be the first over the rails and escape up the course. Sharpe had his work cut out with the racetrack gangs who were out of control and who intimidated bookmakers and punters alike, and witnesses were not always willing to come forward. However, he had his own way of dealing with the gangs. When they surged onto the racetracks, thirty or forty strong, Sharpe would single-handedly step forward, confront them and tell them to, "Clear off." Most times, they did. Anybody who refused or even hesitated found himself flat on his back, courtesy of a right-hander from 'Nutty'.

Sharpe may not have been liked by all the criminals with whom he had dealings but they certainly respected him. One fur thief who had successfully eluded him was finally caught and fearing that he was in for a belting to mark his impudence, quickly said, "Alright, Guv'nor, I won't cut up rough." Exercising his prerogative of mercy,

Sharpe replied, "If you behave yourself, Joe, there won't be any funny business." Joe did, and there wasn't – the fur thief was probably relieved to be let off with three years' penal servitude.

On 27 April 1924, Sharpe married Helen Georgina at St. Michael's Church, in Cornhill, City of London. His bride was fifteen years his junior and came from Windsor. Five years later, their daughter was born. Within eighteen months of his marriage, he was promoted to first class detective sergeant and according to the records he was posted to the Flying Squad on 15 July 1927; in reality, of course, he had been part of the Squad for the previous five years.

Within a few months of Sharpe's official posting, a number of Lea Francis tourers were added to the Squad fleet; the cars were fitted with hoods and mica side-screens to help conceal the detectives inside, and Sharpe ensured that these vehicles, capable of speeds of over 70 mph, were put to good use in the fight against crime. However, it was not too long before Wensley called Sharpe from his regular Flying Squad duties to head up a highly sensitive investigation.

George Goddard was twenty-one years of age when he joined the Metropolitan Police in 1900 and by 1913 he had been promoted to sergeant and posted to 'C' Division's Vine Street police station, which covered the Soho area. There, his duties included the enforcement of the licensing laws as well as all the other statutes needed to bring law and order to that lively district. In 1925, he was promoted to station sergeant and stayed at Vine Street, which suited him very well. But by now, the finger of suspicion was being pointed in his direction, particularly with regard to his dealings with Mrs. Kate Meyrick, the owner of the Cecil Club, situated at 43 Gerrard Street who, it was thought, was paying him substantial bribes to turn a blind eye to her illegal activities.

As a result of Sharpe's enquiries, a number of irregularities at the Cecil Club were proved and Mrs. Meyrick was sentenced to six months' imprisonment. Meanwhile, Sharpe pressed on with his investigations and when he questioned Police Constable 163 'C' John Wilkin, who had been working under Goddard's supervision to keep observation on night clubs, Wilkin cracked and admitted taking backhanders from the clubs' owners, via Goddard. He agreed to give evidence against Goddard, in return for immunity from prosecution, for himself. Goddard, together with Mrs. Meyrick, was arrested in November 1928 and had a hard time explaining how, on a weekly wage of £6 15s 0d (£6.75) he had acquired a house worth £2,000, and an expensive car and two bank accounts, containing funds totaling £2,700. He found it even more difficult to explain how he had managed to gather together £12,500 in a safe deposit box at Selfridges, which he rented in the name of Joseph Eagles (especially when some of the £10 notes therein were traced back to Mrs. Meyrick), and a catalogue of corrupt dealings with several of Soho's inhabitants was uncovered. Goddard was sentenced to eighteen months' hard labour, dismissed from the Force, fined £2,000 and ordered to pay the costs of the prosecution; Mrs. Meyrick was sentenced to fifteen months' hard labour. Although a concerted effort was made to sequestrate the contents of his safe deposit box, Goddard managed to hang on to practically every penny he had dishonestly obtained. While Mrs. Meyrick went on to serve two more six-month sentences for infringing the licensing laws and then lose most of her money in the 1929 Stock Market crash, Goddard completed his sentence and retired to a very comfortable life in the country.

It was therefore a great pity that an investigation – a competent one – had not been launched into Goddard's felonious activities sooner. Seven years previously, Police Sergeant Horace Robert Josling had reported Goddard to the commissioner for taking bribes from bookmakers. During the secret Home Office investigation which followed, Goddard was exonerated and Josling was required to resign. He was then thirty-two years of age and he returned to his former profession of teacher. Following Goddard's conviction, the Home Secretary offered Josling his job back; he refused, continued to teach and was later awarded the large (and well-deserved) sum of £1,500 compensation. He died at the early age of fifty-one.

The case (which received enormous publicity) did the reputation of the Metropolitan Police immense harm. Peter Beveridge, then a detective constable in Whitechapel, remembered that hooligans would shout 'Goddard!' at him, from a suitably safe distance. They were later seen and quietly reminded of their manners; the practice ceased.

Sharpe must have breathed a sigh of relief when the whole distasteful business was over, so that he could return to more regular Flying Squad duties.

"The more crooks a Flying Squad man knows intimately," said Sharpe, "the more he knows about the underworld and the more he knows about the underworld, and what it is thinking and doing, the more he is likely to be of use."

This particular homily was put to good use when Sharpe overheard a fragment of information and followed the men involved. When they met up with a woman who was associated with a well-known warehousebreaker, Sharpe telephoned Birmingham CID with his information. They kept observation on a particular warehouse for a week and at the end of that time the premises were broken into and the warehousebreaker and his accomplice were arrested. They received four years' penal servitude and eighteen months' hard labour, respectively – and apart from yet another commendation, Sharpe was awarded the sum of £5 by the local watch committee. It was one of the few occasions on which Sharpe did not carry out the arrest, himself.

But this did not become a habit. Sharpe was back to his usual tricks when he and 'Squibs' Dance followed a gang of five desperadoes, whom they suspected of daytime breakings into public houses. Deciding that they had enough evidence to sustain a charge of 'being a suspected person, loitering with intent to commit a felony', Sharpe sent Dance ahead to Tottenham Court Road police station to acquire assistance. All five villains put up a tremendous fight and for once, Sharpe was getting the worst of it. Fortunately, Squad drivers in those days had other attributes besides driving skills and just when Sharpe was thinking that all was lost, his driver who had fortuitously discovered a thick length of rubber, used it to crack Sharpe's assailant over the head.

After reports of wholesale pickpocketting at a previous match, the chief constable of Portsmouth City Police asked the Yard for assistance at the forthcoming match against West Ham United. 'Nutty' was sent, and he decided on a little pre-emptive action. Having discovered the hotel at which the pickpockets were staying, he gave orders for his men to surround the building. He then strolled purposefully towards the hotel, was immediately identified by the 'dips' who dashed out of the hotel and were promptly claimed by Sharpe's men. During the match, pickpocketing was down to an absolute minimum; twelve of the most prominent 'dips' were each starting three months' imprisonment.

A man who was stopped as he went to enter a bullion dealers, was found to be in possession of a quantity of jewellery for which he was unable to account. In fact, he had very little to say for himself at all, so when a letter was found in his possession, Sharpe decided to pay a call to the address on the envelope. His knock on the door was answered by a man who was belligerently drunk; not only did he refuse Sharpe access but he also threatened him with a rolling pin. It was not an unusual lack of resolve which made Sharpe back out, into the street, still followed by the occupant, by now roused to a rage and still brandishing the rolling pin; it was simply unwise (and rather unlawful) to carry out an arrest for being drunk and disorderly when the person concerned is not in a public place. So Sharpe waited until his adversary put one foot on the pavement before punching him, very hard indeed, on the chin and knocking him spark out. As a passing constable took the prisoner off to the local police station, so Sharpe searched the premises, to discover a great deal of jewellery and cutlery, which was later identified as being the proceeds of a housebreaking in Surrey. Both men were handed over to the Surrey Constabulary and the confrontational gentleman was sentenced to eighteen months' imprisonment. He was upset with the sentence, so he appealed and was even more aggrieved when the Court of Appeal increased his sentence to one of three years' penal servitude. His companion, who imprudently had in his possession the letter which had led to the search, prudently decided that his own sentence of six months' imprisonment was just right.

Sharpe was promoted to second class detective inspector on 10 March 1930 and still he was retained on the Squad. He led his team on a raid on a garage in Forest Hill, south London where, underneath a tarpaulin he discovered a streamlined 29.1 hp Invicta tourer. Enquiries revealed it had been stolen from the eminent plastic surgeon, Sir Harold Gillies, several months previously. Since Sir Harold had been paid out by his insurance company, the Squad seized the car, put the matter by means of a compelling report to the Receiver, who promptly purchased the vehicle, for Squad purposes, at the knock-down price of £298.

*

Eighteen months later, on 5 August 1931, Sharpe bade farewell – temporarily – to the Flying Squad and was posted to 'C' Division. He settled himself in and on the morning of 2 October 1931, he and his wife were at home, packing to go on holiday when Sharpe's boss, Detective Superintendent George Cornish telephoned; instead of a holiday, Sharpe had a murder to investigate.

'Norma Laverick' was the *nom de guerre* of a prostitute, whose real name was Annie Louisa Norah Upchurch; her body had been found in a shop which was 'to let' in Shaftesbury Avenue. She had been strangled by her cloth belt, and the discovery of the body had been made by the employee of a sign contractor, named Frederick Field. He stated that a few days previously a man had come to his work premises, bearing a written order and asking for the keys of the shop to be handed to him. Later a man was arrested – Field identified him, but the man denied any knowledge of the matter and he was believed; Field was not. Extensive enquiries were made, without success. Sharpe had Field brought in for a general chat and during the course of the conversation casually questioned Field about his knowledge of knots. Field duly obliged by tying a piece of string, using exactly the same knot as had been used on the murder weapon. Nevertheless, it was considered that although he was certainly the prime suspect, there was still insufficient evidence to arrest and charge Field. He was released and later joined the RAF.

On 25 July 1933, Field walked into a newspaper office and confessed to killing 'Norma Laverick', saying that he had committed the perfect murder. He was taken to Marlborough Street police station, where he made a full written statement, admitting everything. At the Old Bailey, he stated that he had only made the statement so that he would be charged and his innocence established; amazingly, he was acquitted.

On 5 April 1936, Beatrice Vilna Sutton was found asphyxiated in her flat in Clapham. Later the same day, a police constable arrested Field for being absent without leave from the RAF and he admitted the killing, saying that he, "just wanted to murder somebody." At the Old Bailey, he again retracted his confession, saying that he had found her body and admitted killing her so that he would be saved the trouble of committing suicide. This time, he was helped on his way by being hanged, and Sharpe had the satisfaction of finally seeing that justice had been done.

George Price was one of Sharpe's detective constables and remembered the occasion when one of the detective sergeants, 'Nunky' Nunn, who was fond of a drink, finally overdid things and wandered into the charge room at Marlborough Street police station stupefyingly drunk only to be put on report by the uniformed inspector. When Sharpe found out what had happened the following day, he was furious that action had been taken against one of his men without his being consulted and decided that a suitable revenge should be taken.

Now, in those days, the prosecution of street bookmakers was strictly a uniform matter but officers were specially employed in plain clothes to detect and arrest them. Sharpe summoned half-a-dozen aids and the 'drag' van, went out and arrested a dozen street bookmakers and their touts, took them to court and saw them sentenced – before informing the uniform branch of his arbitrary action. "Nutty's idea of poetic justice," laughed Price, nearly seventy years later.

Whether this was a contributory factor or not, Sharpe was posted to 'D' Division after ten months' service on 'C' Division but he was as irrepressible as ever, making arrests, being commended by the commissioner and being privately rewarded in a case of larceny.

On 16 April 1934, Sharpe was promoted to detective chief inspector and was posted to C1 Department at the Yard. His promotion was greeted by the *Daily Express* who, with a rush of hyperbole stated that he was:

> A terror to old-time East End gangsters. Stocky, bird-like, close cropped, slow of speech, brusque of manner; wears a stand-up stiff collar, (bowler) hat a size too small; a gourmet, hates publicity. Crooks call him, affectionately, 'Fred'.

He investigated a murder which had been committed in a cinema at Bow on 7 August 1934. The manager had been hit over the head with an axe and the takings, more than £100, stolen. After a fast-paced enquiry, Sharpe arrested nineteen year old John Frederick Stockwell, an attendant at the cinema, who confessed to murdering his employer. Before his trial, the Judge, Mr. Justice Goddard (later to become the Lord Chief Justice) went to the scene of the murder and Sharpe reconstructed the crime for him. Stockwell pleaded guilty to the murder and although the jury recommended clemency due to his youth, he was sentenced to death. His appeal failed, and the night before he was hanged Stockwell was given a pint of beer and proposed a toast: "Here's to the next world." Eleven days after Stockwell's execution, Sharpe was highly commended by the commissioner.

Sharpe's squad was wryly known as the 'Ogpu' (after Stalin's secret police), since, as well as murders, it dealt with all sorts of secret enquiries – forgeries, illegal immigrants, counterfeiters and bribery and corruption; during this time, Sharpe was again commended by the commissioner for his work in one of the corruption cases.

On 24 January 1936, Max Kassel, alias Emile Allard, alias Red Max, Max the Red, Ginger Max and Max le Rouquin was found murdered in Cell Barnes Lane, St. Albans. He had been shot six times. Sharpe took up the investigation and discovered that Latvian-born Kassel had been involved in the white slave trade. Working flat out – Sharpe was going to bed at three o'clock in the morning and getting up again at five – he retraced Kassel's steps and discovered that the murder had actually occurred at a maisonette in Little Newport Street, London. A search of the premises revealed a national insurance card in the name of Marcelle Aubin – she was brought in and questioned. Enquiries showed that the lessor of the property was one Pierre Henry Alexandre and that a tenant was Suzanne Naylor. Alexandre was interviewed and implicated a man named George Lacroix and also Naylor. Aubin was brought in again and now she told the full truth: that Lacroix had shot Kassel and that Naylor had helped dispose of the incriminating evidence. Following the murder, both Lacroix and Naylor had fled to Paris, and Sharpe sent two French-speaking detectives across the Channel where, with the aid of the French police, they traced the pair to a hotel where they arrested them. France refused extradition and the trial was held at the *Assizes de la Seine*, in Paris. The trial was beset with difficulties; before Marcelle Aubin could give evidence, she dropped dead and Suzanne Naylor – real name Bertrand – was acquitted.

Lacroix - real name Roger Marcel Vernon – had a bad criminal record. Aged nineteen, he had been convicted of stealing; at twenty-one, he was sentenced for armed robbery. Later, he was again convicted of armed robbery and on this occasion he was banished from France for ten years, sentenced to seven years' imprisonment and sent to Devil's Island, whence he had escaped.

Arriving in Venezuela in 1928, he later moved to Canada where he busied himself as a ponce and a seller of motor cars and it was there that he first met Max Kassel and discovered that their business interests coincided. Obtaining false identity papers, Vernon now became George Lacroix and travelled to London where he went into the motor trade and met up again with Max Kassel.

Lacroix admitted shooting Kassel, but claimed self-defence – in fact, the real reason was that Kassel had welshed on an unpaid debt of £25, and the three judges now sentenced him to ten years' hard labour, followed by twenty years' banishment from France. Sharpe gave evidence in Paris and at the conclusion he racked up his seventy-ninth and final commissioner's high commendation.

Just prior to Sharpe's appointment as head of the Flying Squad, which would last for the final nine months of his service, he led seven other members of the Squad down to Lewes Racetrack on 8 June 1936 after Ted Greeno had received information that there was to be a pitched battle between the Bethnal Green Gang and the Hoxton Mob on one side, and associates of the Italian Mob on the other.

A bookmaker, Alfred Soloman and his clerk, Mark Frater were attacked by the gang, led by Jimmy Spinks and Charles Spring, who produced hatchets, hammers, knuckledusters and crowbars and although Soloman received minor wounds before escaping, Frater received terrible injuries which might well have proved fatal, had the police not intervened.

At Lewes Assizes, sixteen of the gang were convicted of inflicting grievous bodily harm with intent and riotous assembly and were told by Mr. Justice Hilbery:

> You had armed yourselves with weapons which have been aptly described as villainous instruments to use upon any fellow human being. You showed no mercy to your victim, and you intended to show no mercy. Crimes of gang violence in this country will meet with no mercy. Gang violence is not only a brutal breach of our law, but it also exercises terror on its victims. You men hoped to escape, and I have not the least doubt that in this case you thought that because Frater would not dare, for fear of you, to identify one of you, that you might escape. There is no case here for leniency. You will receive sentences which I hope will teach you, once and for all that crimes of this sort do not pay in this country, and which will teach others who are listening here or who may read what happened in this case afterwards.

> He then imposed swingeing sentences: two of the gang were sentenced to five years' penal servitude, another to four years, five to three years, five more to two years and three (who had no previous convictions) to eighteen months' imprisonment.

The sentences effectively broke the power of the racetrack gangs. In 1923, 110 arrests had been carried out at Epsom racetrack for offences ranging from blackmail and welshing, to pickpocketting. On Derby Day, 1937, the year following Sharpe's intervention at Lewes, the arrests amounted to no more than eight.

The pinnacle of Sharpe's success came on 13 October 1936, when he succeeded Detective Chief Inspector Alec Duncan as head of the Flying Squad. He was heartily welcomed by Detective Superintendent Arthur Askew of C1 Department, himself a well-respected detective who in 1917 had been awarded the King's Police Medal for gallantry, after he single-handedly arrested a gunman in a dark alleyway who had just shot and killed a police constable who was accompanying Askew.

Apart from Askew, Sharpe was in other good company; Bob Higgins was there as a detective sergeant (second class), Capstick as a detective sergeant (first class), and Greeno was a detective inspector (second class), as was the indefatigable Alf Dance. With men of that calibre – plus many more with the same expertise – it would have been impossible for Sharpe to have put a foot wrong; and he didn't.

During Sharpe's short, inspirational reign as head of the Squad, his men worked enthusiastically for him. Detective Sergeant Donaldson (later to become the head of the Squad) led an investigation into a gang of car thieves. Twenty-six stolen cars, with a value of £4,980 were recovered and sentencing the gang's leaders to terms of five years' penal servitude, the Recorder, Sir Ernest Wild said:

> "I strongly commend the splendid detective work done in bringing these men to justice. Infinite pains and care must have been taken by them."

Sharpe also updated the fleet; of the three remaining tenders, he suggested that two might well be disposed of. They were, he declared with considerable irony, well known to the criminal fraternity: and the remaining tender should only be used for conveying either bulky property or large numbers of officers, neither of which cargoes, it could be assumed, would be in a particular hurry to reach their destination. But in a report for the week ending 31 March 1937, he noted, "The supply of the taxi-cab for permanent use by the Flying Squad has proved a most useful addition to the rolling stock."

Sharpe's near namesake, George Sharp was, at that time, a radio operator and because the four-and-a-half-litre Flying Squad Bentley that Sharpe was using was the only one to possess a transmitter, Sharp was appointed W/T operator. Over sixty-five years later, he recalled picking up Nutty at the Yard, in readiness for his journey to Newmarket Races. He had received reliable information that a certain criminal would be attending the meeting and Nutty intended to arrest him.

Resplendent in a top hat and cutaway, a pair of binoculars slung negligently round his neck, Nutty stepped sedately into the Bentley. First, however, a detour had to be made. A 'Race Special' train was due to depart to the races from King's Cross station at nine o'clock; so were a large number of card sharps who, during the hour-long journey intended to fleece the punters for every penny they possessed. Sharpe had considerable experience of dealing with this type of riff-raff; on a previous occasion, he had arranged an unscheduled stop of a Tilbury to Fenchurch Street train – he and his Flying Squad team had boarded the train at Plaistow and arrested eighteen cardsharpers. And now, arriving at Kings Cross station, fifteen minutes prior to the train's departure, Nutty walked slowly along the platform, opening all of the carriage doors. He lived up to his newspaper accolade: 'The man who never forgets a face', as he recognised known card sharps, who were ejected and told to 'clear off'. None of them demurred. Returning to the car, Nutty was whisked away to Newmarket and after a successful day's racing, he returned to the Yard, depositing his prisoner in the cells at Cannon Row, en route. Perhaps referring to this particular episode, Sharpe once ambiguously said, "I do not think there is any place at which an enthusiastic detective can spend a more profitable day than at a race meeting."

Nutty Sharpe retired on 18 July 1937, with an annual pension of £347 17s 2d, having served twenty-six years and one hundred and forty-nine days. When he died at the ripe old age of eighty-four, he had drawn his pension for thirty-seven years; ten years longer than his service in the Metropolitan Police.

The Squad mourned the loss of the hard-faced, hard-fisted man in the bowler hat – Peter Beveridge described Sharpe's record as 'amazing' – who, despite his innumerable brawls with London's criminals, never once charged a crook with assaulting him. "No," he said, shaking his head. "That was all part of the game."

CHAPTER 3

Peter Beveridge

It was pretty-well inescapable that Peter Beveridge would become a police officer. His grandfather had been a policeman, his father was one, as were his two uncles, and in 1913 his elder brother joined the police, as well. Beveridge's initial stay with the Flying Squad as a detective inspector (second class) would last only six months; his next, as detective chief inspector was for five years, and although he was head of the Flying Squad, he was also called upon to investigate provincial murders. Yet it was as the Flying Squad's chief that he was deeply admired and best remembered.

*

Peter Henderson Beveridge was born on 26 June 1899 at Largo, Fife and after leaving school at the age of fourteen (where he dreamt of becoming a professional footballer) he worked as a clerk to a company of linen manufacturers.

Well built, standing just half-an-inch under six feet tall and with flaming red hair, he enlisted in the Seaforth Highlanders on 28 July 1917 and saw active service in France. After being wounded, he was demobilised on 17 January 1919 but by now the thought of spending the rest of his life poring over ledgers had begun to pall and he applied for and was accepted into the Metropolitan Police on 29 December 1919. By coincidence, one of his classmates was George 'Jack' Frost, who would quickly join the newly formed Flying Squad; he would later be Beveridge's driver throughout World War Two.

But for now, they went their separate ways: Frost to 'D' Division and Beveridge, sporting his medal ribbons on the left breast of his brand new serge uniform, to Leman Street, in the heart of London's East End. His weekly wage was £3 10s 0d (£3.50) which, thanks to the police strike of 1919 had more than doubled, from the original weekly 32s 6d (£1.63): and as Police Constable 402 'H' (coincidentally, the same divisional number as Wensley had carried), a winter patrol and a detective constable, there he would stay and learn his trade for the next ten years.

Beveridge checked into the police section house, together with ninety-eight other single police constables, and got to work in one of the toughest areas of London. He learnt the hard way – in those days, the only way – to run his beat; either that, or the local tearaways would do it for him. After two such confrontations, his reputation was assured and within months came his first arrest, for the theft of clothing from a goods depot. It provided him with his first commendation – these would total thirty-eight by the end of his career – and the determination to become a detective, just like his hero, Wensley.

Within six months he became a winter patrol and he and his partner demonstrated their ability by 'borrowing' a horse and van and scouring the streets for thieves, sometimes climbing into the back of the van in order to spring out on criminals whilst they were at work. In four months, they had made over fifty arrests and it is unsurprising that with just twelve months' service under his belt, Beveridge was appointed detective constable.

His divisional detective inspector welcomed him into the department and advised him always to wear a hat. Beveridge did – it looked dignified, it commanded respect and when he became a senior officer himself, he strictly enforced the rule. Anybody who didn't wear a hat was provided with one, free of charge – back in the uniform department.

Beveridge covered everything during his thirteen-hour days; he helped arrest gangs of expert shopbreakers and at the other end of the scale, he arrested juvenile offenders and investigated gas meter breakings. He cultivated informants and used them widely, although in so doing he was also compromised by one of them, something that has happened to detectives ever since the formation of the CID in 1878. He learnt the intricacies of Criminal Records Office (whilst giving grateful, silent thanks that like so many of his fellow detectives, he was never posted there) and used it frequently, especially 'Method Index' where the peculiarities and descriptions of criminals were recorded.

He teamed up with fellow 'H' Division officer Ted Greeno and the pair of them waged a private war against the pickpockets of the area. This proved so successful that they were told now to concentrate on the prostitutes who lured half-cut, well paid sailors into alleyways before relieving them of their wallets. This practice was so prolific that during one particular evening in the space of ninety minutes they made five separate arrests.

Promoted to second class detective sergeant on 27 May 1929, Beveridge was posted to Kings Cross Police Station – it was then part of 'G' Division and another very tough area. The following year, he returned to his native Fife and married Margaret, his long-term sweetheart. The name of Caledonian Road was the only thing vaguely Scottish to the young girl who had never been out of Fife before, and the four rooms and the environment into which they moved, must have been a profound shock to her. The following year, their only child, also named Margaret was born.

On 13 June 1932 Beveridge was promoted to first class detective sergeant and posted to 'E' Division – by now, his career was moving very fast and in under two more years, he was again promoted, to second class detective inspector, and posted to the Flying Squad.

*

It is somewhat surprising that Beveridge's first tour on the Squad lasted only six months; nevertheless, he appeared to make a success of it. He was surrounded by some of the best Squad officers – Dan Gooch was the head of the Squad and his old friend, Ted Greeno who had been there for over six years, was a detective sergeant. Alf Dance (who had never really been away from the Squad) was one of the detective inspectors and Claud Baker (posted there one week before Beveridge's arrival) and Henry 'Nobby' Clark, both of whom would serve on the Ghost Squad, were making themselves busy.

As was everybody. *Police Orders* dated 15 October 1934 noted that Beveridge, together with his fellow inspector, Cyril Woodcraft and other officers had shown 'marked skill, courage and determination' in tackling three dangerous mobile criminals, one of whom was armed, and who were actively engaged in country housebreakings. Beveridge had spotted them and their car at a south London garage; following them, with Woodcraft in a separate car, they had carried out 'leap-frog' tailing before finally arresting them on the driveway of a country house near Guildford.

Beveridge took over as detective inspector at Great Marlborough Street and made his presence felt; he notched up commissioner's commendations numbers thirty-one and thirty-two on the same day, the first for the arrest of two men for inflicting grievous bodily harm, the second, following some astute work by a patrolling police constable, resulting in Beveridge clearing up a substantial shopbreaking in Bond Street where a large number of ladies dresses had been stolen. The three men, responsible for the theft and the three men who received the goods were all sent to prison.

"In my estimation," said George Price, some sixty years after the event, "Peter Beveridge was amongst the top coppers of his era." Price, an aid to CID at the time recalled that Beveridge was, "a man well-known to be unapproachable until after 11am, but after that, a good guv'nor."

But a strict one. George Sharp was the wireless operator on the 'C' Division 'Q' Car, call sign '5 Q', a Humber, which had appeared at the 1933 Paris Motor Show, and he remembers reporting to Beveridge every Monday morning, to check the crime map. If there were, for example six extra 'G' flags (representing six larcenies from unattended motor vehicles) that week and no arrests, Sharp recalls, "there was hell to pay!" However, if there were six 'J' flags (representing the arrest of six suspected persons for loitering with intent to commit a felony) this tended to balance matters out and, as Sharp told me, "everything was sweet."

Beveridge later recorded this posting as being, "the happiest time of my career" but within twenty-one months, he was on the move again, back to 'H' Division, this time as first class or divisional detective inspector. He arrived slap-bang in the middle of a tide of political disorder where the police as usual, found themselves right in the middle between the opposing factions.

Sir Oswald Mosley, 6th. Baronet, had formed the British Union of Fascists in the autumn of 1932. A First World War veteran, he had been a Tory, then an Independent and then a Labour MP. Now, he was a Fascist rabble-rouser and had raised a large army of so-called Blackshirts. The public meetings, at which Mosley roared his hatred of the Jews, inevitably degenerated into brawls between his men, Communists and anti-Fascist demonstrators. At Olympia in 1934, anyone in the audience who heckled Mosley was set upon by anything up to twenty Fascists and was manhandled, punched and kicked.

Jack Comer, also known as Jack Spot, had been born in Whitechapel in 1912 and as a very tough Jewish boxer he had built up a reputation as a man not to be crossed; this, in no small part, was due to the fact that he had been running protection rackets throughout the East End, forcing shopkeepers and stallholders to pay an unofficial excise. So although he and Mosley had never met, the 6th. Baronet was about to do Spot the most enormous favour. On 4 October 1936, Mosley organised a march which would take him right through the East End. Six thousand police stood by and within a very short space of time, what became known as 'The Battle of Cable Street' broke out. It was not, in fact, a fight between Fascists and Jews; it was more a fight between the anti-Fascists and the Police. Casualties were many and the damage to the nearby (predominantly Jewish) property was enormous.

Spot immediately capitalised on this and put about the story that during the wild mêlée he had taken a lead-filled chair leg and felled Mosley's enormous bodyguard. He may have been in the vicinity but the story was pure fiction. Nevertheless, it did Spot's reputation as a protector amongst the Jewish community no harm whatsoever.

Following the Cable Street incident, Parliament pushed the Public Order Act, 1936 on to the statute books and this forbade the wearing of quasi-military uniforms at public meetings, the carrying of offensive weapons and provided periods of imprisonment for those convicted of threatening, abusive or insulting behaviour; the latter offence under the provisions of Section 54(13) Metropolitan Police

Act, 1839 had prerviously carried a maximum penalty of just forty shillings.

Beveridge dealt with over 400 arrests arising from the persistent disorder during his stay in the East End and after receiving another commissioner's commendation in a case of larceny, he was transferred back to his beloved 'C' Division, on 10 January 1938; he described it as being, "like going from the jungle to apparent civilization." So Beveridge and Spot did not meet on that, or in fact any other occasion in the East End – that pleasure would be reserved for the West End, nine years later.

*

There was plenty to do. At Vine Street police station his junior detective inspector was Bob Fabian; together they collected a commissioner's commendation each for their work in the case of an abortionist. And when Beveridge was called away from a friend's wedding to return to Vine Street on 24 June 1939, it was because Fabian had dismantled an IRA explosive device close to Piccadilly Circus; it was on Beveridge's recommendation that Fabian was later awarded the King's Police Medal for gallantry. Pausing only to make a significant contribution to the murder investigation of Rose Muriel Atkins in Wimbledon, which would ultimately send George Brain to the gallows, Beveridge now concentrated on a murder case of his own, again assisted by Fabian. This was the murder of Georgina Hoffman, a prostitute who had been stabbed to death; a witness picked out Arthur James Mahoney from the photographic albums at the Yard as having been with Mrs. Hoffman, prior to the murder. The rather pathetic Mr. Mahoney had been an engineer's steward on board ship prior to being conned out of the £6 he had in his possession by his victim. Torn between the desire to reform her and get his money back, he purchased a sheath knife in Brixton, returned to Mrs. Hoffman's flat and during the ensuing row, he stabbed her to death. Sentenced to death, Mahoney was later certified insane and sent to Broadmoor, where he died shortly afterwards.

World War Two broke out, although because of the initial lack of hostile activity, many people dubbed it 'the phoney war'. Meanwhile,

Beveridge had his hands full with crime, particularly with gangsters who were running protection rackets.

The four-year sentence that he had received, courtesy of Ted Greeno on 2 July 1926 for assault and blackmail, had done little to curb Jack 'Dodger' Mullins' lawless ways. Now, he was trying the selfsame tricks on Vine Street's manor, and Beveridge would not tolerate it.

Beveridge met up with Mullins in a pub, fined the shaken bully a large scotch and told him his fortune. He also informed him of the boundaries of Vine Street, so that Mullins would be sure to stay away in future. Although Mullins continued to be a thorn in the side of the authorities for many more years before dying in his seventies, he never again crossed Beveridge.

On 12 February 1940 Beveridge was promoted to detective chief inspector and a week later he was posted as head of the Flying Squad.

*

Just as Beveridge was settling into his new posting, a notorious criminal named Charles J. Sparks, better known as 'Ruby' Sparks, was slipping out of his, namely Dartmoor Prison which was where he had been sent on 10 February 1939 to commence a sentence of five years' penal servitude for burglary. So when Sparks decided to arrange a little private parole, exactly eleven months to the day since he had commenced his sentence, it was to represent a reduction of five months and sixteen days, which was a record at the time. It was by constantly following his companion Lillian Goldstein, who had been born Lillian Rose Kendall some thirty-seven years previously but who was known as 'The Bobbed-haired Bandit', that it was discovered Sparks would be going to the Ritz Cinema, Neasden. Suddenly, the street erupted with police officers and Sparks, who was wearing dark glasses, was seized. A rubber-faced master of disguise, Sparks refused to admit his identity and unsuccessfully attempted to bluff his way out of this undeniably tricky situation.

Sparks had been using Goldstein's address and she was charged with harbouring him. A little later, at the Old Bailey, the Recorder of London, Sir Gerald Dodson, perhaps a little surprisingly sentenced

Sparks to a humane twelve months' hard labour, to run concurrently with his existing sentence. Goldstein was sentenced to six months' hard labour; a sudden change of heart prompted the Recorder to bring her back to court, where he varied her sentence so that she was bound over in her own recognizance for a period of three years – "a leniency she does not deserve," sourly commented Detective Superintendent Alec Bell of C1 Department.

*

Since the Flying Squad was still part of C1 Department (and would continue to be for the next eight years) the detective chief inspectors were expected to carry out investigations into provincial murders, as part of the C1 Murder Squad. Beveridge got his first murder case on 9 July 1940. It was an extraordinary case that due to an injudicious press photograph thrust Beveridge into the police limelight, and it is still referred to today. The offence was brilliantly investigated and the person responsible, who lied and lied throughout, was convicted on purely circumstantial evidence; yet Beveridge received no official recognition for it whatsoever. This is what happened.

Three bodies, those of Mrs. Dorothy Fisher, her daughter Freda and a maid, Charlotte Saunders had been discovered at a cottage at Matfield, near Tonbridge, Kent. All three had been shot at close range with a shotgun and after an examination the pathologist deduced that due to the nearness of the blasts, the murderer must have been known to the victims.

Beveridge made his way to Kent, taking with him his official car and Jack Frost, who was considered to be the best driver on the Squad. This roused the fury of his senior officers, since it was normal for officers on provincial duties to travel by train and then be provided with a car and driver by the Force concerned: they furiously demanded that both car and driver be returned immediately. Beveridge ignored them. He wanted a driver, skilled at working in the blackout and able to drive fast and safely when necessary, and he simply dismissed their rantings. It caused considerable amusement to the tubby detective sergeant, Bert Tansill, who was very experienced and who accompanied him as his bag carrier. Tansill had joined the Metropolitan Police almost fifteen years previously and the year prior to this investigation had been promoted to detective sergeant (first class) and posted to C1 Department.

The Fisher family was a curious set-up. Walter Lawrence and Dorothy Saunders Fisher had lived with their two daughters in Rosslyn Road, Twickenham. Just before the war, they became estranged, both of them took lovers, the eldest daughter, Joan left for India to marry a doctor and the family broke up. Nevertheless, Mr and Mrs Fisher and their respective lovers all remained on good terms and Mrs. Fisher, daughter Freda and the maid, Miss Saunders, (Mrs. Fisher's lover, a Dane named Westergart, lived separately in London) went to live in the cottage at Matfield. Mr. Fisher and his mistress, a widow named Florence Iris Ouida Ransom, who was aged thirty-five, moved into a farm at Piddington, near Bicester, Oxfordshire. Friendly relations were still maintained and Mr. Fisher would often visit his wife and daughter. For the time, it was an extraordinarily liberated way to behave; and to confuse matters even further, the family insisted on using nicknames for each other; thus, Mrs. Fisher was 'Lizzie' or 'Mrs. Kelly', her estranged husband was 'Peter' and the striking looking Mrs. Ransom was known as 'Julie'. Small and slim, she dressed flamboyantly, used a considerable amount of cosmetics, had brightly painted fingernails and a mop of red hair; she was quite unmistakable. Beveridge met her, exchanged a few words with her and then discovered from one of the servants at the farm that Mrs. Ransom had been learning to use the cowman's shotgun and that he had been teaching her to ride a bicycle, albeit with limited success.

Beveridge carefully inspected the scene of the crime. The cottage appeared to have been ransacked and on the floor of the kitchen was a tea tray, surrounded by a quantity of smashed crockery. Beveridge had every fragment collected and pieced together; there had been four cups, saucers and plates on the tray, as though four people were going to be served tea. Could the fourth person have been the murderer, pondered Beveridge. Between the bodies of Mrs. Fisher and Freda, Beveridge found a white hogskin glove – if he could find the person to whom this glove belonged, he felt sure he would have the murderer. A bicycle, identified as belonging to Mrs. Fisher, was found, slightly damaged, close to the scene.

Witnesses were now found who stated that a woman, exactly fitting Mrs. Ransom's description had been seen in and around the vicinity of the cottage on the day of the murders; moreover, the same woman was seen carrying a long, narrow brown paper parcel under her arm, boarding the 4.25pm train to London.

Beveridge now urgently wanted to interview Mrs. Ransom but upon his arrival at the farm, he discovered that Mrs. Ransom had already left for London, taking with her the cow-man's wife, in order to meet Mr. Fisher. It is fairly certain that Beveridge arranged for an intercept to be put on Mr. Fisher's office telephone, since Detective Inspector Black from the Flying Squad was able to keep him informed of the varying times throughout the day when Ransom, the cowman's wife and Mr. Fisher were to meet at a solicitor's office at High Holborn, with one appointment after another being cancelled. But the final appointment at six o'clock was kept, and as she arrived Beveridge stepped forward, politely raised his Homburg and said, "Mrs. Ransom, I believe?" Mrs. Ransom pretended that she had never seen him before and the look of annoyance on her face was perfectly captured in the photograph taken by a Fleet Street photographer. Taking Mrs. Ransom to the Yard, Beveridge blocked publication of the photograph – identification was going to be a key issue in this case, which would have been seriously compromised if the photograph had appeared in a newspaper.

Mrs. Ransom stated that she had not been to the cottage on the day of the murder; in fact, she asserted, she had been at the farm all day and this would be authenticated by the servants. Except that it wasn't. More than that, a statement was taken from the cowman's wife who surprised everybody when she stated that her husband was none other than Mrs. Ransom's brother and that the elderly housekeeper at the farm was Mrs. Ransom's mother. Beveridge questioned Mrs. Ransom on this point; she denied it. She was detained, prior to being taken down to Tonbridge where it was intended to put her up for identification.

Her brother – for so the cowman proved to be – admitted lending her the shotgun the day before the murder and receiving it back the day afterwards. The white glove, which she denied ever seeing before, fitted her perfectly. She was picked out by several witnesses on the identification parade. A doctor found a graze on her knee which could well have been attributed to a fall from a bicycle. The stationmaster at Bicester remembered her boarding a train for London early on the day of the murder and recalled that she was carrying the long, brown paper parcel. All of the connecting train times gelled, a witness stated that on the morning of the murder she was wearing white hogskin gloves and another stated that afterwards, she was not, and Beveridge had little hesitation in charging her with all three murders. One month later, after a three day trial she was found guilty and Mr. Justice Tucker put on the black cap and sentenced her to death. Mrs. Ransom had a history of mental illness; she was reprieved and certified insane.

The stunning photograph of Beveridge raising his hat whilst arresting a murderess was flashed around the world and it made him famous. As a footnote to the story, on 4 March 1948, the *Evening Standard,* under the heading, 'Broadmoor puts on a play' revealed that a production entitled *The Earl and the Girl* had been staged by the inmates of Broadmoor Criminal Lunatic Asylum. The last paragraph read:

> One of the most outstanding performances of the night was given by Daphne Brent. She played the part of a fairground dog trainer's girl friend and did so with an aplomb that would have startled many experienced actors and actresses.

No prizes for guessing that 'Daphne Brent' was the pseudonym of one Florence Iris Ouida Ransom. She was finally released in January 1967, at the age of sixty.

In September 1940 Beveridge had paid a visit to West End Central police station and had gone for a drink to a pub across the road with the local officers, when a parachute mine exploded, destroying his Railton saloon, killing four police constables and injuring twenty-six more at the station. A month later Beveridge lent a team of Flying Squad officers to 'C' Division, to assist the already overworked West

End officers who were dealing with 4,584 reported cases of looting, and they achieved tremendous successes. They also helped in the six-month-long task of tracing and arresting a gang of handbag snatchers, who were taking full advantage of the blackout to ply their trade.

Beveridge was called to the office of the Assistant Commissioner (Crime), Sir Norman Kendall, who told him to concentrate on cracking down on black market offences. Since just about every saleable commodity was on ration, thieves were cornering the market in stolen clothing, petrol coupons and ration cards. Deserters from the armed forces, including those from the Commonwealth were crowding into the capital, bringing firearms with them and becoming organised. Gun crime, as well as smash-and-grabs, robberies and looting were daily occurrences and were steadily rising. Arrests were going up, too; 663 in 1940, rising to 767 in 1941 and 862 in 1942. But the Flying Squad, in spite of their successes, were fighting a losing battle. Nevertheless, under Beveridge's leadership, the Squad fought back; they made impressive inroads into the stolen and forged coupon rackets and when a gunman in the West End threatened Flying Squad officers with his pistol, he was flattened by three of them and was sentenced to two years' hard labour for his pains. When a gang obtained employment for a young woman as a kennel maid at Wembley Dog Track and then tried to persuade her to dope the dogs, the girl took fright and reported them to the Flying Squad. There followed a long series of observations and 'dry-runs' by the gang, with the girl acting as a participating informant before sufficient evidence was gathered and the gang's West End flat at Bryanston Square was raided. One of the gang who was over the wall from prison put up fierce resistance and had to be subdued. The other two came along more peacefully, and the officers also seized boxes containing Corytone, a drug which acts on the nervous system of dogs. Three men were convicted at the Old Bailey of conspiracy to cheat and defraud and the Judge sentenced the jailbreaker to two years' imprisonment, to run consecutively with his existing, albeit interrupted sentence. The other two gang members were sentenced to two years' and nine months' imprisonment, respectively, and Beveridge was commended by the Director of Public Prosecutions and the commissioner.

*

In 1943, Beveridge was called to Barnsley, after a girl had been murdered. A hammer had been used and the striking end had obviously broken off some time previously, judging by the rust, and was missing – as was her fiancée, a young man from a thoroughly decent family. Searching through the coal cellar at his parents' house, Beveridge discovered the missing part of the hammer. The youngster confessed to the murder – he had been jealous of a supposed rival, a jealousy which turned out to be completely unfounded. A young girl, as decent as her boyfriend, had had her life snuffed out and, following a date with the hangman, so was his.

Later that year, in November, Beveridge was off to Yeovil in Somerset to investigate what had originally been thought to be a case of child abandonment. In fact, it turned out to be a child murder and Beveridge sent a deeply unpleasant army sergeant to the gallows.

By August 1944, the excitement which had once gripped Beveridge at the prospect of investigating murder cases had somewhat palled; he had been looking forward to taking his wife and daughter up to Scotland for a well-earned (and much needed) holiday. Instead, he was called to Bedfordshire to assist in the investigation of a murdered man and as his bag carrier he took with him Detective Sergeant Herbert Hannam, known as 'Suits' Hannam, because of his natty attire. Initially, all that was known was that it was the body of a man; the August heat had done its work well in assisting the decomposition of the body. Near the body was the torn-up photograph of a girl – she was traced and stated that she believed that the clothing that the dead man had been wearing had belonged to her cousin, Robert Smith. He had been employed by a firewood merchant and had been friendly with the proprietor's son. Beveridge interviewed the son who stated that he had never been to the area where his friend's body had been found. It took a lot of patient work for Beveridge to prove that he had, and that he had killed Smith following a silly and pointless quarrel. Following a trial for murder at Leicester Assizes, the young man was convicted of manslaughter.

For this, plus the previous two investigations, Beveridge was commended by the commissioner: with the grand total at thirty-eight, these were the last commendations he would receive. But it would not signal the end of his career, which was still ten years away, nor would it be the last killing that he would investigate; not by any manner of means.

*

On New Year's Day, 1945, Beveridge was promoted to detective superintendent and placed in charge of No. 4 District, which covered one quarter of the Metropolitan Police Area in the south-east of the capital. Living, as he did, in Francklyn Gardens, Edgware, in north-east London, this made travelling to and from work very difficult, so when, eight months later, a vacancy appeared for the same job at No. 2 District, his long-term friend, Ted Greeno, who up until then had been a leading light on the Murder Squad, took the reins of No. 4 District and Beveridge slipped gratefully behind the desk at a headquarters far closer to home.

Beveridge had known the self-styled 'Boss of Britain's Underworld', Billy Hill for some time. As head of the Flying Squad he had drunk with Hill and had told him, "It's going to be put on you sooner or later so make the most of it while you can. Because when I feel your collar, you're going to stay nicked for a long time." (Ted Greeno had held a similar conversation with Hill, although he was not nearly so polite.) Nor did politeness feature in the run-up to the Joe Baksi/Bruce Woodcock fight at Harringay Arena on 8 April 1947. Gang warfare, involving Hill, Jack Spot and the White family had reached boiling point and a confrontation was planned between the various combatants and their allies at Harringay on that date. Beveridge was tipped off, together with the information that all of the interested parties had a large number of firearms and other assorted weaponry at their disposal. Beveridge had Spot brought in and very quietly and firmly informed him that he was simply not prepared to tolerate armed gang warfare on the streets of London. Spot was shaken; no one, police officer or otherwise had ever spoken to him like that. Beveridge then repeated the same speech to Hill. The weapons were disposed of and, for a time, peace reigned.

Bruce Woodcock, incidentally, fared less well – Joe Baksi battered him so badly that he was nearly blinded by bone splinters from his smashed jaw; he was put into hospital and out of the ring for eighteen months.

In the 1948 New Year's Honours list, Beveridge received a well-deserved MBE but six weeks later, his pleasure at receiving the award turned sour with the news that a patrolling police constable, named Nathaniel Edgar had been shot dead. PC 807'Y' Edgar, who had joined the Metropolitan Police in 1939 and had volunteered for war-time service with the Royal Navy, had been on an anti-burglary patrol on 13 February in Wade's Hill Road, Southgate. He had stopped a suspected burglar and jotted down the details from his identity card before the man, one Donald George Thomas, who had been a deserter for exactly four months, shot him three times.

Thomas was nowhere to be found; Beveridge discovered that he had run off with one Noreen Winkless, whose husband, Stanley had reported her disappearance three weeks previously. Mr. Winkless provided a photograph of his wife, and following a discussion with the commissioner it was decided to publish photographs of the couple in the press, asking the public for help in tracing them. It paid off. Three days after the murder, Mrs. Connie Smeed who was running a boarding house in Clapham picked up her morning paper and realised that the couple whose photographs were staring out at her were ensconced in her top-floor room.

The fully loaded .33 Luger pistol that was snatched from Thomas' hand as Inspector Moody of 'L' Division and his men – all of them were later awarded the King's Police and Fire Services Medal for gallantry – crashed through the door, was proved to be the murder weapon. More ammunition was found, together with a number of identity cards. Mrs. Winkless who had initially vowed to stand by Thomas but probably decided that he was not quite as attractive as she had first thought, made a statement to police, outlining how Thomas had admitted the shooting of PC Edgar to her. In turn, Thomas stated that he had shot the officer because he thought that as a deserter he would be sent to prison for three years. He was luckier than he knew; Parliament was debating the possible abolition of the death penalty at the time and Thomas, who had originally been sentenced to death by Mr. Justice Hilbery at the Old Bailey on 20 April, had his sentence commuted to one of life imprisonment. The man who in answer to Inspector Moody's question as to whether the gun was loaded had replied, "Yes, full up – and they were all for you," was released from prison in April, 1962.

A two-month enquiry in Bogota, Colombia, with Bert Tansill followed, and then it was one of Tansill's informants who gave Beveridge a lead in the strange case of Stanley Setty, aged forty-six, who had been born in Baghdad with the name of Sulman and who had been working as a car dealer in Warren Street.

He was originally reported as being a missing person at 12.45pm on 5 October 1949 at Albany Street Police Station by his brother in law, Ali Arum Ouri, but since he had last been seen the previous evening, this report not unnaturally, failed to push the local police into a state of frenzied activity. But Tansill told Beveridge that Setty could have been murdered; the informant had said that he had a large amount of money with him when he went missing. Enquiries revealed that this was so – Setty had withdrawn £1,005, in £5 notes from his bank the day before his disappearance, to secure the purchase of a three-and-a-half litre Jaguar which was for sale in Watford.

The days went by. Setty's distraught family offered a reward of £1,000 for information leading to his whereabouts but of 'Honest Stan', as Setty was erroneously known, there was no sign.

Then on 22 October, a headless, legless torso was recovered from the mudflats at Tillingham Marshes, Essex. Fingerprints confirmed it was Setty – he had served a term of imprisonment in 1928 for obtaining credit as an undischarged bankrupt – and the post mortem revealed that he had sustained a number of stab wounds to the chest. Most importantly, the pathologist was certain from the other injuries to the body that it had been dropped from an aeroplane. Enquiries were made at airfields and on 24 October Elstree Aerodrome reported that a man named Hume had hired a plane for £20, which he had paid in £5 notes, on 5 October. He had arrived in a car with two parcels and refusing offers of assistance, had put them on board the plane.

Brian Donald Hume, who had been convicted of false pretences in 1942, was arrested and whilst he admitted hiring the plane, he denied putting parcels on board. He later changed his story, saying that he had been approached by three men who promised him £150 if he hired a plane and disposed of some parcels, by dropping them into the sea.

Traces of blood, the same group as Setty's, was found at Hume's flat. A large stain on the back of a carpet in the flat might have yielded clues, had it not been thoroughly cleaned on 5 October. Also on that date, Hume had paid to have a large carving knife sharpened – now it was blunt. Hume, who was known to have money difficulties, paid a large sum of money into his bank on 5 October. And when items were discovered in the flat, which had been paid for with some of Setty's £5 notes – the investigators had obtained the consecutive serial numbers, M.41039801 to M.41040000 in respect of £200 from the total amount taken from Setty's bank – Hume was charged with murder.

He faced three juries at the Old Bailey; the first had to be discharged, the second failed to agree and when the third was sworn in, the prosecution offered no evidence on the charge of murder and Setty pleaded guilty to being an accessory after the fact. He was sentenced to twelve years' imprisonment.

Released in February 1958, Hume went to the offices of the *Sunday Pictorial* and admitted that he had indeed murdered Setty; none of the investigating team was particularly surprised. In January 1959, he went to Switzerland where during the course of a robbery he killed a Zürich taxi driver and was sentenced to a long period of imprisonment in Regensdorf Penitentiary. In 1975 he was transferred to Broadmoor; he died in 1998.

*

Bert Tansill (now promoted to detective chief inspector) featured again in the case of a double murder: when Beveridge managed to pull out and extinguish burning blood-soaked clothing from a stove, it provided evidence which led to the killer being hanged.

Beveridge's rank was regraded to that of detective chief superintendent and eventually, after serving thirty-five years, one month and three days, his career came to a close, when he retired on age limit. He took with him his 'exemplary' certificate of service, his annual pension of £906 13s 4d and a lot of memories. Within a week he had moved right out of London, to Edinburgh.

He died, aged seventy-seven on 6 January 1977, sadly missed by his family and friends. His old friend Bert Tansill lived on for another twelve years, dying at the age of eighty-one.

Beveridge was a "great name" amongst detectives, said Leonard 'Nipper' Read QPM. In Jack Capstick's words, Peter Beveridge would always be remembered as, "the tough, red-headed Scot who had supreme control of the Flying Squad."

CHAPTER 4

Greeno – Master Detective

During the 1930s and through to the 1950s the press elevated several of the Yard's murder investigators to the status of household names. One of them was a child of the East End; physically, he was very tough, he was fearless, remarkably well informed and completely unorthodox. His name was Ted Greeno.

*

Born in Walthamstow on 14 September 1900, Greeno was the youngest of five children – four boys and a girl, whose ages ranged from three to fourteen – of Charles and Susan Greeno. Charles was a stationer's warehouseman and the Greenos were of Huguenot descent, having been employed as silk weavers, cigar-box makers and shoe makers. Ted Greeno joined the Merchant Marine as soon as he was able and saw out the last month of World War One as a wireless operator on board the ammunition ship, the *SS Rother*. At the end of February 1920 he returned home and went into his brothers' Surrey-based cartage and car-hire business. But the war had whetted his appetite for a life of adventure and although he developed a passion for studying form and betting at racetracks all over England, this alone failed to satisfy his craving for excitement. In fact, it was the racetracks that would be responsible for moulding his future. As young Greeno attended the race meetings with his father, he quickly noticed that the genuine racegoers, the jockeys and trainers were only a small part of the scene. The racetracks were also infested with thieves, racketeers, gangsters and pickpockets. Protection rackets abounded against the bookmakers; in turn, the bookmakers hired thugs to protect them. Violence was endemic. Why, wondered Greeno, didn't the police stop it? With fatalism, born of years of experience, Charles Greeno shrugged his shoulders. "Easier said than done."

Ted Greeno decided to do something about it.

On 10 January 1921 this brawny young pugilist joined the Metropolitan Police. His new employers provided him with warrant No. 111283 and a blue serge uniform to cover his five feet ten inch frame which weighed in at 11st. 6lbs: they decided that the East End of London would be an excellent testing ground for him.

In the 1920s, 'H' Division was probably a daunting prospect for many probationers, although possibly less so for one with Ted Greeno's talents, and it would be his hunting ground - for the next eight-and-a-half years. He was a tough fighter and was hugely disinclined to accept abuse, whether verbal or physical, from anybody. "I've given some villains some awful hidings," he once said; it is not thought that he said it with any sense of contrition. He was also shrewd and supplemented his weekly wage of £3 5s 0d (£3.25) with rewards of £1 or 10s 0d (50 pence) from the Commercial Gas Company for arresting meter thieves and awards ranging from 5s 0d (25 pence) to £1 which often accompanied commissioner's commendations, as well as revenue from horse racing tips. Within nine months of joining the Metropolitan Police, Greeno hung up his uniform for the last time, became a winter patrol and started his career in plain clothes.

On 17 September 1923 Chief Constable Wensley congratulated Greeno upon his appointment to the CID. He had built up an encyclopaedic knowledge of the gangs who infested the racetracks and the pickpockets who frequented them and as a result he was frequently loaned to the Flying Squad. At Epsom racetrack he faced up to Charles 'Darby' Sabini, the head of the Italian Mob and told him and his henchmen to "clear off". They went. John 'Dodger' Mullins (who would later take a significant part in the 1932 Dartmoor mutiny) and Timmy Hayes, two gangsters with a well-founded reputation for mindless violence, were terrorising local publicans. Greeno arrested the pair of them single-handedly for blackmail and saw them sentenced to terms of penal servitude. Greeno attended one race meeting the day before he was about to start his holiday. He spotted a troublesome member of Sabini's gang and told him to leave; the gangster refused. Now this presented a problem for Greeno, because if he arrested the man, it would mean that he would have to take him to court, thereby ruining his holiday; but to back down was unthinkable. Greeno solved the problem with commendable presence of mind. Without another word, he simply raised his large, clenched fist in front of the gang member's face. The thug quickly got the message and, without another word, he left.

On 15 July 1929 Greeno married Jessie Stone, who was five years his junior, at Stepney Registry Office. A son, also named Edward, was born the same year and another, Ronald, was born four years later. From 1928, Greeno had been on permanent loan to the Flying Squad and on 6 August 1929 the Squad was completely reorganised under a detective superintendent of C1 Branch. Greeno was one of forty officers posted to the Squad, where he would remain for eleven years.

Within eight months of joining the Squad as a detective constable, Greeno was promoted to detective sergeant (second class) – and stayed. As the years went by, Greeno worked with the indefatigable Detective Sergeant Bill Salisbury, later, like Greeno to become a highly successful murder investigator and together, they were responsible for smashing scores of international gangs of swindlers and pickpockets, as well as the racetrack gangs. High speed chases in Squad cars resulted in the arrests of smash and grab artists; in one case, Greeno used a substitute Squad car after the future head of the Squad, 'Nutty' Sharpe and his team had spotted three men trying to break into a warehouse. The gang also spotted Sharpe, leapt into a stolen car and roared off. One of Sharpe's sergeants flung his truncheon through the windscreen of the stolen car, to no avail and the gang had such a start on the Squad car that they might have got clean away; except that Greeno, completely oblivious of what had happened was strolling along the road when the stolen car flashed by him. Realising something was amiss – there were not as many black drivers in England as there are today – Greeno stopped and commandeered a passing car, pursued the gang and eventually forced them to stop. When Sharpe arrived in the Squad car, Greeno, following a terrific fight, had subdued one of the gang, and the driver was sitting, terrified in the roadway, waiting to be picked up: the following day, the third gang member was arrested.

*

For many years, it was the practice of CID officers to pay informants out of their own pockets, in order to start them working. This had always been expressly forbidden, even though it was a well-known fact. When Percy Worth MBE, the chief constable of the CID submitted his report outlining the feasibility of what became known as 'The Ghost Squad' to the Assistant Commissioner (Crime), Sir Ronald Howe, in it he stated:

> 'We all know that many informants are helped financially by CID officers without the knowledge of their superior officers...'

The correct way to address matters was for the informant to provide information leading to the arrest and charging of a person or persons responsible for a crime: only then, could he be rewarded from the Yard's informants fund; later, perhaps, an additional reward could be paid from the loss adjusters acting for the losers in the case. However, many informants required funds to kick-start them into life.

In the 1930s, payments from the Fund were less than generous; the standard was 5s 0d (25p) for each piece of information. In his excellent book, *The Ghost Squad*, John Gosling, referring to an informant named 'Stringy', mentioned the practice:

> 'It was cash I could ill-afford – ten bob meant a lot to me in those days and Stringy was keeping me poor. All my beer money was going on him and I couldn't collect from the informants fund until I could make an arrest following one of Stringy's tip-offs.'

Had Gosling been caught doing that, it would have been the end of his brilliant career. Five shillings? Ten bob? So this is what Greeno did.

With a win at the races, Greeno would pull in his informants and from his winnings, he would lavish £25, perhaps £50 on them. It was little wonder they gave him the best jobs. Just how well this unorthodox way of dealing with informants paid off, can best be gleaned from some of the commissioner's commendations that Greeno was awarded during a twelve-month period during the 1930s.

On 31 March 1933, a commendation for a case of stealing and receiving a motor car and conspiracy, and effecting two arrests: six weeks later, another for the arrest of three men for larceny and receiving and two men for loitering to steal from unattended motor cars: and on the same day, for the arrest of four persons loitering and Aliens Order offences: the following day, for the arrest of two men for warehousebreaking.

Ten weeks later, for the arrest of six men for warehousebreaking where he sustained personal injury, and where he was also commended by the Chairman of the County of London Sessions: and on the same day, for detective work in dealing with a number of thieves, followed four months later by another commendation for excellent detective work in dealing with a number of thieves.

On 28 February 1934, as well as being commended by the commissioner for zeal and ability in a difficult case of conspiracy to steal motor cars, he was also awarded the princely sum of £2 and was additionally commended by the chairman of the County of London Sessions. On the same day, he was again commended by the commissioner for 'a heavy case' of housebreaking, larceny and the recovery of stolen property.

The following day, Greeno was promoted to the rank of detective sergeant (first class) and then, astonishingly, just six months later, promoted again, to detective inspector (second class). He paused just long enough to take and pass a special course of instruction before being posted to Deptford on 'M' Division; this posting lasted under three months, but was time enough to identify, trace and arrest a bookmaker for passing forged ten shilling notes and to be commended by the commissioner, before he was back at the Flying Squad on 5 November 1934, running his own team.

When Bob Higgins had gone to the Squad as a newly promoted detective sergeant (second class) ten months previously, he had been on 'Chesty' Corbett's team, but as Corbett was posted to 'N' Division, so Greeno took charge of his old team, which included Higgins.

"Ted Greeno was the Daddy of 'em all," Higgins told me. "His knowledge of East End criminals was unsurpassed. I consider him to be the best detective the Squad ever had. He believed in working hard and playing hard; his idea of playing being horse racing or greyhound racing, and where better to meet informants than at race meetings? Many times I was phoned at home, off duty but ready to go out and assist in the capture of some miscreant. Often in the middle of the night, to go up to the East End and meet up with another officer to act on information obtained by Mr. Greeno."

Often, the 'other officer' would be Detective Sergeant (First Class) Ted Renson, Greeno's right-hand man. On one particular occasion, Greeno had received information at Newmarket which he passed on to Renson. It was that a convicted and violent criminal named George Anthony Smith was planning an armed hold-up at a jeweller's, somewhere near the Strand. After hours of surveillance, Higgins and Renson saw Smith loitering outside a jeweller's in Maiden Lane, which runs parallel to the Strand, at closing time. Pulling up his coat collar and putting on horn-rimmed glasses, Smith went into the shop. The two officers hurried forward and peering through the window they saw Smith robbing the occupants, at gunpoint. Crashing in through the door, Higgins and Renson threw themselves on Smith and during the ensuing struggle the gun went off. Luckily for everybody concerned, the gun had been loaded with blanks. Smith had previously appeared before the courts and had been convicted of burglary whilst armed with a loaded Webley revolver. Perhaps he thought that on this occasion, by having his gun loaded with blanks, it would substantially mitigate his sentence, should he be unlucky enough to be arrested again. It could be he was right. A poor specimen, observed the Judge at the Old Bailey the following February, as he read a report stating that Smith was not physically fit enough to be flogged, and mercifully sentenced him to five years' penal servitude. Higgins and Renson were complimented for their courage by the commissioner, who also made then richer with an award of £2 apiece. The snout who provided the information in the first place got rather more, of course.

"Why was it," I asked Higgins, some sixty years later, "that you didn't include that story in your memoirs, *In the name of the Law?*" Higgins was affronted. "It wasn't my case," he explained. "It was from information supplied by Ted Greeno," adding indignantly, "I'm not a poacher!"

Tailing a pair of burglars brought Greeno to an MP's house in the prestigious Woodcote Road, Wallington, where a short, sharp fight resulted in the burglars receiving three years and eighteen months' imprisonment respectively, and Greeno, his sixty-first commendation.

Thinking that an active team of receivers would never suspect a constable meandering about on his beat, Greeno got Detective Sergeant Harry Stuttard to revert temporarily to the status of uniformed police constable. The ruse worked; the Squad was led to a warehouse containing thousands of pounds worth of stolen cigarettes. The assistant commissioner (crime) was mildly scandalised at the thought of the possibility of bringing the uniform into disrepute; then swallowed his misgivings and ensured that Stuttard notched up his fifteenth commissioner's commendation and Greeno his sixty-fifth.

Greeno was unstoppable, roaring through the underworld, being commended for the arrest of two alien pickpockets, for his ability in a case of warehousebreaking and receiving, the arrest of five aliens for larceny and receiving, and in a case of shopbreaking: in a case of larceny (trick) and conspiracy, he was also commended by the Chairman of Plymouth Quarter Sessions. Promoted to detective inspector (first class) on 25 May 1937, Greeno scarcely drew breath as he was commended in a case of larceny, receiving and conspiracy and also by the magistrate at Old Street Police Court, plus the Trial Judge at the Old Bailey – on the same day, he was also commended for making an arrest in a case of warehousebreaking. Still, he was retained on the Flying Squad – with such a record of successes, any other course of action would rightly have been considered madness.

With the advent of 1938, Greeno was commended in a case of shopbreaking and receiving, then in a case of officebreaking followed by a case of factorybreaking and receiving. These commendations were followed by others, in a difficult case of procuration and in a case of housebreaking and receiving.

Above all, Greeno was renowned as being a hard man, although having a reputation as a tough guy was not without its drawbacks. Whenever Greeno's reputation was challenged, whether it was in a pub, a racetrack or a street market, the matter was settled there and then. Off would come his jacket, a makeshift ring would be hastily formed and the challenger would be taken on and thrashed. At the conclusion of the fight, Greeno and his adversary would shake hands and that was the end of the matter. There was, of course, no question of the challenger being arrested. Greeno's reputation, not only as a hard case but a sport as well, remained unsullied.

*

By 18 November 1938 Greeno had acquired some excellent information concerning a gang of safeblowers. The gang, he had been told, intended to break into a store in Cranbrook Road, Ilford, Essex and blow the safe. At the appointed time, Greeno, together with Detective Sergeant Cyril Green was secreted in the darkness of the store. Outside were more Flying Squad officers, waiting to swoop once Greeno gave the signal. After the officers had spent hours patiently waiting, at 9.15pm the gang broke into the store and made their way to the safe. Greeno waited just long enough for the gang to satisfy the requirements of the Larceny Act, 1916 and then he called out to his colleagues. It was at that point that matters became a little tricky.

The doors through which the Flying Squad had intended to enter became jammed: and now that Greeno had called out to his men, the gang also knew that they were not alone in the office. Mistaking him for the night watchman, the gang leader shouted at the others to, "Do 'im!" It was a classic mistake. Greeno drew his truncheon and went into action. As the figures loomed out of the darkness at him, Greeno hit out with studied ferocity. He accounted for two of the gang; Sergeant Green settled the third. The night air echoed with the sound of wood smashing on skulls, the howls of the safeblowers and the frantic hammering on the door from the Squadmen, who were still trying to gain access. With a final crash, the door flew open, the squad officers fell into the room and one of them put the lights on. Greeno, panting from his exertions, looked around. He later admitted that he was horrified when he saw the three inert bodies on the floor. The whitewashed walls were covered in so much blood that he described the scene as rather like standing in the middle of an enormous jam sandwich. The night duty at Ilford police station were suitably shaken when the Squad officers hauled the blood-spattered gang into the charge room; but it was an ashen-faced Greeno who had to sit down when one gang member was found to be in possession of eight and a half sticks of gelignite and a second was found to have a number of detonators in his pockets. It was a minor miracle that Greeno's thrashing had not caused his and the gang's detonation.

In sentencing James Robertson to three years' penal servitude, John Fairley to five years' penal servitude and James Paynter to be bound over in his own recognizance in the sum of £5 for three years and to be placed on probation, the Justices at Stratford Petty Sessions warmly congratulated Greeno and Green, and after they were each awarded a commissioner's high commendation they were additionally awarded £10 from the Bow Street Police Fund. Presenting the cheques to the two officers, the Magistrate, Sir Rollo Graham-Campbell said:

> "I think there can be no doubt that both officers are deserving of the highest commendation for their courageous action. I am sure they acted in a way in which we expect all Metropolitan Police Officers to act and I congratulate them and wish them all success in their further career in the Force."

It is clear that Sir Rollo intended that his words should act as a catalyst for Greeno and Green to receive well-deserved gallantry awards for their actions; sadly, none was forthcoming.

The case was just one of a long string of safeblowings during 1938; between March and November that year, thirty-six such cases had been reported, and Greeno was hot on the trail of one of the main gangs. Eddie Chapman, George Darry – he was also known as Anthony Latt – and Hugh Anson were just three members of a team of safecrackers who travelled the country blowing safes, often those contained in Odeon cinemas, and making a healthy living from it.

Greeno's elation was short-lived when the gang were arrested in Scotland; taken before Edinburgh High Court, they were inexplicably granted bail for fourteen days in the sum of £150 and neither Greeno nor anybody else of reasonable intelligence was particularly surprised when Chapman & Co. skipped bail and continued to crack open safes all over the country. But thanks to Greeno's persistence, the net was tightening around Chapman's gang, who fled to Jersey. Greeno discovered their whereabouts and the island police raided their hotel; Anson and Darry were arrested and were shipped back to the United Kingdom where Greeno and long prison sentences awaited them. Chapman, meanwhile, escaped – a few days later, he broke into a safe in a club and was arrested; he was sentenced to two years' imprisonment, the maximum allowed by Jersey law.

It was while Chapman was serving his sentence that war was declared, the Germans invaded the Channel Islands and Chapman, ever the opportunist, offered to work for them as a spy. Later, he was parachuted into England where, knowing that Greeno was looking to hang about ten years' penal servitude around his neck, offered to become a double agent, providing, of course, that all of his outstanding crimes were expunged from the record.

The offer was accepted and Chapman was lucky enough to finish the war with a generous bounty, the Iron Cross and most important, escape from Greeno's clutches.

*

"Greeno was one of the best murder investigators the Yard ever had. He was also one of the best thief catchers." A commonplace tribute from a fellow police officer, or perhaps a newspaper reporter, except that these were the words of Billy Hill, the self-proclaimed 'Boss of

Britain's Underworld' who had served terms of imprisonment totalling over twenty-three years. A more conventional accolade came from Bob Higgins who later retired as a detective chief superintendent, after a spell as deputy head of the Flying Squad. "He was a hard taskmaster who expected, and got total loyalty," said Higgins.

Greeno was promoted to detective chief inspector on 9 September 1940. So far, he had collected seventy-seven commissioner's commendations, mainly for catching professional criminals. Now he was going to concentrate his efforts on murder investigations

*

The first did not take long to arrive. On 17 October 1940, Gwendoline Louisa Cox was serving behind the counter at an off-licence in Wood Green when three youngsters staged a hold-up and Miss Cox was shot through the heart. Greeno organised a huge search for the youths, which was carried out in the middle of an air-raid, utilising officers from all over the Division. Four were arrested – one was the getaway driver – and all confessed their various roles in the robbery. Nor was that all. They also admitted robbing a man to whom they had given a lift and, following the killing of Miss Cox, they had gone on to break into an electrical retail shop where they stole a quantity of radios. Greeno was understandably furious when they were convicted of the manslaughter of Miss Cox and even less impressed when two were each sentenced to terms of three years' imprisonment, the other two receiving eighteen months each.

Next, Greeno investigated the murder of the seventy-one-year-old pawnbroker, Leonard Moules, who was discovered at his shop in Shoreditch, having been savagely battered on the head. He lay unconscious in Bethnal Green hospital for eight days before he died. Greeno questioned 300 men from in and around the immediate area, and it was not too long before Samuel Dashworth and George Silverosa were identified, arrested and charged. Each blamed the other and after Mr. Justice Wrottesley sentenced both of them to death, the duo swaggered from the dock, with Silverosa waving to a woman in the public gallery who had called out, "Hard luck, George."

Greeno once said, "In the West End, you could buy anything and see everything and you could get your throat slit more promptly than in a pirate ship on the China Seas." To emphasise his words, February 1942 saw the commencement of a series of gruesome murders. The first was on 9 February when the body of Evelyn Hamilton was discovered in an air-raid shelter in Marylebone. She had been strangled. The following morning, the body of Evelyn Oatley was discovered in a flat in Wardour Street, Soho, appallingly mutilated. Within the week, a third body was found, that of Margaret Lowe. She, too, had been butchered. It was whilst Greeno was making enquires at the scene and the noted pathologist, Sir Bernard Spilsbury was making a preliminary examination of the corpse, that Greeno was informed that a fourth body had been discovered, in Sussex Gardens. This was Doris Jouannet, who had been strangled with a silk stocking just one hour previously and then mutilated.

The murders had occurred on Sunday, Monday, Tuesday and Thursday; why, wondered Greeno, had nothing happened on the Wednesday? But at the same time that Greeno and Spilsbury were at Doris Jouannet's address, another girl was attacked in the street; and this one lived to tell the tale. Moreover, the young airman who had attacked her had dropped the gas mask he was carrying. Inside was service number 525987. It had been allocated to one Gordon Frederick Cummins. He was traced to his billet in St. John's Wood, arrested and, because he had not been connected with the murders, was charged with inflicting grievous bodily harm and remanded in custody at Brixton Prison.

Because some of the victims had been prostitutes, Greeno questioned many of them in the West End – in war-time, there were a lot of them – and eventually, this paid off. He found a girl who had been picked up by a man, between the time that Doris Jouannet had been murdered and the other girl attacked. The man had accompanied her back to her flat, where he had tried to throttle her. The woman fought back and the man had given her some money and fled. Greeno interviewed Cummins in prison, who denied everything and said that he had lost his gas mask on the Thursday evening when it was mistakenly taken by somebody else; therefore, this other man, said Cummins, was the attacker.

At the billet Greeno discovered that entries in the pass book revealed that Cummins had returned long before the murders had been committed; he also discovered that the whole system was a shambles, with other airmen being duped into covering for Cummins. More than that, he discovered property from the murdered women in his possession and a mass of forensic material. Two of the pound notes he had given as appeasement to the woman that he tried to strangle were traced back to him. Best of all was that several of his fingerprints was found in the rooms of Mrs. Lowe and Mrs. Oakley. The evidence was enough for the jury to take just thirty-five minutes to find him guilty and for the Judge, Mr. Justice Asquith, to send Cummins to a rendezvous with the hangman.

During the course of his investigations, Greeno discovered why no woman had been attacked on the Wednesday of that fateful week. That night, Cummins had been on fire picket duty and could not get out.

Three weeks after Cummins' execution on 25 June 1942, Greeno was called to Lewisham, after a little girl had been reported missing. Suspicion fell on one man, who promptly went missing himself. His house, which had already been searched, was searched again. Buried in the cellar was the body of the child, who had been sexually abused and strangled. The suspect returned and confessed everything; he too was hanged.

But it was not all murder. Chief inspectors at the Yard had to deal with all sorts of unusual crimes, including one where pupils at Eton College received a series of obscene letters. Greeno investigated this case with the same thoroughness as he investigated anything else – his investigations led him to Bournemouth where he made an arrest and also seized the offending typewriter that had been used, together with the carbons containing details from the original letters. The Judge at the Old Bailey took a very dim view of this offence; congratulating Greeno for his work, he sentenced the very strange prisoner to three years' imprisonment and Greeno notched up his eightieth commissioner's commendation. Greeno's next case became known as 'The Wigwam Murder', and initially he was unaware of the victim's identity. Halfway through the morning of 7 October 1942, Marine William Moore was crawling across Hankey Common, Surrey during an army exercise when he was horrified to discover a girl's arm sticking out of the mud. Greeno arrived on the scene during the late afternoon and ensured that his bag carrier, Detective Sergeant Fred Hodge (with whom he would score seven out of seven murder investigations) had not neglected to put a bottle of whisky in the murder bag. It was much needed; murder scenes are often inhospitable places and the whisky is a solace. Moreover, it was useful to break down any misgivings that constabulary officers might have mistakenly felt about a smart Londoner arriving to try to teach them their job. The body of the unfortunate victim was in pieces – the skull alone was in thirty-eight sections – and the area was painstakingly sifted for weeks afterwards, gathering up teeth, bone and articles of clothing. There were three army camps in the area, housing English, American and Canadian troops, and Greeno knew that anyone of those tens of thousands of soldiers could have carried out the murder and then simply moved on.

It was discovered that a girl, a highly-sexed vagrant named Joan Pearl Wolfe had been associating with one of the Canadian soldiers, a mixed-race Cree Indian named August Sangret and she had not been seen for some considerable time. Greeno did not want to interview Sangret – at that time, the corpse had not been positively identified and he did not have enough information about the murder – but Sangret had been granted fourteen days' leave and Greeno decided he would have to interview him there and then. Greeno waited until Sangret had spent an unusually long time washing his hands and then commenced the interview. Sangret admitted living with Joan Wolfe in a wigwam he had constructed – another GI had told Sangret to "stop using her like a Goddam Squaw" – but she had vanished on 14 September, perhaps, said Sangret with another soldier. After questioning Sangret for five days, Greeno realised he could not detain him any longer so he released his prime suspect.

But Greeno had managed to piece together how the girl had been chased and killed; a branch that had been found fitted the hole in her skull exactly. There was one other wound unaccounted for – a round hole, right in the top of her skull, almost like the mark of a drill. What could have caused it? As Greeno fitted the pieces of the jigsaw puzzle of murder into place, there came the last clue he had been waiting for. A knife had been pushed down the waste pipe of the shower, behind the guardroom where Greeno had first interviewed Sangret – the same shower room where Sangret had spent an overly long five minutes washing his hands prior to Greeno's interview. The knife point which had been ground down, almost into a curve, fitted the hole in the skull exactly, the knife was positively identified as belonging to Sangret and he was arrested and duly hanged at Wandsworth Prison. Before he died, Sangret admitted killing Joan Wolfe but never said why. Did she want to marry him? Perhaps. Was she pregnant? Possibly, but her remains had deteriorated to such a degree that it was impossible to say. Joan's mother stated that she was riddled with venereal disease; perhaps that was a contributory factor to her early demise. So whilst the *Daily Express* called the investigation, 'the detective achievement of the century', and the Director of Public Prosecutions congratulated Greeno and the commissioner highly commended him, there were still questions that remained unanswered.

Poor dirty, diseased and deeply unhappy Joan Wolfe, a former convent girl who spoke like a duchess had taken to wandering the streets at the age of nineteen and always carried a Bible with her. In a deserted cricket pavilion where she and Sangret had spent many hours, she wrote in pencil on the wall:

'O holy Virgin, in the
midst of all thy glory we
implore thee not to forget
the sorrows of this world
cast a look of pity
upon all those who are
suffering against lifes
difficulties and who cease
not to feel all its
bitterness. Have pity on all

who have been separated
from those they love. Have
pity on the lonely and the
friendless. Pardon the
weakness of all our faith.
Have pity on all those
whom we love. O Holy
Mary show a mothers
compassion towards the
sorrowful to all who
pray and to all who
tremble at lifes
afflictions and give
them all hope and peace.

Could those words have softened Sangret's heart? Probably not. The mixed-race Crees were chosen for service in the Regina Rifles because, as their Brigadier said, they were great fighters, "and sometimes with a streak of the real savage." That was one reason. The second was that Sangret could not have read them in any event; the reason that he had been sent to the camp was to learn how to read and write.

*

On to Greeno's next case; to Halifax this time, on 4 April 1943, after the body of eighty-two-year-old Mark Turner had been found, stuffed in his folding settee. His ration and identity cards were missing and Greeno immediately suspected a deserter. He was right. Mervyn Clare McEwen had conveniently left his Canadian uniform, complete with army number, jammed behind the boiler, and after that it was the long slog of a ten-week manhunt which brought McEwan to Leeds Assizes and execution.

Next, the theft of 5,000,000 clothing coupons: the use of surveillance and informants brought about the undoing of a larcenous army major. The coupons were recovered and the major went to prison for five years.

Iris Miriam Deeley, an attractive WAAF was murdered and robbed on 14 February 1944 at Eltham, South London. This time it took Greeno just one week to trace her killer, after making his normal painstaking enquires. Ernest James Harman Kemp, a gunner in the Royal Artillery and a deeply insecure person, made the mistake once too often of wearing decorations to which he was not entitled. It brought him to Greeno's attention, and he then discovered property belonging to the strangled girl in Kemp's possession; moreover, his shoes fitted exactly the footprints found at the scene of the crime.

Winifred Mary Evans was another WAAF who met an untimely end on 8 November 1944 after she was savagely attacked. It took Greeno no time at all to finger Leading Aircraftsman Arthur Heys for the crime; proving it took a month, after meticulously gathering all the evidence.

Daphne Jean Bacon was just thirteen years of age when she was found dying in a corn field in Suffolk. She had suffered atrocious injuries to her head after she had been battered with a thick stick and as she died she told the detectives that it had been a British soldier who was responsible. There were 300,000 British soldiers in the area but Greeno had them all confined to camp and had them fill in questionnaires as to their movements. At the end of the investigation's second day, the war ended, making the men in the camps even more eager to get out: but all the time the questionnaires were checked and double-checked. Greeno needed to find the stick that had been used for the murder, although it was tactfully pointed out that in Suffolk, *everybody* carried a stick. Greeno never did find the stick, but he found his man. His army camp was just 100 yards from where he left the body of Daphne Bacon.

*

Promotion, long overdue, to detective superintendent arrived on 3 September 1945 and Greeno was posted to No.4 District headquarters. There were to be no more commissioners' commendations; he had bowed out with eighty-six, of which the last four had been for murder investigations. Much of his time was spent behind a desk, dealing with administrative matters and selecting new entrants for the CID, although he still managed to visit the races and at the 1947 Derby, when *Pearl Diver* romped home at 40-1, he collected a cool £5,000.

But Greeno still retained his contacts and they were as reliable as ever. In November 1948, when the snooker champion, Joe Davis had his prized cue stolen at Victoria Railway Station, it was only natural that he should turn to his friend Superintendent Greeno for help. Telling the distraught champion (who was already considering premature retirement) that he would, "have it back in no time," Greeno put out his feelers in the underworld; two days later, Davis and his cue were reunited.

On 10 June 1949, Greeno was appointed MBE, a thoroughly deserved honour, and when he collected his police long service and good conduct medal four years later, they, together with his First World War medals made an attractive collection; one month later, his rank was regraded to detective chief superintendent.

As one of 'The Big Five', Greeno was regarded with awe by his subordinates. He would be seen arriving or leaving the two-storey building that was the District headquarters, situated behind Balham police station in Cavendish Road, in his personal car with his driver. As an aid to CID, Peter Elston would often see him; he had no idea that his first encounter with Greeno would propel him not only into the CID but also to C1 Department at the Yard.

Elston received a tip from an informant that both the perpetrator of a robbery and the proceeds were to be found at a certain address in Brixton. A check with the crime book revealed that there had indeed been a robbery, although the proceeds amounted to no more than a few pounds. However, Balham is not only a considerable distance from Brixton, it was also on a completely different Division; but aids to CID were impetuous and inventive young men in those halcyon days of police work, and Elston and his partner soon found themselves knocking on the door in a block of council flats at Brixton Hill which was as grubby as the occupants were villainous. Entering the bedroom, Elston discovered a suitcase containing £50,000 in a cupboard; which, it transpired was the result of the robbery of a payroll clerk in the north of England. The money and three prisoners who turned up at the flat were transferred to the constabulary dealing with the robbery and a few days later Elston and his partner were told to report to Greeno. "We went to his office, expecting to be congratulated," Elston told me, fifty years later. "However, it turned out to be almost the opposite; we got a dressing down because we had not reported the information to the Flying Squad." Both officers left Greeno's office feeling a little deflated; but matters turned out very well for Elston. A few months later, he appeared on a board for acceptance into the CID; Greeno was a board member and prompted Elston to recount the circumstances of the arrest, the telling of which took up most of the interview. Greeno grinned throughout the narrative, no mention was made of his strict words following the arrest and Elston was the only candidate to pass the board. Posted to the Yard, Elston told me, with masterly understatement, "I must put some of the success down to Ted Greeno's support".

One of the cases with which Greeno was always associated was what became known as 'The Francasal Affaire'. In fact it was not his case, but thanks to his deep knowledge of horse racing, his input into the investigation resulted in the case being cleared-up far quicker than the investigating officer could have hoped for.

A race horse, running as Francasal won the two o'clock Spa Selling Plate at Bath Races on 16 July 1953. Previously, the horse had been unplaced in five of its races and had finished third in a sixth – hence it's odds of 10-1. Thirty minutes before the race began, enormous amounts of cash began to pour in to bookmakers all over England. In turn, the bookmakers attempted to hedge their bets with the bookies at Bath, which would have resulted in the starting price on Francasal being reduced. They would have been successful, had the telephone line of 'the blower' not been severed, not, as had been originally thought by lightning, but by means of an oxy-acetylene cutter. The National Sporting League advised the bookmakers to withhold the £250,000 which represented the punters' winnings, Francasal was proved not to be Francasal at all, but another, far faster horse named Santo Amaro, and the Yard was called in to investigate.

Detective Superintendent Reginald Spooner, (formerly of the wartime MI5 and later to head the Flying Squad) was recalled from holiday to deal with the investigation. In fairness, Greeno would have been a far better man to investigate the case, because he knew the racing world inside out and it was there that his best contacts existed, whereas Spooner knew nothing about racing whatsoever. But as one of 'The Big Five', Greeno was the detective chief superintendent in charge of No. 4 District headquarters and as a detective superintendent Spooner was 'in the frame' on the Murder Squad, so it was he who was selected.

Six months before the event, Greeno had heard that people were trying to open bookmakers' accounts all over England and he guessed, quite rightly, that a large-scale fraud was going to be perpetuated – so when the Francasal fraud came to light, he knew who was responsible. So it was fortuitous that Spooner's assistant was Fred Hodge – the same Fred Hodge who had been Greeno's war time bag carrier. It was Hodge who met up with Greeno, who imparted the information to him, and Hodge, in turn, passed it on to Spooner.

But knowing someone has carried out a crime and proving it are two entirely different matters; and Spooner and his team deserve full credit for carrying out a meticulous and enormously complex two month investigation which resulted, the following February in four men receiving sentences of three years, two years, two years and nine months at the Old Bailey.

The press heralded it as Spooner's finest case – except many thought it was Ted Greeno's case. Perhaps it was a bit of both. It matters little; supporters in both Greeno's and Spooner's camp will badger away at the facts to this day – and ne'er the twain shall meet.

On 3 January 1955 Greeno took control of No.1 District and within a month he was in the thick of it. Martins Bank in St. James was tunnelled into, the safe blown and £20,300 stolen. In fact, it was Detective Superintendent Bert Sparks' case, but Greeno, unable to resist a blown safe, extracted himself from behind his desk and got thoroughly involved. Press photographs taken at the time show Greeno leaving the bank, with a huge grin on his face; Sparks trails along behind, looking less happy. Good, old fashioned coppering paid off – a search of the suspects homes revealed some of the stolen money, whilst their clothing revealed incriminating particles, linking them with the scene of the crime and they went away for seven and ten years.

Although Roger Lane's father referred to Greeno as "Uncle Ted" and Lane grew up believing that Greeno was his great-uncle, this was not the case; in fact, he was a distant relation, Lane's grandfather having married into the Greeno family. But the Lane and Greeno families greatly admired their distinguished relative and he was frequently the topic of conversation, due to his name being mentioned so often in newspaper reports.

Roger Lane recalls Greeno occasionally visiting his grandfather's house in Chadwell Heath when Lane was staying there on holiday with his family. Greeno and Lane's father would discuss racing form at the dining room table, although Lane's mother was less than impressed with the distinguished visitor; this was because Greeno used to tell her son thrilling stories of police derring-do, usually with gruesome embellishments, just prior to bed-time.

Greeno had served thirty-eight years, seven months and twenty-seven days when on 5 September 1959 he retired – or perhaps it would be more correct to say that he *was* retired – not on service, but because of his age, which was fifty-eight. I imagine he was dragged screaming and kicking out of the Police Force, which he loved and to which he devoted most of his adult life. He took his annual pension of £1,805 and from his Croydon home stated that he would devote the rest of his life to his first love, the turf. There was not enough time. He barely had time to draw his state pension before he died, on 30 April 1966. Jessie, his wife, lived on for another twenty years and died at the age of eighty, in February 1986.

Many hardened, vicious criminals must have uttered a sigh of relief at the demise of the man that the crime reporter, Percy Hoskins referred to as, "The Underworld's Public Enemy Number One."

*

Finally, one more anecdote which serves as a fitting tribute to a great detective and a great sportsman: Greeno and the members of his Squad had spotted a gang of international forgers who had just arrived in Harwich from the Hook of Holland. The gang boarded the train for Liverpool Street and as they were followed onto the train by the Flying Squad officers, Greeno gave careful instructions to his Squad driver, PC 383 Bob Edney. As the train slowly pulled out of the station, Edney jumped into the Squad Lagonda and gunned the engine. As the Hook Continental thundered across the Essex countryside, Edney tore past it, covering the seventy-one miles to Liverpool Street Station, in record time, and as the train pulled into the station, Edney was waiting at the barrier. The gang were rounded up, the counterfeiting ring was smashed, sentences of four, two and two years' imprisonment were imposed, and on 29 June 1934, *Police Orders* noted that Greeno was one of two officers to be highly commended by the commissioner – the other was Bill Salisbury – for their initiative, perseverance and ability. Bob Edney did not receive a commissioner's commendation. Instead, he pocketed a £10 note which constituted his winnings after Ted Greeno, unable as ever to resist a bet, had wagered against Bob Edney beating the train to its destination.

CHAPTER 5

Fabian of the Yard

Every now and then, someone enters a profession and becomes successful at it, so successful that by a combination of ability, luck and simply being in the right place at the right time, they become a household name. Such a man was Robert Honey Fabian. Even though over thirty years have passed since his death, he is still known world-wide as 'Fabian of the Yard'. This is how it came about.

*

Born on the last day of January, 1901 in Ladywell, south-east London, Fabian attended an elementary school in Catford and at twelve years of age went to the Borough Polytechnic to train as an engineering draughtsman. He was subsequently employed in a succession of offices as a drawing office clerk and thoroughly disliked the work. It was while he was working at the Royal Arsenal, Woolwich, that he met and was extremely impressed by a police inspector, who was a friend of the family. It was not long before young Fabian was fitted into a suit of the Metropolitan Police's finest blue serge and on 11 July 1921, having been allocated warrant number 111858, he moved in to the Section House at 42 Beak Street, Soho and commenced duty at Vine Street police station on 'C' Division. It was there, for the next eight years, he would serve as Police Constable 118 'C', an aid to CID and a detective constable.

At twenty years of age, Fabian stood just under five feet ten inches tall and weighed 10st. 4lbs. Rapidly concluding that the West End of London was a tougher area than (at that time) the semi-rural Ladywell, Fabian supplemented his rudimentary boxing experience by attending the Polytechnic boxing club on Tuesday and Thursday evenings, plus ju-jitsu classes: whenever his duties permitted, he also played rugby at weekends. His devotion to exercise paid off. His

Fred Wensley

Steinie Morrison on
trial for the murder
of Leon Beron,
1911

Freddie Bywaters (left), Edith Thompson and Percy Thompson, the latter later murdered by the two former

Fred 'Nutty' Sharpe

Vernon and Bertron on trial in Paris for the murder
of Max Kassell

Max Kassell

Kate Meyrick after a visit to Holloway

Peter Beveridge

Beveridge arresting
Mrs Ransom

Jack Spot at the races

Billy Hill outside his lock-up

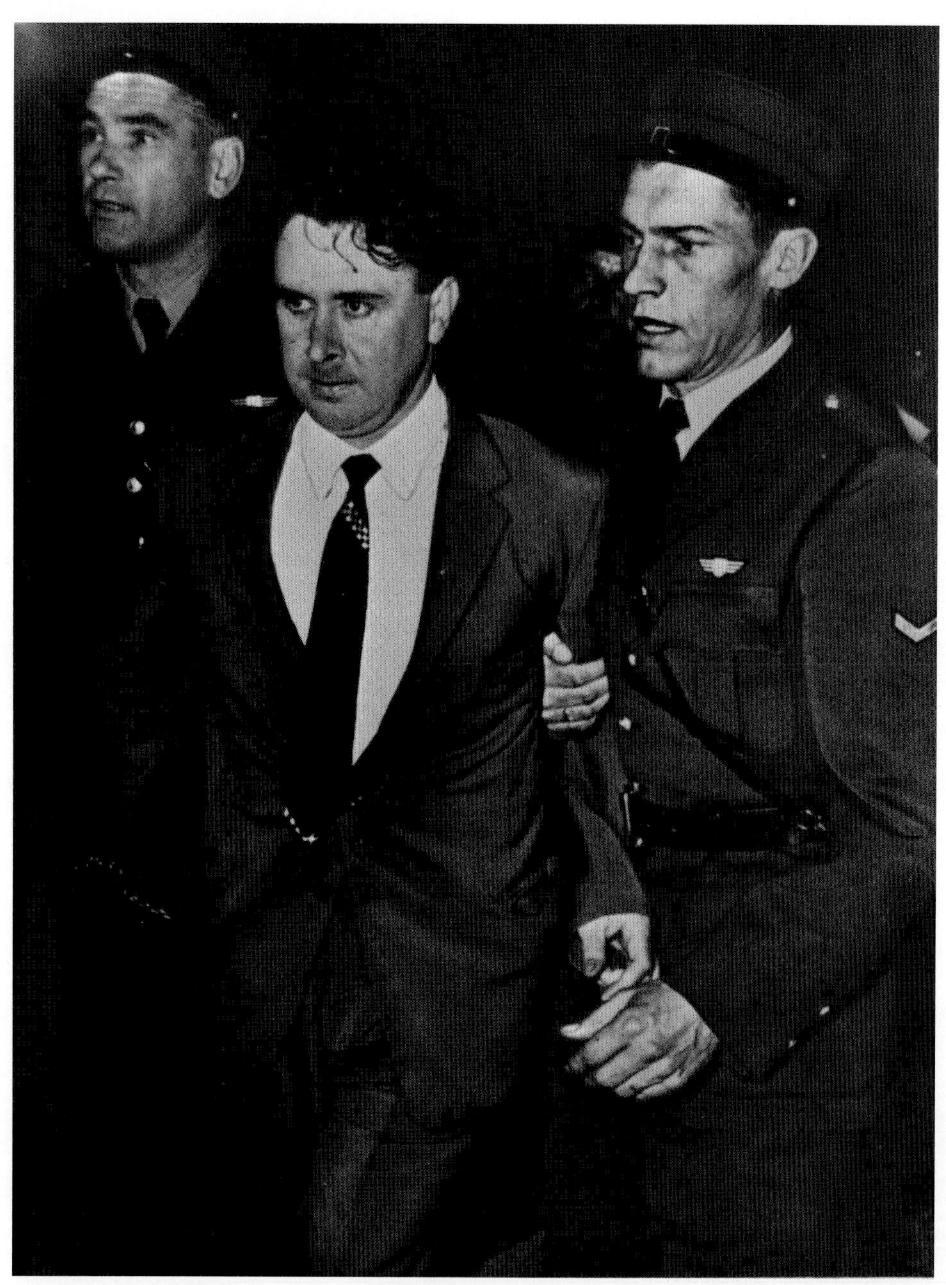

Donald Hume arrested for murder in Switzerland

Ted Greeno, 'Master Detective'

August Sangret,
hanged for the
murder of Joan
Wolfe

Robert Fabian, 'Fabian of the Yard'

Eddie Manning in the dock at Bow Street Court

The murder of
Alec D'Antiquis

James Hynes

Jack Capstick,
'Charlie Artful'

Peter Griffiths, hanged
for the murder of June
Ann Devaney

nie 'Hooter' Millen

Harry Clapham

Alice Wiltshaw

Leslie Green, hanged for the
murder of Alice Wiltshaw

Tommy Butler,
'Mr Flying Squad'

Tommy Butler (right) and Peter Vibart, the 'Terrible Twins'

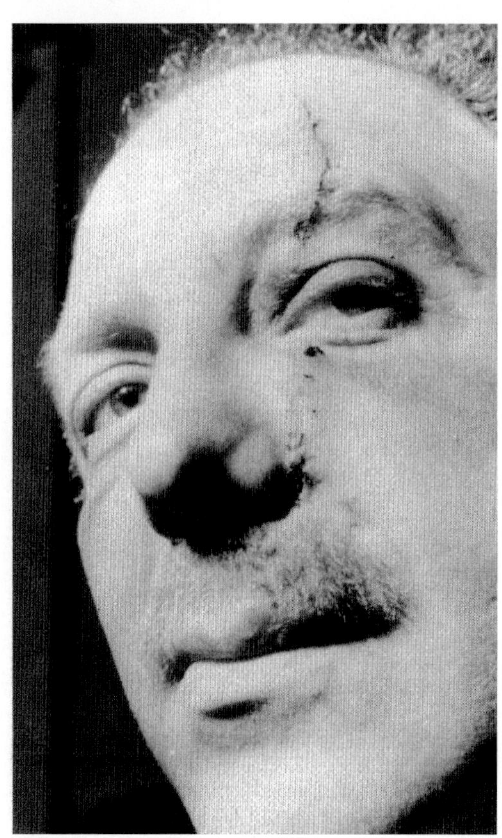

Jack Spot after
the razor attack

Bruce Reynolds

Ian Forbes, 'the Tarland Ploughman'

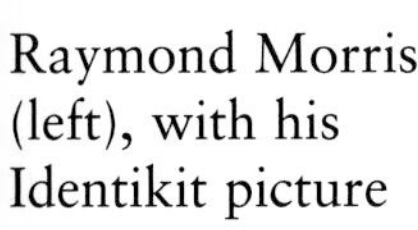

Raymond Morris (left), with his Identikit picture

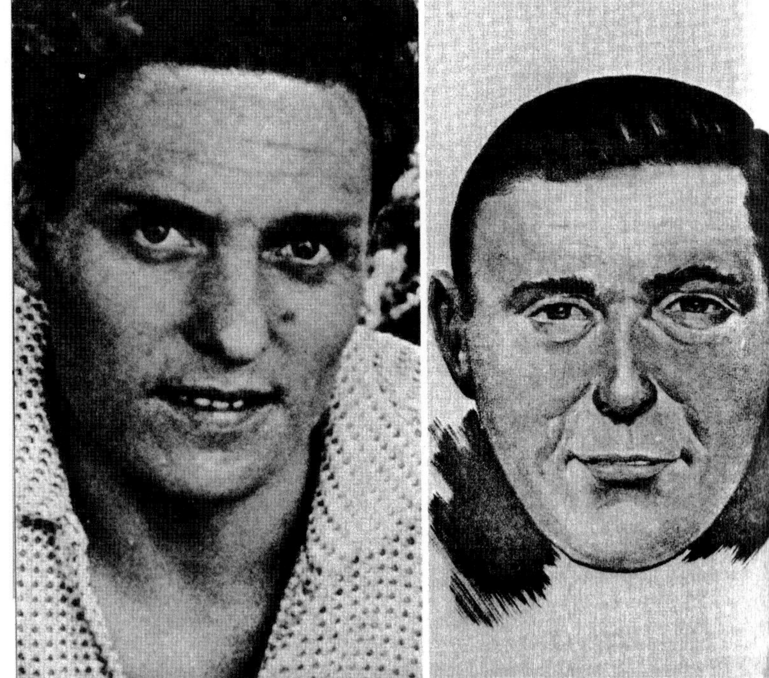

Bert Wickstead, 'the Gangbuster'

Jimmy and 'Rusty' Humphries

shoulders broadened, his chest filled out and he developed a crushing grip. He became a formidable adversary; little wonder that during the course of his career, he was attacked only on three occasions – and those who carried out the assaults, lived to regret them.

His first arrest came when he was off-duty. He was squiring a girl friend, Winifred Stockwell, around the West End when he spotted two young men who were taking a studied interest in unattended motor vehicles. He decided to follow them, and his patience was rewarded when he arrested them for stealing a rug from a car in Sloane Street.

Fabian probably initially regretted mentioning his former trade or calling, because although not withstanding the glow of pleasure he received when he was commended by a Magistrate for the clarity of his plan of a traffic accident which, the Beak stated, "had materially helped clear up proceedings", Fabian was also quickly conscripted into preparing plans in order to assist with raids on illegal drinking clubs. Yet the time he spent in those clubs was turned to his advantage, because it became very useful in identifying the local criminals and getting to know their haunts and associates.

It was as an aid to CID that Fabian enthusiastically threw himself into the cauldron of crime that was known as Soho, where he arrested murderers, burglars, fraudsters and the petty thieves and racketeers of the area. He was quite fearless; when a raid was planned on the Quadrant Club and no obvious means of speedy entrance into the premises could be found, Fabian solved the problem by climbing onto the roof and jumping in through the skylight, oblivious to any dangers which might lie below.

Fabian picked up some interesting information regarding Eddie Manning (also known, with considerable justification as 'Eddie the Villain') who ran a chain of prostitutes and supplied drugs. Manning, whose real name was Freddie Simpson, had arrived in the United Kingdom from Jamaica several years previously and he first came to the notice of the authorities in 1920 when he was sentenced to twenty months' imprisonment for shooting three men in the legs. There was little Fabian could have done on his own with the information he received – he was still an aid and his experience was limited, certainly in dealing with a villain as sophisticated as Manning, but he took his intelligence to the CID. As a result, Manning was arrested in possession of an opium pipe and capsules of cocaine and when it was revealed in court that two girls had died in Manning's flat, one through an overdose of heroin, the other from cocaine poisoning, these facts undoubtedly contributed materially to his sentence of three years' penal servitude.

All the time, Fabian was learning, and discovering the value of informants, upon whom he relied all through his career. As a measure of his success, in just eight years, Fabian was commended by the commissioner on no less than fifteen occasions; by the time he retired, the number would have swollen to forty. It was little wonder that he was appointed detective constable within three years of joining the Force – quick work, indeed. As a new detective constable, Fabian distinguished himself by arresting Robert Augustus Delaney, a persistent cat-burglar who in the space of a few weeks had helped himself to jewellery from the homes of the wealthy in Mayfair's Park Lane, valued at more than £30,000. His first conviction – although certainly not his last – earned Delaney three years' penal servitude at the Old Bailey.

The following year, Fabian married his girl-friend, Winifred on 9 May 1925 and they settled into 138 Harvist Road, in Kilburn; their son, Peter, was born one year later.

During his retirement years, Fabian would fondly recall his times with Scotland Yard's Vice Squad, adding that he eventually rose to become its chief: but this was something of a misnomer. During Fabian's career, the 'Vice Squad' was an *ad hoc* organization, run out of Vine Street police station, not Scotland Yard. Much later the unit became Clubs Office, which operated from West End Central police station. Perhaps Fabian wanted to distance himself from the disgraceful antics of Station Sergeant George Goddard, who was at Vine Street at the time and who came to grief a few years later. But in any event the unit was effective and Fabian from an early part of his career was part of it. The squad developed a great deal of intelligence regarding the prostitutes and pimps who frequented the area, as well as the owners of the illegal clubs and pubs, and the clientele who visited them.

Casimir Micheletti was a violent French pimp, nicknamed 'The Assassin', due to his expertise with a knife, who owned a club known as 'Le Mirage'; his sworn rival was Juan Antonio Castanar, a Spaniard who was credited with introducing the tango to Britain. He owned a Rolls Royce and had a dancing school in Archer Street, which served as a front for acquiring prostitutes, before shipping them out to the Middle East. Each of them had his supporters and one of Castanar's was a Frenchman, named Emile Berthier, otherwise known as 'Mad Emile'.

On Easter Monday, 5 April 1926, Fabian was called to The Cochon Club in Frith Street, where there had been a shooting. The victim was a French pimp, Charles Baladda, also known as 'Charles Bateleur' – 'Charles the Acrobat' – although *bateleur* also means mountebank or buffoon. Whatever the interpretation of his nickname, Baladda, who was playing billiards in the club, was neither sufficiently nimble nor clever enough to evade Berthier, who shot him fatally in the chest. A fellow billiards player cracked Berthier over the head with a cue, but he escaped, bleeding copiously.

Fabian was instructed to make enquiries at the hospitals and railway stations to see if Berthier had gone to the former to have his injuries tended or the latter in order to escape. At Victoria Station he struck lucky; a washroom attendant remembered a bloodied foreigner asking for the next train to Newhaven, and it was on the ferry which left that port for France that Berthier was arrested by Special Branch the following day.

Berthier claimed that whilst he had indeed shot Baladda, it was a case of mistaken identity; he had thought he was shooting Casimir Micheletti, although he denied that this was on Castanar's instructions. At the Old Bailey he was found guilty but insane and was later transferred to France.

There was insufficient evidence to prosecute Micheletti or Castanar for any offence although both of their premises were firebombed and there followed a spate of shootings and stabbings between the two factions. In 1929 both were deported, the former to

France, the latter to Spain. The following year, the men met up in Paris, for the last time. In the Rue Petrograd Micheletti reached for his knife, alas, too slowly; Castanar shot him dead and was sentenced to life imprisonment on Devil's Island, a penitentiary which figured large in Fabian's next case.

Fabian never lost sight of the old adage that a detective 'should give his eyes a treat', so when he spotted an old lag in the foyer of a hotel, hanging around a group of suitcases, he arrested him for the offence of 'loitering with intent' and saw him sentenced to three months' imprisonment. It transpired that the old thief, who was well and truly down on his luck, was none other than the legendary Eddie Guerin, who in 1901, together with his girl-friend, 'Chicago May' Churchill had dynamited the safe of the American Express office in Paris and escaped with $30,000. Guerin was caught on the train to Calais and 'Chicago May' was sentenced to four years' hard labour – Guerin was sentenced to life imprisonment on Devil's Island. In 1905 he was one of the few men to escape from that sun-baked penitentiary alive. Nor were his adventures completely over – when he went to London in 1907, he was spotted by 'Chicago May' and her latest paramour, Charles Smith, who promptly shot and wounded him. Smith was sentenced to penal servitude for life and 'Chicago May' received fifteen years' penal servitude. Since then, Guerin had existed by means of petty thieving and at the time of his arrest by Fabian, he was sixty-eight; he died in poverty, twelve years later.

As his time on 'C' Division drew to a close, Fabian once again distinguished himself by arresting a fraudster who, upon arrival at the police station, drew a loaded gun on Fabian who managed to wrestle it from him; the gunman was sentenced to eleven years' imprisonment.

Fabian's last posting as a detective constable commenced on 3 July 1929. It lasted for eighteen months and he regarded it as the dreariest of his career but he was not alone. A posting to the Yard's Criminal Records Office (CRO) was viewed with dismay by all working detectives. Fabian had passed his examination for detective sergeant (second class) in 1925 – and having failed his first class educational examination in both 1926 and 1927, he now buckled down at CRO and finally passed the exam in 1930. Meanwhile, Fabian, like everybody else, learnt from the posting at CRO. In answering the ever-ringing telephones and also indexing cards, he learnt the way that criminals' minds worked, their *modus operandi*, how their traits, quirks, habits and peculiarities were recorded and how one could make an input into the system and make use of it.

Promotion to detective sergeant (second class) and a posting to 'D' Division's Marylebone Lane coincided on 5 February 1931 and both were highly welcome – escape from the detested CRO and out to practise his detective skills again, plus the additional money from his promotion. The Fabian family moved shortly afterwards to a police flat, situated above Marlborough Street Police Court. On rare family visits to the flat on Sundays, his nephew Paul never saw his uncle; Fabian was fast asleep, having spent the previous evening out, catching criminals.

The skills that Fabian had acquired in CRO came in handy to catch a burglar who had used his experience of amateur theatricals to change his appearance with each offence. What he did not change was his method of carrying out the crimes; Fabian painstakingly put them together, much like a jigsaw puzzle, which resulted in the young thespian asking for over 100 cases to be taken into consideration at the Old Bailey, where he was sentenced to five years' penal servitude. Some clever detective work, coupled with the use of informants resulted in Fabian arresting a man who had carried out an armed robbery at a jeweller's in Oxford Street in 1932. The man, a former member of the Palestine Police, was sentenced to three years' penal servitude and twenty strokes of the birch. Fabian was commended for good detective work in a difficult case of larceny, and when precious stones were stolen from the National Geological Museum, informants were once again utilised, as was surveillance, detective ability, and a little kindness to the family of the man responsible for the break-in. The thief was sentenced to seven months' imprisonment; Fabian was commended by the Recorder at the Old Bailey, a commendation that was echoed by the commissioner on 29 December 1933, making it Fabian's twenty-third.

As his three years service at Marylebone Lane came to an end, Fabian was commended by the commissioner for effecting the arrest of a man wanted by a provincial police force and was awarded the sum of £1 5s 0d. He was again promoted, to detective sergeant (first class) and a posting across the river, to 'M' Division's Kennington Road police station. It was short-lived – just over a year – although in that time, he collected commendations for the arrest of two men for warehousebreaking, a case of larceny and receiving, two violent criminals for receiving and for smashing a gang who were stealing from the railways, plus their receiver, before being posted to C1 Department at the Yard. This posting was even shorter – just eight months later, he was promoted to detective inspector (second class) and posted back to his beloved 'C' Division. It was at about this time that Fabian and his family moved again, this time to a house at Manor Drive North, New Malden, Surrey.

With so many successes to his credit, it is difficult to pin-point the most triumphant time of Fabian's service but it was probably this posting on 'C' Division that was the pinnacle of his career. He was certainly well liked. George Sharp, who at that time was the wireless operator on the local 'Q' Car, call-sign '5Q', recalled, almost seventy years after the event, that when his wife became involved in legal proceedings against Southern Railways at Barnes Railway Station, Fabian immediately introduced Sharp to his legal representative. The prominent King's Counsel acted for George Sharp and his wife at no charge whatsoever.

James Hynes (also known as Willie Goodman) had been a close associate of Jack 'Legs' Diamond; so close, in fact, that when John 'Snake Eyes' Dillinger, then rated 'Public Enemy Number One' by the FBI, ordered Diamond's demise (and very nearly succeeded) Hynes was close enough to absorb four machine gun bullets in the stomach – another associate was not so lucky. After a few weeks recovering from his injuries, Hynes slipped out of hospital, slipped out of New York and with the help of a false passport and an associate named Harry Kleinz, slipped into England. There, Hynes and Kleinz were part of a gang who travelled north to Newcastle where they started tunnelling into a jeweller's. Disturbed by two young police officers, the gang attacked them with iron bars, severely injuring one officer, but the constables nevertheless managed to arrest three of the gang. Hynes was not amongst them. He escaped to London where he was arrested. Taken back to Newcastle, he unsuccessfully tried to escape from the speeding train and both he and Kleinz were sentenced to five years' penal servitude. Hynes was bitter that the rest of the gang had persuaded him to carry out the job without a gun; never, he vowed, would he be so unprepared again.

So when Hynes and two associates broke into the flat, of a millionaire's daughter, he certainly had a gun with him. He was also masked but he could not disguise his pale green eyes, and after he and his companions had fled, taking with them jewellery worth £20,000 and cash in French and English currency to the value of £200, it was the victim's description of those eyes that would lead to his arrest. That, and the fact that he had been heard to complain that English prisons, unlike their American counterparts were so uncivilized, they did not possess Turkish Baths. Fabian assisted a fellow Detective Inspector, Arthur 'Nat' Thorp in the investigation and they had every Turkish Bath in England searched. Hynes was spotted by a Detective Sergeant Barrett in such an establishment in London's East End – not by his eyes, since his face was swathed in towels, but rather by the four holes in his naked stomach – and the gun was recovered from the pocket of his jacket in the cubicle. The officers' enquiries led them from a railway cloakroom ticket to a suitcase which in turn led them to Dublin thence, to a safety deposit box in Liverpool, which had been hired in a false name and address, by Hynes' girl friend, who was arrested when she came to inspect the box, and the jewellery was recovered intact. Charged as an accessory after the fact, she received nine months' imprisonment; Hynes did rather worse, having the misfortune to appear before Mr. Justice Goddard, who sentenced him to twelve years' imprisonment. Hynes gloomily prophesied that he would never emerge from prison alive and he was right; he died in Parkhurst, five years later.

But no sooner were the arrests made in that case, than Fabian was off again, once more dealing with armed robbers. Less than six weeks after the attack on the millionaire's daughter, four men were waiting at the Hyde Park Hotel for the arrival of a jeweller, whom they had duped into turning up carrying jewellery valued at £16,000. The unfortunate man was taken up to the robber's suite, where he was savagely attacked and his jewellery stolen. The four men became known as 'The Mayfair Playboys' and after some smart detective work they were all arrested. The leading toff, Peter Martin Jenkins was sentenced to seven years' penal servitude, which he served in Dartmoor, together with twenty strokes of the cat o'nine tails – the others to a total of almost ten years' imprisonment and penal servitude. Fabian received a commissioner's high commendation – his thirtieth. Other commendations followed, for his work in a case of procuring an abortion and in a case of conspiracy and receiving, but within a year, Fabian's actions would ensure that his name was on everybody's lips.

Just prior to the commencement of hostilities in the Second World War, Londoners received a taste of what was to come. Beginning on 12 January 1939, there was a rash of fifty-nine bombing and incendiary incidents, courtesy of the IRA. The vast majority of these matters were dealt with, then, as now by Special Branch; however, Fabian had one such incident thrust upon him. At ten o'clock in the evening of 24 June, a bomb exploded in Piccadilly Circus. Fabian ran from his office at Vine Street police station – he was, by now, heading the Vice Squad – to the junction of Glasshouse Street and Piccadilly to discover a scene of devastation. Shop fronts had had their windows blown out and their wares scattered all over the pavements. Fabian carefully looked around him and his eyes settled on a brown paper parcel. Slowly unwrapping it and realising it was getting hotter by the second, Fabian discovered ten sticks of gelignite, inserted in one of which was a detonator. Pulling the detonator from the stick of gelignite and putting it in his pocket, Fabian burned his hands on acid contained in a balloon in the parcel; then, to ensure there were no other detonators concealed in any of the other sticks, he took his pocket knife and hacked them to pieces. Because the Fire Brigade, who had just arrived, possessed no fire buckets, Fabian put the pieces of gelignite into cigar boxes blown from a tobacconist's window during the explosion, and conveyed the lot back to Vine Street where he tipped it into a row of fire buckets. His actions were rewarded with a commissioner's high commendation, an award of £15 from the Bow Street Police Court Reward Fund and in the New Year's Honours for 1940, the award of the King's Police Medal for gallantry. It was probably no coincidence whatsoever that one month after the award he was promoted to detective inspector (first class) and posted to C1 Department at the Yard.

So was that Fabian's finest hour? Well, for breathtaking courage there was little to touch it, but his greatest case would take another seven years to arrive.

After a year at the Yard, where he again distinguished himself by being commended by both the commissioner and the Common Serjeant at the Old Bailey for his actions in a difficult case of conspiracy, Fabian was transferred to 'B' Division. At once, he successfully investigated a murder resulting from an abortion, followed by a difficult case of unnatural offences: he was commended by the commissioner in both cases. Next, he busied himself with the investigation of a string of housebreakings and by carefully collating all the information he also cornered five of the gang with the proceeds in a flat and bluffed them into thinking that assistance was on the way; it earned him his thirty-seventh commissioner's commendation. Speaking to me over sixty years after the event, Arthur Stevens recalled being on a board for detective constable on 'B' Division and being astonished when Fabian jocularly remarked to him, "You will meet many temptations – but never admit anything!" It was precisely the type of remark guaranteed to put a nervous applicant at his ease – and it worked.

On 1 January 1945, Fabian was promoted to detective chief inspector and posted to head the Flying Squad, in lieu of his old 'C' Division boss, Peter Beveridge. But as Beveridge had discovered five years previously, this posting would not mean that all of his energies would be directed at the Squad to the exclusion of all else; as a chief inspector, he would be on call as part of C1 to be sent to investigate serious crimes in all parts of the country. In fact, Fabian hardly had time to get behind his desk before he was off to Warwickshire.

The murder of Charles Walton was one of the most baffling and certainly the most exasperating of his career; it was one of the few cases that he failed to clear up. Although Walton was seventy-four years of age and in poor health, he still worked full-time as a hedge cutter. On the morning of 14 February 1945 he set off, carrying his pitchfork and slash hook to attend the hedges bordering the farm belonging to his near neighbour, Alfred Potter. When he failed to return home by six o'clock that evening, his niece, Edith with whom he lived, became concerned and, fearing that due to his rheumatism he might have had a fall, she went to Potter's farm. Potter stated that he had seen Walton cutting his hedge earlier that day, and he and Edith Walton set off in the general direction of where Potter had last seen him. It was Potter who found Walton's body; it was a gruesome sight. The two prongs of Walton's pitchfork had been thrust through his throat with such force that they had impaled him to the ground; signs of the cross had been cut into his face, throat and body and his walking stick had been used to beat him mercilessly around the head. Warwickshire police lost no time in requesting the Yard for assistance, and Fabian set to work. That he was unsuccessful was not through lack of effort. Four thousand statements were taken. Two miles away was a camp containing 1,043 prisoners of war – all of them were interviewed. A prime suspect was found close to the murder scene, hurriedly washing blood out of his coat. He turned out to be a poacher; an analysis of the blood revealed it to be that of a rabbit. But Fabian's biggest problem came in dealing with the local population. The whole area was steeped in a history of witchcraft. An almost identical murder had occurred in 1875 when a youth had killed a woman, thought to be a witch. And a book, written by a local parson in 1930, described how a boy had met a black dog on nine consecutive days and on the final occasion a headless woman in a silk dress had rushed past him. The following day, the boy learnt of his sister's death.

The name of the boy was Charles Walton – same as – the murdered man.

Within a few days of the murder, a black dog was found hanged from a tree, close to the murder scene. As Fabian walked through the villages, doors were slammed in his face. In the end, he simply ran out of clues and returned disenchanted to London, leaving the file on the murder still open. Not that he was completely baffled by it. Just before he died, Fabian mentioned to a crime historian that he believed, as he always had, that Alfred Potter was responsible. Potter died in 1974 and if he was the murderer he took that secret to the grave with him. Witchcraft? No, Fabian thought it was far more mundane than that. Potter had borrowed a large sum of money from Charles Walton and Walton had been demanding that the loan be repaid. It was all a matter of proof, which Fabian simply didn't possess.

Back in the Flying Squad office, Fabian decided that if he was not on call, he would go out and do what he did best; catch criminals. In the autumn of 1945, he participated in an investigation into two men posing as officials from the Russian Embassy, accompanied by his tough aid, Detective Sergeant Arthur Robert Veasey. Nicknamed 'Squeaker' because of his high tenor voice, Veasey had served in the army during the First World War and had joined the Metropolitan Police the year prior to Fabian. The fraudsters had substituted steel ingots for platinum ones in a classic con trick with a greedy businessman as the mug, and earned themselves over £20,000. They also earned themselves three and five years' imprisonment, respectively and for Fabian and Veasey, commendations.

Then it was back to more murder investigations. One such case was the murder of Dagmar Peters whose body was found, minus a yellow string handbag, which had been crocheted for her by her sister-in-law. Fabian asked her to make another identical bag and this was photographed and circulated in *Police Gazette*, which led to the discovery of the original. That, and other painstaking enquiries brought Harold Hagger, a lorry driver with a conviction for attacking a woman, to the gallows.

In fact, the lady responsible for the manufacture of the two bags became the mother-in-law of Ron Goodall who, as a probationary police constable on his CID attachment a few years later, met Fabian in the Sherlock Public House, by the Embankment. He remembers the disparity between his demob suit and Fabian's Savile Row counterpart; but the friendly meeting did his career no harm at all. And by coincidence, years later, as editor of *Police Gazette*, Goodall found the copy which contained the photograph of the reconstructed handbag – a keepsake of a meticulously investigated crime.

The assault on off-duty Police Constable Arthur Collins, attacked by five men who were breaking into a shop, brought Fabian back to Warwickshire, together with Veasey to investigate the case, since PC Collins was so badly injured that it was thought he would die. The only clue was a piece of material, which PC Collins had torn from the lapel of one of the attackers. Fabian discovered that it was cloth from a demob suit, made for returning British soldiers from the war. Identifying first the piece of cloth, then the stitching, and finally the owner of the suit, Fabian saw him sentenced to four years' penal servitude at Northampton Assizes. The other gang members were traced and sentenced, PC Collins eventually recovered from his injuries and Veasey received his thirty-seventh and Fabian his fortieth and final commissioner's commendation.

In the meantime, Fabian settled back into running the Squad. Following the end of the Second World War, the Flying Squad's fleet was in an abysmal condition and urgently needed repair or replacement. The only van used by the Squad was a V8 Ford Tender, which had first been brought into service in February 1934; it now had 97,434 miles on the clock. Fabian went out as a passenger in the van; in his subsequent report in October 1946 to the detective superintendent, he noted that the maximum speed did not exceed 30 mph, the brake drums were oval and huge pressure was required to bring the vehicle to a standstill. He added that the doors, seats and windscreens rattled continuously and that rain leaked in through the roof and windows.

In addition, Fabian reported that a Flying Squad four-and-a-half litre Bentley had chased a criminal's car, of the same make, at speeds of up to 85 mph over a distance of five miles but had finally lost it. When the driver lifted the bonnet of the Bentley, he discovered that one of the twin carburettors was hanging off the engine and was held on only by the petrol pipe.

Fabian's report found its mark. The Minister of Supply promised the commissioner that twenty of the Flying Squad fleet would be replaced within eight weeks; in addition, the Home Secretary authorized an increase of Flying Squad personnel, from fifty-five to eighty-one officers.

In 1947 Fabian moved from the Flying Squad, back to the Central Office of C1 Department. Also on the move at this time was his family, who moved into Bramley Way, Ashtead, Surrey, just north-east of Leatherhead

On 29 April of that year, Bob Fabian was acting detective superintendent in charge of No. 1 District headquarters. As he set off for a late lunch on that Tuesday afternoon just before two o'clock, several miles away three masked men had rushed into Jay's, a jeweller's shop at 73-75 Charlotte Street, W1, vaulted the counter and attacked the director of the company, viciously coshing him with a gun barrel. The seventy-year-old manager threw a wooden stool at the gunmen, one of whom fired, fortunately missing him. The robbers ran outside empty-handed but found that their stolen getaway car had been hemmed in by a lorry and ran off on foot. It was then that Alec d'Antiquis, a motor mechanic who was married with six children, drove around the lorry on his motorcycle. Seeing what was going on, he skidded his machine into the path of the escaping gunmen. Callously, they shot him through the head, and he died shortly afterwards.

Alerted by his deputy, Detective Inspector Bob Higgins, Fabian arrived at the scene. On the face of it, there appeared to be an abundance of clues – the abandoned getaway car, a discarded revolver, the discharged bullets and a large number of witnesses, all of whom wanted to help. The redoubtable Detective Superintendent Fred Cherrill from the Fingerprint Branch arrived but despite a painstaking search no useful marks were found on the revolver or in the shop or the car. Unfortunately, all of the descriptions given by the witnesses were contradictory.

Two days later, the manager of Brook House, a block of flats at 191 Tottenham Court Road reported finding a key in the flats – it fitted the getaway car. A search of the flats was carried out which revealed a raincoat, a cap, gloves and a mask. Inside the seam of the raincoat Fabian discovered a stock ticket, and a check with the manufacturers in Leeds revealed that the coat had been delivered to one of three shops in Central London – enquiries showed that the coat was connected to a villainous family named Jenkins, who lived in the Bermondsey area of South London. Meanwhile, the murder weapon was discovered in the Thames at Wapping. Charles Henry Jenkins, who had been released from Borstal just six days before the murder, was brought in but admitted nothing. A check at the Criminal Records Office revealed that he associated with Terrence John Peter Rolt and Christopher James Geraghty.

It was Geraghty who as the leader of a gang of armed robbers, had carried out two raids in 1945; sentenced to three years' Borstal Training, he had been released after serving half of his sentence. He and Rolt were also arrested, they similarly denied involvement and were later released. Jenkins was put up for identification but when none of the twenty-seven witnesses picked him out, he was also released. A couple of days later, Jenkins was brought in again and was asked for an explanation regarding the raincoat. Jenkins now made a fatal mistake: he told Fabian that the raincoat had been lent to a man named Bill Walsh, just prior to the murder. Walsh could not be found – the homes of his associates were thoroughly searched and in one of them were found two watches which had been stolen during the course of an armed robbery, which had occurred four days before the murder. Walsh was arrested and denied ever borrowing the raincoat. Fabian believed him but pressed him regarding the watches and Walsh eventually admitted taking part in the armed robbery, in company with Geraghty and Jenkins. The robbery, which had taken place at a jeweller's in Queensway, had netted the robbers property valued at £4,500; it had occurred on Jenkins' second day of freedom from Borstal.

It transpired that Walsh had kept all of the stolen jewellery – for revenge, since Jenkins had attempted to frame him for the murder. Geraghty was brought in again and skillfully interrogated – he admitted the robbery and then the attempted robbery at Charlotte Street where d'Antiquis had been murdered, and in doing so he implicated Rolt. Rolt, too was re-arrested and faced with Geraghty's statement, he also confessed and in his statement, implicated Jenkins. In addition, Rolt also admitted that two days before the murder, the three of them had broken into F. Dyke & Co, a gunsmith's in Union Street. It was one of the guns which had been stolen that Geraghty had used to murder d'Antiquis. Now Jenkins was arrested and all three were charged with murder.

Rolt was ordered to be detained at His Majesty's Pleasure, because he was too young to hang. Jenkins and Geraghty were not, and both were executed at Pentonville Prison on 19 September 1947. There is a curious footnote to this deeply disturbing story.

Two years previously, Captain Robert Binney RN tried to stop a car containing a gang who had carried out a smash and grab in the City of London and was killed doing so; the Binney Medal was struck in his memory to be awarded each year to the civilian performing the bravest deed in assisting the police in London. Three men were arrested; Ronald Hedley was sentenced to death, but was later reprieved and sent to penal servitude for life. The second man arrested was Thomas Jenkins, the elder brother of Harry Jenkins and he was sentenced to eight years' imprisonment.

The third man was not charged with the murder. Just prior to being put up for identification, he attacked a police sergeant and, unsurprisingly for those days, received a thorough beating in return, to such an extent that his facial injuries required sticking plaster. He demanded that every other participant on the identification parade should have their faces similarly obscured with sticking plaster and he was not picked out. He was, of course, charged with attacking the police officer and he was sentenced to Borstal Training, which was rather better than being hanged. It was a pyrrhic victory because it only delayed the inevitable.

The name of this third man was Harry Jenkins.

Still Thomas Jenkins did not learn a lesson from his and his brother's misdeeds, because following his release he was part of an armed three-man team who, on 6 February 1953 went to rob a wages clerk. Police arrived on the scene and chased the gang, one of whom produced a revolver and fired three shots at the pursuing police officers. Jenkins was arrested after a struggle and was lucky to receive just five years' imprisonment; two of the police officers were awarded the George Medal.

So the d'Antiquis case was a fitting end to a tremendous career and one for which Fabian received no official recognition. Commendations were not awarded to acting superintendents in 1947.

Fabian finished his career, fittingly, 'at the Yard'. His office was on the third floor of the old Yard building and he was one of several senior detectives at CID Central, under the control of George Hatherill. John Swain (later to be detective chief superintendent of the Flying Squad and awarded the Queen's Police Medal) was a very new detective constable co-opted on to Fabian's team, about a month before he retired. "Morning, young man," said Fabian, as Swain entered his office. Swain viewed Fabian's extended hand with suspicion. He knew about his crushing grip from his own father, who had served with Fabian, so he accepted the handshake, at the same time pressing his middle finger against Fabian's wrist. "Cunning monkey!" laughed Fabian.

Fabian was promoted to detective superintendent on 1 July 1949; he retired two weeks later, having served twenty-eight years and five days with an exemplary certificate of conduct and a pension of £687 per year. He wrote two books – *Fabian of the Yard* and *London After Dark* – and the books gave rise to a series of memoirs on BBC Radio. Shortly afterwards, thirty-nine *Fabian of the Yard* films were produced for television, starring Bruce Seton. The real Fabian appeared in each episode, just to add an encouraging homily to the story-line, but it was rather a wasted exercise; for a man who was such an amusing raconteur, his televised appearances depicted him as a rather wooden-faced individual. Fabian had already featured in a documentary film, *A Routine Job* which dealt with Flying Squad work. He devoted himself to journalism, contributing a weekly column in the *News of the World*, wrote a third book, *The Anatomy of Crime* and later became Chief Security Officer at Thompson House.

He was especially good with children, and his nephew Paul, recalled the looks of pleasure on the faces of the children at his brother's old school in the Old Kent Road, when Fabian came along to present the awards on Prize Day. And his kindness became indelibly imprinted on the memory of Paul De Langhe. Returning with his parents from Belgium to live permanently in England in 1952, young Paul was initially dismayed at the thought of a three-quarter of a mile walk home from the railway station in driving snow. Fortunately, Mr. De Langhe Senior remembered the nearby Malden Manor Public House where he had once worked and where he had met Fabian. Help was enlisted to carry the family's luggage, and seven-year-old Paul's transportation was the shoulder of fifty-one year old Bob Fabian. "It must have rubbed off," he told me, over fifty years later, "because I eventually joined the Met and enjoyed every minute."

Being a household name certainly had its advantages. As a nineteen-year-old police constable at Bow Street in 1960, John Loader was out on his first week's patrol with a more experienced officer to show him the ropes. In Great Queen Street, alongside a very large white building, is a thoroughfare named Wild Street. To Loader's joy, there were a number of illegally parked cars there and he eagerly produced his brand new pocket book, together with his brand new pencil. But as Loader told me, the older officer stopped him. "'See this building?' said the experienced and worldly-wise officer. 'This is Freemasons Hall. See all these cars? These belong to CID men. This car here? That belongs to Fabian. Shall we go somewhere else?' Believe me," said Loader, "I went!"

In 1961 Fabian went to South Africa for a lecture tour which had been sponsored in Johannesburg by the Institute of Race Relations. His nephew, Donald Fabian was at the opening lecture, which was hosted by Mr. Justice Schreiner, the President of the Institute and also Chancellor of the University of the Witwatersrand, and the City Hall was packed to capacity with an audience of 2,000 who were eager for the lecture to commence. Unfortunately, Judge Schreiner spoke for so long in his introduction that the audience became fidgety, then bored: Fabian realised that something fairly dramatic would have to be done. As the Judge droned on and on – the audience by now had stopped rustling their papers and were openly talking amongst themselves – Fabian slipped silently away behind the scenes and went to the opposite end of the stage. Finally, Judge Schreiner's peroration came to an end and flinging out an expectant arm to the left of the stage, he dramatically announced, "And now, I have great pleasure in introducing ex-Superintendent Robert Fabian." In full view of the audience, but unseen by the Judge, Fabian tip-toed on to the stage from the right hand side, tapped the Judge on the shoulder and said in a loud Cockney accent, "Ere I am, mate!" The audience howled with laughter and, as Donald Fabian said, "From then on, he had the audience in the palm of his hand. He spoke without notes for an hour and you could have heard a pin drop."

But retirement did nothing to change Fabian's hard-line views on law and order. Two men who participated in a mutiny at Wandsworth Prison received eighteen and six strokes of the cat o'nine tails on 6 July 1954; three days later, a nineteen-year-old prisoner, serving a sentence of thirty months' imprisonment for robbery with violence at Lewes Prison, received six strokes of the birch for attacking a warder. The cases raised a certain amount of controversy, although not with Fabian, whose views were unequivocal on the matter. Writing in the *Empire News* on 11 July 1954, he stated: "…the 'cat' must stay. And it must be used. It is the only protection prison officers have."

Fabian's toughness was certainly not confined to the written word. It was whilst he was working at Thompson House that he was urgently called to the messenger's room in the basement. There, one of the motorcyclists who had come to collect a delivery was creating a disturbance and terrorising the staff. Old habits die hard. Fabian – he was over sixty years of age by now – grabbed hold of the abusive biker and threw him out of the building. That, he thought was the end of the matter. He made the mistake of turning away and suddenly collected an almighty punch in the face from the biker, which put him in hospital.

Upon hearing the news, one of Fabian's nephews rushed to the hospital and asked the Matron the whereabouts of his uncle. She pointed in the direction of the general ward and smiled. "Just follow the sound of laughter," she replied.

Unfortunately, much of the laughter had gone out of Fabian's marriage and he and Winnie drifted apart. They never divorced and he moved to Ewell in Surrey where he lived with 'Billie', who had been married to the jockey, Steve Donoghue and who was described as 'a charming lady', who sometimes, rather inaccurately, introduced herself as 'Mrs. Fabian'. They were very happy together although Billie decided that a watchful eye had to be kept on her 'spouse'.

This was demonstrated when Steve Engel, a young officer in the mid-1970s was invited to a Rotary meeting in Richmond. There, now in the twilight of his years and surrounded by be-suited Rotarians was the very dapper Fabian. Upon learning that Engel was a police officer and ignoring everybody else, Fabian introduced himself to the young constable, bought him a drink and proceeded to regale him with details of some of his famous cases. Four pints later, the furious Rotarians managed to sit Fabian down to dinner, which was now running an hour late: to add insult to injury, Fabian promptly nodded off. Upon being awoken, Fabian launched into the same stories that he had been recounting to Engel. His account became rather jumbled, interspersed with brief periods of slumber although he did manage to complete the details of one of those cases. Repairing to the bar, Fabian then gained his second wind and was about to delight Engel with a fresh round of stories when Billie walked in, fixed him with a glare and said, rather sharply, "Bob, time to get you home!" With a sigh of resignation, Fabian replied, "Yes, dear," shook hands with Engel and left, without a backward glance at the stunned Rotarians.

Towards the end of his life, Fabian's eyesight started to deteriorate, and he died in Epsom Hospital on 14 June 1978, aged seventy-seven; sadly, his son, Peter died four years later at the early age of fifty-seven from a heart attack, and two years after that Winnie died, too.

Fabian's death, which was proclaimed on newsagents' billboards, saw the end of a vastly popular, immaculately dressed, courageous and able detective, who was nicknamed 'Fun and Games' because of his propensity for playing practical jokes on his colleagues. He was a detective through and through – he knew his job inside out, could run informants, knew how to squeeze the crumbs out of every bit of information and would never give up while lines of enquiry existed. Most of all, he knew how to talk to people and was able to inspire confidence in others to come and tell him what they knew. Fabian was a master murder investigator and young detectives wanted to be just like him; I know I did.

Just a few years before his death, I strolled by the Clockhouse in St. Mary's Lane, Upminster, close to where I used to live, and I saw a poster, stating that 'Fabian of the Yard' would shortly be giving a talk at Romford Town Hall. I didn't attend – I believe I was posted on the late-turn 'Q' Car – but how I've regretted that decision, ever since.

CHAPTER 6

'Charlie Artful'

Cunning used to be a much admired commodity amongst detectives – once upon a time. John Capstick was one of the Yard's top investigators but he looked like nobody's idea of a detective. Short, at five feet nine, with a waistline that expanded until he weighed fifteen stone, he looked more like a gentleman farmer who had strayed up to London for the day to visit his club, with his wavy hair, twinkling eyes, his large bowled-pipe and the inevitable rose in his buttonhole. But appearances can be deceptive; Capstick was a brilliant and a very tough thief-taker who nevertheless inspired confidence in the underworld. He served several tours on the Flying Squad, headed the Ghost Squad and, as head of the Murder Squad, solved many of the Yard's most baffling crimes. Associates called him, 'Jack' or sometimes, 'Cappy'. But to the underworld he was universally known as 'Charley Artful', and what follows, explains why.

*

John Richard Capstick was born into an affluent family in Aintree, Liverpool on 24 August 1903. His father was a dairy farmer, and young Jack was obliged to help out with the milk deliveries – something that was not to his liking. How he must have chuckled to himself when he informed the Metropolitan Police that his previous trade or calling had been that of traveller; it was not entirely true but then again it was not a blatant lie. It did reflect a rather troubled and somewhat rebellious childhood. Deserting the family milk round and wearing a suit stolen from his elder brother, he had run away to sea, serving as a deck boy on board a cattle boat bound for Argentina. It taught him a number of salutary lessons; the first two were toughness and self-reliance. The experience also cured him of his wanderlust but most of all, seeing the flagrant dishonesty of some of the inhabitants of the Argentinean port of Rosario and also of many of his shipmates, he developed a serious dislike for criminals.

He returned to the bosom of his apprehensive family who, after the sale of the dairy business had settled in the prosperous Heswall Road, Aintree. Capstick's anxious mother sought the services of the famous phrenologist, Professor Best, to examine the bumps on his head, in order that some clue could be found as to what the contours on her wayward offspring's cranium might portend. His examination complete, the pompous old charlatan looked up. "Madam," he exclaimed. "Your son will either be a great detective or a great thief!" As far as Capstick was concerned, those words effectively settled his choice of occupation.

Capstick completed his six-week training course for entry into the Metropolitan Police on his twenty-second birthday. His smart new uniform bore the Divisional number 402'E' and Police Constable Capstick, weighing in at ten stone dripping wet, was ready to commence his career at Bow Street police station. It was an inauspicious beginning. His boots, which had cost him the princely sum of thirty shillings (£1.50), were promptly stolen from the locker room. Just as promptly, he put on a pair of shoes and slackened his braces, and for his remaining twelve months in uniform, no-one was any the wiser. Next, he was tricked into an ambush at the very tough area known as Seven Dials. Just off Shorts Gardens was the dingy Neal's Yard, and it was there that four or five members of the feared 'Titanic Mob' handed out a severe thrashing to him, sending him tottering back to Bow Street, minus his helmet, whistle and truncheon. He received little sympathy from his peers – it was commonly accepted that that was how all young coppers were indoctrinated into the real world of policing – but as the eponymous hero of James Hilton's novel, *Goodbye Mr. Chips* said, after a ragging from his unruly class, "It will not happen again, I assure you."

It didn't; Capstick heeded the helpful words of Detective Sergeant (First Class) Jerry Johnson, soon to become a Flying Squad officer (and in Capstick's words, "one of the greatest detectives of all time") and made a friend of 'Johnny Wood' - his truncheon. He quite gratuitously handed out a lot of punishment to those who merited it, and not in the style approved by the recruits' *Instruction Book*, which suggested tapping a recalcitrant subject on the shoulder, arm or leg. Not so Capstick. "I have hit quite a number of ruffians on top of the head, and they have gone over all right," he once wrote, "but the best place to catch a man is right across the ear. That is the place I have always aimed for," adding, "it sounds brutal, I know."(!)

So the young probationary police officer, who had initially been dubbed 'Baby Face' by the local tearaways, began to get a justifiable reputation as a tough character. He had a number of fights with some of the Covent Garden porters who wanted to see how far they could push young constables, and with Capstick, they found out. In so doing, they began to admire and trust him; in the years to come, it would stand him in good stead. He was also acquiring a reputation as a thief-taker. He had been commended by the Bow Street Magistrate, Sir Ronald Graham Campbell for his ability in arresting two men for attempting to break into a shop: this led to his first commissioner's commendation. His next commendation by the same Magistrate, again for the arrest of two men for attempted shopbreaking, made whilst off-duty in company with a friend who had not yet joined the Metropolitan Police, resulted in both of them being taken to the Yard, where they were personally commended by the Commissioner, Brigadier-General Sir William Horwood and also the Chief Constable of the CID, Fred Wensley. Two commissioner's commendations in as many months; a very good omen, indeed. Within one year of joining, Capstick became an aid to CID and had passed his second class Civil Service Examination. His arrests, particularly of pickpockets, soared.

An expert in the arrest of pickpockets was Henry Finbar Corbett, who joined the Metropolitan Police after four and a half-years' service with the Canadian Forces during the First World War. He was known as 'Chesty' because of his enormous physique which he kept honed by daily use of a chest expander and two 56lb weights. His knowledge of pickpockets was so encyclopaedic that he had been accepted on to the Flying Squad, before half of his two-year probationary period as a uniform constable had expired. Now he spent all of his time watching pickpockets at court, following them and their associates and carrying out a lone patrol, often walking immense distances to arrest them, bagging them single-handedly, four, five or six at a time. Capstick's first meeting with Corbett was when he saw him, disguised as a Spanish seaman, waiting by a bus queue: thinking he looked suspicious, Capstick decided to keep an eye on him. Corbett was, in fact, keeping observation on a team of pickpockets and as soon as Capstick was close enough, Corbett muttered, "Get away, you fucking fool. Corbett here!"

A rather more cordial welcome was given by Frank 'Squibs' Dance, whom Capstick spotted in naval uniform. Having followed him for a considerable distance, Capstick suddenly realized that Dance was himself following a suspect and went to ask if he could help. "You're from Bow Street, aren't you?" said Dance. "I'm Dance of the Flying Squad – follow on behind!" So he did, and within a couple of hours, they arrested two men who were caught in the act of breaking into a silk warehouse.

On 17 August 1928, he was appointed detective constable, and whilst his career looked very bright, it was about to receive another tremendous boost.

*

Walter Hambrook had been the first divisional detective inspector of the newly-formed Flying Squad and he was certainly aware of Capstick's growing reputation as a thief catcher. When the Flying Squad was completely reorganized on 6 August 1929, one of Wensley's last actions before retiring one week earlier was to ensure that Hambrook, now promoted to detective chief inspector, headed the Squad. Hambrook wanted a young, capable officer to assist him and he chose Capstick. It was a wonderful opportunity for Capstick and he not unnaturally seized it with both hands. He was not bogged down with mounds of paperwork, he saw how major enquiries were conducted and he was introduced to a number of senior officers. As the first 'Q' Car pulled out of Vine Street police station, it was crewed by Capstick. Every waking hour was spent getting to know the faces of the thieves, the pickpockets and the shoplifters who infested central London, and he was commended for smart work in dealing with two confidence tricksters and also for the arrest of suspected persons.

Promoted to detective sergeant (second class) on 13 September 1933 he was posted to 'D' Division; this clearly did not suit him, and ten weeks later he was posted to 'C' Division. Again, he threw himself into his work and again, it was not too long before he was back, crewing the 'C' Division 'Q' Car, a smart looking Humber, driven by Police Constable Geordie Plaice with George Sharp as the wireless operator. It was later replaced with a very rough looking beige six-cylinder Commer van. As the 20.9hp, fifteen-hundredweight van lumbered through the West End streets, untruthfully stating that it was the property of Oxford Street's prestigious department store, *Bourne & Hollingsworth*, two of the crew, curtained off from the driver, sat in the back of the van and peered out through the one-way glass at the sides and rear of the vehicle. On one particular occasion, the van had been parked up in Compton Street, Soho, and Capstick and Sharp were keeping watch from the back of the van. Suddenly, recalled Sharp, Capstick's head jerked up as he looked out of the rear one-way window. "Hey, George, you see those two coming towards us?" exclaimed Capstick. "Well, one is Izzy Solomon." This was a well-known fence, though the other man was unknown to Capstick. "I wonder what they're up to?" he mused, but did not have to wait long before he found out. The two men suddenly stopped, with their backs to the van, right beside one of the one-way windows. As Capstick and Sharp peered out of the window, Solomon furtively took a small parcel from his pocket, opened it and displayed to his companion a glittering selection of stolen jewellery. The pride on Solomon's face and the admiration of that of his companion lasted as long as it took for the van doors to burst open and unfriendly hands to pull them inside, where they were deprived of both the jewels and their liberty.

Spotting members of the infamous 'Hoxton Mob' at work, Capstick arrested five of them for larceny and for being suspected persons and was commended for it, as he was when he received the rather unusual commendation for 'sustained vigilance resulting in a large number of arrests over a short period.' During the following two weeks, he received two more commendations from the commissioner, for the arrest of six thieves and suspected persons and then the arrest of eleven suspects loitering; six weeks later, there was another for the arrest of ten men for various offences.

In spite of this sustained activity, within one year of his promotion, Capstick passed his first class Civil Service Examination and with only seventeen months in the rank he was promoted to detective sergeant (first class) and posted to the Flying Squad.

*

Capstick arrived at the Flying Squad with impressive credentials: a meteoric rise to first class detective sergeant with under ten years' service, a well deserved reputation as a thief catcher and twenty-six commissioner's commendations to his credit.

All through his career, Capstick met men who would become his mentors and he was generous in his praise of them. Detective Inspector 'Chesty' Corbett, whom he had already met on 'E' Division was there, as was Ted Greeno. Walter Hambrook had moved to another section of C1 Department and Dan Gooch was the head of the Flying Squad. 'Squibs' Dance had already left the Squad, never to return, but his brother Alf who remained on the Squad for twenty-three years and was commended by the commissioner on ninety-two occasions was there, as one of the detective inspectors. Capstick described Alf Dance as being "a natural-born leader of men" and as he went on to achieve greatness in the world of criminal investigation, he freely admitted that almost all of his success stemmed from his association with Dance. Rather than rush in and make an arrest for 'suspected person' when he saw someone up to no good, around a shop or a house, Dance would always wait until the thieves had stolen property in their possession before carrying out an arrest – and sometimes not even act then. He would often defer an arrest until such time as the thieves led Dance to their 'run-in', where even more stolen property might be found, or until they led him to their receiver.

It was Dance who provided Capstick with his nickname. Capstick had spent days tracking down the thieves and receivers of a huge consignment of bales of stolen silk. Dance congratulated him on a job well done and asked Capstick how he had achieved it. Capstick replied that whilst Dance kept his men on duty for fourteen hours a day, he and his men worked eighteen hours a day – including early-closing days. "Hark at him," laughed Dance. "Old Charlie Artful, himself!" The nickname stuck.

The first of Capstick's sons was born when he joined the Squad; the next, two years later and a third in 1942. Not that his wife or young family saw much of him at all. Capstick was roaring through the underworld, being commended for the arrest of three active thieves; two months later, he had ventured to 'J' Division, on the boundaries of the Metropolitan Police District to effect the arrest of an international pickpocket and was commended again: two weeks later he received another commendation for the arrest of three persistent thieves, also being commended for their arrest at Lambeth Police Court.

Capstick teamed up with Ted Greeno, Bob Higgins and others for the tailing and subsequent arrest of a team of burglars in Wallington, Greeno administering the *coup de grace* on one of the struggling suspects by cracking him over the head with his truncheon: the arrest brought them all another commissioner's commendation. Six weeks later, another commendation was awarded for the arrest of 'three cunning aliens, for larceny trick': six weeks after that, yet another was won after days of observation led to the arrest of a gang for the manufacture of counterfeit half-crowns. The coins were very convincing. The gang leader had used the melted-down caps of soda water siphons to provide him with the metal for the coins and in consequence, they were actually worth more than the genuine article.

Three months later, the arrest of four expert criminals for housebreaking, conspiracy, larceny and receiving won him another commissioner's commendation, and now his first tour on the Flying Squad was drawing to a close. On New Year's Eve, 1937 he received his final commendation, in a case of warehousebreaking, incidentally, it would be his last commendation for the next four years.

Promotion to detective inspector (second class) on 2 May 1938 was very welcome; his posting to 'J' Division was not. It was one thing to arrest an international pickpocket there but quite another to make a habit of visiting the place. Capstick kicked up a fuss and lasted there all of two weeks; then he was posted back to his beloved 'E' Division, as Guv'nor at Bow Street.

The Coach and Horses was a market pub in Wellington Street, Covent Garden, and when Morrie Scholman, a very popular local character who served in the pub was murdered in December 1940, everybody wanted to help. Capstick went straight to the market porters whom he had befriended as a young constable and told them what had happened. The description of the gunman that he obtained from them was not very promising; just a man in service uniform, no regiment, or country of origin – and wearing a muffler round his throat. Capstick took the simple expedient of telephoning the provost marshal's office and arranged for every serviceman within a one-mile radius of Bow Street to be brought in. And they were – 200 of them, with Capstick leading the way, from the streets, pubs, clubs and railway stations – with none of them being told why. The servicemen were in a mutinous mood as they overspilled from the cells, charge and waiting rooms and into the exercise yard at Bow Street police station. It was only when Capstick identified the culprit and arrested him in a prostitute's room that he telephoned the staff at Bow Street and gave them the order to open the gates – and then run for their lives!

As the murder trial came to a close, Capstick received a telephone call from his old mentor, Alf Dance at the Yard. The Squad had been told to go all-out to arrest the thieves and black marketeers who were ruining the economy by flooding the market with stolen and forged coupons of every description. Would Capstick return, to lend a hand, asked Dance? Capstick expelled a sigh of relief. "When do we start?" was all he wanted to know. The date was 20 January 1941.

*

Little had changed during Capstick's two-and-a-half year absence from the Flying Squad. Peter Beveridge was now in charge, Alf Dance was there, as always, and Greeno, like Capstick had left, been promoted and returned, as had Bob Higgins. On the day that Capstick had left the Squad, a tall, thin detective constable had moved in. His name was Matt Brinnand and he later teamed up with a giant of a man who had also arrived on the Squad during Capstick's absence. He was Detective Sergeant (Second Class) John Gosling, and the two of them were making themselves extremely busy, making vast inroads into the black marketeers. They would figure prominently in Capstick's life, a little later on.

But now, Capstick, like everybody else had his hands full with his own team of men and his own work. They were working around the clock, meeting informants, keeping observations and smashing gangs of thieves and burglars. In 1942, he was commended for the arrests which resulted from a difficult case of warehousebreaking and receiving; four months later, he broke up a gang of lorry thieves, and their receiver, a very oily gentleman who had eluded capture for a considerable time was now awarded five years' penal servitude for his endeavours; Capstick was commended both by the Trial Judge at the Old Bailey and by the commissioner. The double commendation was repeated the following year in a case of shopbreaking and receiving and then five months later, he won a triple commendation by the Justices at Stratford Petty Sessions, the Trial Judge at the Old Bailey and the commissioner in a case of attempted shopbreaking.

Capstick used an informant to act as a buyer – this was a part of police work at which he was particularly adept – for a colossal amount of stolen cloth. He sent a couple of very large, menacing Squad officers along with the informant to act as his minders (having first ascertained that the villains were not known to the police officers), and the deal was agreed. With only an hour to spare, the informant telephoned Capstick to provide him with the meeting place, and the hastily assembled party of Flying Squad officers crashed into the house at Homerton, front and back simultaneously. There was more than a little gratuitous violence, but the bales of cloth were recovered from the premises as were the other rolls which the gang members, who seldom if ever could resist a little 'creaming-off', had taken to their home addresses. Following a hotly contested trial at Kingston Assizes, the men received sentences of penal servitude and Capstick another commendation.

Capstick had been promoted to divisional detective inspector in 1943 and had been retained on the Squad; now he received his fortieth and final commissioner's commendation for his work in a case of shopbreaking just two weeks after his posting to 'W' Division on 8 January 1945. However welcome this posting might have been, away from the rigours of four very tough wartime years on the Flying Squad, it would last one day short of a year. A revolutionary concept of police work was being hatched which would represent a rather large challenge, and it was advancing in Capstick's direction.

*

With six years of war at an end, Londoners sat back and licked their wounds. During the war, crime – and in particular, violent and sexual offences – had increased dramatically. Whenever spirits and cigarettes were available, they carried heavy customs duty. These, and food supplies, consumer goods and clothing became the target for thieves and receivers. Normally law-abiding men and women stole goods from work, obtained ration coupons using false names and purchased stolen or forged ration coupons. Companies overcharged on Government contracts, accounts were falsified and civil servants were bribed to secure contracts. Desertion from the forces, ration coupon and black market offences became very prevalent. In a fiercely patriotic report, an exasperated chief constable of the CID wrote to the assistant commissioner (crime):

> Black Market offences have been the main cause of the extra work and it is pleasing to see that the <u>sewer rats and traitors</u> who impede the war effort by committing this class of offence are being brought to justice.

But not enough of them were. With rationing still in place – and before long it would substantially increase – the situation was tailor-made for a crime explosion to become inevitable, and so it did; with the Metropolitan Police 4,000 men short, indictable offences for 1945 reached a record level of 128,954. Circumstances dictated that a revolutionary concept be implemented in order to deal with this predicament. Percy Worth MBE, the chief constable of the CID, provided the answer.

Worth suggested that a small group of experienced officers with proven sources of information be detached from ordinary duties to infiltrate gangs of thieves and black marketeers and that sufficient funds be made available to reward the informants. The officers, said Worth, were not to get involved in carrying out the arrests themselves (although, for obvious reasons, it would later become clear that this was not always possible) but to hand the work over to Flying Squad and divisional CID Officers.

Capstick was chosen to lead the team; in turn, he selected Detective Inspector (Second Class) Henry Valentine Clark – he kept quiet about his middle name, and was known always as Henry or 'Nobby' – who was one of the best informed officers in South London and who possessed a punch like the kick of a mule. The third and fourth members of the team were Capstick's Flying Squad contemporaries, John Gosling and Matthew Brinnand. Gosling had served a very tough apprenticeship in east and north London; he had dozens of informants whom he could call upon. They queued up to provide information to the genial giant who would invariably turn a blind eye to the lesser of their misdemeanours. Brinnand had served for years in London's West End; he loathed criminals, especially pimps, but as with Gosling, his informants provided Brinnand with top-class information. The difference was, that informants gave Gosling information because they liked him; with Brinnand they were too terrified of him not to.

On New Years Eve, 1945, Capstick sat in one of the dark, heavy leather armchairs in the Assistant Commissioner (Crime), Sir Ronald Howe's office and puffed contentedly at his pipe, in the way his hero, Wensley used to. He glanced idly round at his surroundings. Howe was there, of course, as was Worth, as well as the three other officers who would make up what would become known as 'The Ghost Squad'.

Ronald Howe surveyed the four men, glanced at Percy Worth and nodded briefly. If anybody could crack the present crime wave, he thought, these four could. Fixing them with his striking grey eyes, Howe leant his slight frame across his desk and addressed them in almost conspiratorial tones, telling them why they were here and what he wanted them to do. They would infiltrate the underworld, he told them, run informants and gather as much information as possible, in order to pass it on either to the Flying Squad or Divisional CID Officers to act upon. They would not get involved in the arrests personally, he said, and added that never would they be required to divulge their sources of information. Howe told them that they would be released from their present duties and, in an unprecedented move, the room allocated to them would come with a key. A car would be provided for them, they would be able to go anywhere at any time and they would not be required to book on or off duty.

A report would be required in six months' time to judge their successes or indeed, the lack of same; but Howe was a believer in sending his troops out on to the field of battle with their heads held high. "This Special Duty Squad has got to succeed," he said forcefully, and as he shook hands with all of them, he added, "I know you won't let me down."

They didn't.

During the three years and nine months of its existence, the Ghost Squad was responsible for 789 arrests, the solving of 1,506 cases and the recovery of stolen property valued at £254,106.

How had these tremendous results come about? The cunning Capstick managed to infiltrate the gangs who worked with receivers of stolen property – men who until now had quite rightly considered themselves to be untouchable by the law – with not one, but a pair of informants. Capstick felt that two informants were more inclined to bolster each other's confidence and courage in gleaning the required information: and whilst there were always some informants who preferred to work alone, he felt that if they could accept his invitation to work with another twice as much work would be obtained from each of them. This system proved to be highly successful, although having the same pair of informants working with two different gangs, based in the same district was discouraged; when it was unavoidable, Capstick would ensure that different Divisions made the arrests. On some occasions, pairs of informants were split up and each introduced to different informants in different districts: then continued to enjoy further successes. Capstick, for all of his experience, never once lost sight of the fact that informants are a dangerous breed and required (as he put it) 'tactful handling'; otherwise, they would be running the officer instead of the officer running them. In walking an unsteady tightrope with informants, he was aware of those who would give police information as a cloak to their own criminal activities: yet the squad was obliged to encourage the informants to associate with thieves up to the border-line when the informants had to think of their own safety and communicate with the squad, as soon as possible.

Capstick recognized the difficulties faced by informants, since the thieves and receivers were playing for such high stakes that they were very careful in whom they confided when they had committed or were contemplating committing an offence. The thieves were highly secretive concerning the location of their run-in, the place where stolen property could be stashed prior to it being disposed of to the receiver, and it was usual for no more than two members of a gang to be aware of the location of the run-in.

But although the Ghost Squad continued to flourish until September 1949, Capstick was not there to see it; on 27 January 1947 he was transferred to other duties in C1 Department.

*

Capstick was promoted to detective chief inspector on 9 June 1947 and was retained at C1 Department; he was now 'in the frame' for the Murder Rota. The first call took him to Wattstown, South Wales after a seventy-six-year-old widow, Mrs. Rachel Allen had been found murdered on 12 October 1947, near to her house in Hillside Terrace. She had been kicked to death, and so ferocious were her injuries that her face was unrecognisable. Who could be responsible for such a dreadful crime? Charley Artful went straight to the village constable and asked him, difficult though it might be, to write down a list of names of people in the village who might conceivably have done such a thing. Unwillingly, the constable agreed; the following morning, he handed a list to Capstick. There were few names on it, but the one that headed the short list was 'Evan Haydn Evans'. When Capstick discovered that Evans had argued with Mrs. Allen in the

Butchers' Arms pub shortly before her death, he paid a visit to him. The young colliery worker admitted that he had drunk about ten pints of beer that night and that he had argued with Mrs. Allen. Capstick took possession of his shoes which had been painstakingly polished and now he asked to see the brand new brown suit which Evans had been wearing in the pub that night and which had been the subject of comment; Evans denied ever possessing such a suit. Capstick later found the suit which had been hidden in the family settee; the bloodstains on it and the seized shoes matched the blood grouping of the victim, and the following February, Evans was hanged for the murder. There was no real motive, save that of a few sharp words, to account for the crime.

Detective Sergeant John Stoneman had accompanied Capstick on that investigation; he did so again when Capstick's investigations took him to Lancashire following the murder of a young boy. The investigation was extended when June Ann Devaney was found murdered in May 1948. June had not yet reached her fourth birthday. She had been abducted from her bed at Queen's Park Hospital and had been bitten, subjected to a violent sexual assault and swung by her feet against a wall. When Capstick looked down at her pathetic body lying in the mud, his iron resolve temporarily left him. It is worth quoting Capstick's words from his autobiography, *Given in Evidence*:

> I stared down at the pitiful form of June Anne Devaney. I am not ashamed to say I saw it through a mist of tears. Years of detective work had hardened me to many terrible things; but this tiny, pathetic body, in its nightdress soaked with blood and mud was something no man could see unmoved, and it haunts me to this day. I swore, standing there in the rain, that I would bring her murderer to justice if I had to devote the rest of my life to the search. I would find him if he hid himself in the bowels of hell.

The best clue appeared to be a winchester bottle, which had been moved from the hospital ward and was found underneath the murdered child's cot; thumb- and fingerprints were found on it. Whilst Capstick and his team launched an enormous enquiry, he also arranged for the entire male population of the area – 123,000 of them – to be fingerprinted.

Almost three months later, fingerprint card No. 46,253 revealed a match with the prints of Peter Griffiths, a twenty-two-year-old former guardsman. His home was kept under observation, and as he left to go to work Griffiths was seized by Capstick and the local officers. He admitted his guilt and his statement was corroborated by a mass of forensic evidence. There was a chilling addition. In Griffith's bedroom was found a piece of paper. On it, he had written:

WARNING

For lo and behold, when the Beast
Looked down upon the face of beauty
It staid its hand from killing
And from that day on
It were as one dead.

The Terror

The defence tried to prove that Griffiths was suffering from schizophrenia at the time of the murder, but after a twenty minute adjournment the jury found him guilty. He was hanged at Walton Prison on 19 November 1948. It was this case more than any other that brought Capstick to the public's attention; and rightly so.

On 1 July 1949 Capstick's rank was regraded to that of detective superintendent; he was, of course, retained on the murder squad and on 28 January 1952 he was sent to York to investigate the murder of seventy-two-year-old Walter Wyld. Capstick soon discovered that Wyld, who had been found stabbed to death in the kitchen of his house in Huntington Road, had been in the habit of lending friends and relatives sums of money. One such person had been John Dand, who had lived near to Wyld and whose alibi was found to be full of holes; the bottom part of his mackintosh and the lower part of his trousers were found to be stained with blood, of the same group as Walter Wyld's. Capstick faced a cross-examination at Leeds Assizes that was so fierce as to be almost unheard of in those days, but it left his reputation intact, and Dand was found guilty of murder. All for the sake of a £3 debt.

When Patricia Cullen, the daughter of a High Court Judge, was found murdered outside the family home, Glen House, Whiteabbey, Northern Ireland on 13 January 1952, it was originally thought that she had been shot in the face at very close range with a shotgun. In fact, as Capstick discovered, she had not; she had been frenziedly stabbed with a knife. A young aircraftsman had been speaking to people about the murder in a way that it was thought that only the perpetrator would have done so. Capstick was convinced of it, and the suspect made a full confession. He was found to be guilty, but insane.

Fifty years later, the Court of Appeal (Criminal Division) decided that he was not guilty and in gratuitously destroying the long-dead Capstick's character, quashed the conviction.

Between 13 April and 1 May 1953, Capstick attended the Police College at Ryton-on-Dunsmore before returning to C1 Department. John Swain, then a detective constable, recalls driving him in those days, usually to take a short statement or clear up a point in one of his cases to ensure that the evidence was completely watertight. He recalls Capstick as being a quiet, deep-thinking man.

Deep thought was certainly needed when farmer John Harries and his wife Phoebe disappeared from their property, Derlwyn Farm, Llanginning, Carmarthenshire. The last time they had been seen by anybody was on 16 October 1953. Anybody, that is, except their nephew, Ronald Harries who stated he had taken them to Carmarthen Railway Station on the morning of 17 October, so that they could start a secret holiday in London: he said that he was to mind their farm whilst they were away.

When no trace of them was found by 6 November, Sir Ronald Howe sent Capstick to investigate. As the express train thundered west, Capstick protected himself against the bitter weather by wrapping up in a travel rug with old rabbitskin slippers on his feet. Quickly changing into more suitable footwear, Capstick commenced his investigation by gaining access to the farm. As the son of a dairy farmer, Capstick knew that no farmer would go on holiday, leaving his cows unmilked – cows that had suddenly reappeared at Cadno Farm, which belonged to Ronald Harries' father. And when he discovered that Phoebe Harries had left an uncooked joint of meat in the oven, he was convinced that both of them had been murdered.

Then there was the question of John Harries' £9 cheque which Ronald Harries had presented at the bank, and which the bank had rejected after they discovered it had been altered to read £909. There was also the fact that it had been ascertained that neither John Harries nor his wife had boarded the London train on the morning of 17 October. When Capstick decided to search the 100 square miles of countryside around the Harries' farm, the one place he did not search was Cadno Farm. Instead, Capstick paid a visit in the dead of night and fastened black thread around all the exits to the farm. In utilising this old Alf Dance trick, he wanted to see if anyone living at the farm was also making nocturnal journeys, perhaps to the scene of a crime. Someone was. Discovering some broken threads led Capstick into a field on the farm where a crop of kale had been recently disturbed, and there he gave his men the order to start digging. Media attention to the whole case had been acute and one of the reporters from the *Daily Mirror* was in the company of Ronald Harries whilst the excavation was underway. He was astonished when Harries blurted out, "People are talking about me and they thinks I battered them." When the bodies were found and examined, it was established that both John and Phoebe Harries had indeed been battered to death. Worse still, it was discovered that Ronald Harries had borrowed a large hammer on the night of the murder and had failed to return it. It was discovered, four days after his arrest, pushed shaft first into the ground at Cadno Farm; it was later established that the indentations on the skulls were caused by that hammer. No one was really surprised when Ronald Harries was hanged for the murder.

*

Capstick was promoted to detective chief superintendent on 3 January 1955 and took charge of the CID personnel in No. 4 Area.

As such, he could have relegated the investigation of murders to the detective chief inspectors and the detective superintendents under his control, and to a certain extent he did. However, as the Guv'nor, he had to be seen to be in charge of major investigations, as he was on 26 February 1955 when the lifeless body of Mrs. Freda Kathleen Carwadine was discovered on Wandsworth Common.

By some clever detective work, Capstick discovered that on the evening prior to her death she had been in the company of a man who claimed that he was employed as a film cameraman and who was traced to a Salvation Army hostel. He admitted killing Mrs. Carwadine by "giving her a good shaking" following a row over bad language: but after the defence showed that the victim was frail and that the slightest pressure could have brought about her death, the man was sentenced to eighteen months' imprisonment for manslaughter.

Right at the end of Capstick's career came the murder of four-year-old Edwina Marguerita Taylor who walked out of her family home in Tudor Road, Upper Norwood on 31 August 1957 – and completely vanished. Capstick immediately got together 100 police officers – including those off duty and Special Constables – and commenced a search of the area. Two weddings had taken place at a church near to Edwina's address at round about the time of her disappearance; working on the assumption that little girls are often attracted to wedding ceremonies, Capstick got the photographers at both weddings to hastily provide prints to see if she – and possibly anybody paying attention to her – was featured in any of the photographs. She was not. Capstick ensured that the widest publicity was given in the national press to the little girl's disappearance, but all of the calls received were fruitless. And all the time, the search continued.

One week after Edwina had gone missing, two aids to CID were routinely searching premises for her and at a house in St. Aubyns Road they asked the occupier if they could take a look in the basement. There they found Edwina's body; she had been strangled. The tenant of the ground floor flat was one Derrick Edwardson, and a check at Criminal Records Office revealed that he had eight previous convictions, including some for indecency. His latest conviction had been obtained five months previously at the Old Bailey, after he had written threats to murder his wife and published an obscene libel, saying that he wanted to entice a little girl aged between five and eight years of age into his flat and indecently assault, rape and kill her. Despite being informed by the medical officer at Brixton Prison that 'there was always a chance that persons of that mentality might implement what they had written', the Judge decided to accept the advice of a probation officer, who disagreed. Placing Edwardson on probation for two years conveniently left the door wide open for him to offend again.

Four days later, Edwardson gave himself up and made a full confession to what is every parent's nightmare. The forensic evidence was overwhelming, and on 25 October 1957 at the Old Bailey, he pleaded guilty to Edwina's murder and was sentenced to life imprisonment.

*

After three years in the post, Capstick retired on 5 January 1958. He had served thirty-two years, four months and thirteen days, and I find it astonishing that no recognition of his work was forthcoming in the Honours List.

His son, who attended his father's retirement party, told me that Capstick told the assembled company, "This is the happiest day of my life": and indeed, he looked forward to a long and happy retirement with his wife Babs at their home in Norwood. He spent his days playing bowls at Norwood Sports Club and cultivating the beautiful roses which habitually adorned his buttonhole. But the strains and stresses of the job which he loved had left their indelible mark on him. His appetite would be reduced to nothing for two or three days at a time during murder investigations, and at night, he would retire to the spare bedroom so that nobody else in the family would have his suffering inflicted upon them. He did not live long enough to collect his State pension and died on 4 June 1968.

John Gosling, his colleague from the Flying Squad and the Ghost Squad said he was, "one of the greatest murder investigators in the

… history of Scotland Yard." His death was a sad loss to the Police Force to whom he had devoted most of his adult life.

CHAPTER 7

'Hooter' Millen

To 'Nipper' Read, he was brusque and rude. Her Majesty's Inspector of Constabulary, Frank Williams hinted that he shielded dishonest CID officers. Tommy Butler had a furious row with him concerning the investigation of the great train robbery. But although he could not have been described as a quintessential Flying Squad officer, when he headed the Squad Ernie Millen was admired and respected by his officers. He was called 'Hooter' either because of his imperious nose or because, disdaining the use of internal telephones or intercoms, he would bellow orders from his office at the Yard.

Millen knew police work inside out. He had time enough to learn it, because he was a constable and a sergeant for the first twenty years of his service; in the nine years that followed, he jumped to the rank of deputy commander of the CID and six years after that, to deputy assistant commissioner. He spent a total of six years on the Flying Squad and became its head; and after his preliminary training as a detective constable, he spent only four months of the remainder of his service on division, thereafter. It's easy to see why; top investigators and, later in his career, great administrators were needed at New Scotland Yard.

*

Ernest George William Millen was born on 24 June 1911 at Westgate on Sea, Kent, and if he had had his way, he would have become a doctor. Like so many other police officers before and after him, financial constraints (his father was a railway worker) precluded any further education necessary to gain the requisite qualifications. But Millen's education at the local Church of England school was certainly good enough and it inspired in him a love of mathematics and science – hence his appointment as an apprentice to Boots the

Chemist where he stayed until he was twenty-three years of age. For several years his father had encouraged him to secure employment that was more stable and financially rewarding, so when young Millen saw an advertisement in one of the national newspapers for applicants for the Metropolitan Police, he applied and was immediately snapped up. Millen was half an inch over six feet with a sturdy build, and the Metropolitan Police was always on the lookout for sportsmen – he had excelled at swimming and boxing and he effortlessly passed the examinations which were set for him at Peel House. On 23 July 1934 Millen was posted to 'B' Division's Gerald Road police station.

Within his first eleven months' service, he made two impressive arrests for housebreaking, and his application to be an aid to CID was promptly accepted. During the next two-and-a-half-years, Millen was an active aid; his first commissioner's commendation was for the arrest of two persistent thieves and the next was for the arrest of three of the same, this time on neighbouring 'F' Division. Best of all was a third commendation, for the arrest of a burglar; in those days, under the Larceny Act 1916, a burglar was one who broke into a dwelling house under cover of darkness, as opposed to nowadays when burglary covers a multitude of breaking and entering offences. It was that arrest probably more than anything else which saw him sail through his selection board to become a detective constable.

On 31 January 1938 Millen was posted to Arbour Square police station, on 'H' Division. He moved from the police section house in Gerald Road to another in Violet Road, Bethnal Green. Nine months later he passed the examination for detective sergeant (second class), passed a course in Criminal Law procedure on 9 August 1939 and was awarded another commissioner's commendation when he arrested a thief who had stolen the gold cup at the Chelsea Flower Show. Millen had been off-duty at the time and had been in the company of his schoolteacher girlfriend, Ena Joyce – the following year, they would marry. They moved into a rented flat in East Ham, which overlooked Plashet Park, and their daughter Jean was born soon after the outbreak of war.

Millen was working hard and learning his trade, fast. A further commissioner's commendation for an arrest for larceny was awarded, followed by another for harbouring a prisoner who had escaped from an internment camp. With just over three-and-a-half-years' service as a divisional detective constable, Millen was posted to C1 Department at the Yard, and there he would stay for the next eight-and-a-half-years – at C1 Department, that is. For the remainder of his service, Millen would spend just four months back on divisional duties.

He came under the supervision of Detective Chief Inspector George Hatherill who at six feet six was a colossus of a man and in addition, a shrewd murder investigator who spoke six languages, including Polish. Hatherill tended to growl at his subordinates and had a stern look, but after a few weeks in the office, Millen summoned up his courage and told him that he felt underemployed. Hatherill smoked silently for a moment – he was a chain-smoker – and looked down at Millen from his great height and nodded slowly. Millen's love of mathematics was about to be put to the test.

*

The Reverend Harry Clapham was portly and bespectacled as well as being very well dressed and shod, surprisingly so given the modest £400 per annum stipend that he received for being the vicar of St. Thomas' Church, Kennington. The sanctimonious Reverend Clapham gratefully accepted donations from his parishioners over a period of fifteen years, which totalled £117,000. Just one percent went to the poor; the rest to a far more deserving cause – himself. His series of expensive cars, his holidays on the continent and cruises in the West Indies eventually became the subject of comment amongst the members of the Charity Organisation Society, but Clapham steadfastly refused to show them his accounts. Millen took a close look at Clapham's activities and was able to prove conclusively one small case of obtaining money by false pretences; that was all that was needed for him to gain access to Clapham's account books. What Millen found staggered him. Clapham had dozens of bank and building society accounts in London alone; with the others, dotted all around the country, they totalled ninety-seven; this was in addition to his nine houses. Money had been donated from all over the country,

Clapham had cooked his books to perfection and Millen had to call in the services of an accountant to assist in unravelling the fraud. After six months work, Clapham appeared at the Old Bailey before the Recorder of London, Sir Gerald Dodson, facing twenty-one charges of fraudulent conversion and falsification of accounts, charges which he strenuously denied. Found guilty of every offence after a three-week trial, Clapham was sentenced to three years' penal servitude and was unfrocked: following his release from Parkhurst, he moved to Canada, where he died, aged sixty. Millen was commended by the Director of Public Prosecutions and then by the commissioner. But more than that, Millen had learnt a valuable lesson. He undertook a course in accountancy and banking, something that would stand him in good stead later in his career.

All the time, his expertise was growing. He received two more commissioner's commendations for dealing with cases of procuring abortions – his training at Boots the Chemists helped considerably – and another two, both for his work in cases of conspiracy to defraud. On 3 June 1946, after twelve years' service, he was promoted to detective sergeant (second class) and was retained at C1 Department.

Shortly after his promotion, he was co-opted onto the newly-formed City and Metropolitan Fraud Squad and was sent to Australia, accompanying Detective Chief Inspector Wilfred Daws (known as 'Flaps' because of his protruding ears) to investigate the activities of Claude Albo de Bernales, who had masterminded a goldmine fraud involving £9 million. After seven months' work, statements and exhibits weighing one-and-a-half hundredweight and containing an cast-iron prosecution case were brought back to England. A number of highly respected (and doubtless very well paid) doctors and specialists testified that de Bernales was too ill to stand trial, and the following year Millen gave evidence of the case at the House of Commons. No prosecution was ever brought against de Bernales who gamely managed to battle on, in the face of his debilitating illnesses, right up to his death, aged eighty-seven, in December 1963. He had managed to live a full, and certainly a rewarding life

*

Millen was sent to Lancashire to assist in Jack Capstick's investigation into the brutal murder of little June Ann Devaney; he later wrote down Peter Griffith's confession to the crime. There was a curious incident when Millen had been accompanying Griffiths from prison to court. Griffiths had asked for a glass of water, and a local officer poured water from an earthenware jug into a glass. As he passed it to Griffiths, Millen inexplicably and suddenly leaned forward and knocked it from his hand, and the glass fell to the floor and smashed. "Let him drink it from the jug," growled Millen to the astonished officer: but Griffiths later admitted to Millen that he had intended to crunch the glass with his teeth and swallow it.

Millen learnt to his dismay that he would have to give evidence against Griffiths on the same day that the examinations for detective sergeant (first class) were being held – there was no way on earth that he could possibly sit the exam on time. Telephone calls were made and a special dispensation granted, so that Millen could sit (and subsequently pass) the examination in Lancaster Town Hall under the supervision of an invigilator.

Millen received a belated Christmas present on 28 December 1948 with his twelfth commissioner's commendation for 'excellent work' in the investigation but this was a busy period for Millen and his services were much in demand.

On the evening of 4 October 1948, the news vendors were shouting that an enquiry had been undertaken by the Yard which threatened to bring down the Government. Seven months previously, in what became known as the Lynskey Tribunal, Viscount Jowett, the Lord Chancellor, had asked the Yard to investigate a number of serious and potentially damaging allegations. The man appointed to head the enquiry was Detective Superintendent Arthur 'Nat' Thorp, the head of the Fraud Squad, who had relinquished a promising career as a boxer after becoming a CID officer in 1925.

The enquiry was an enormously complex one. Sidney Stanley – otherwise known as Solomon Kohsyzcky (or perhaps Solomon Wulken) – had arrived in the United Kingdom, at the age of twelve from his native Poland and from an early age had poked his finger into a number of lucrative pies. The proprietor of Sherman's Football

Pools complained that a cheque for £27,000 which Stanley had given him had been stopped by the bank, on the grounds that it was stolen. Then the director of a woman's clothing store stated that Stanley had offered to bribe Board of Trade officials in order to acquire trade permits. And then Harold Wilson, at that time President of the Board of Trade reported that attempts had been made to bribe its officials.

Stanley had thrown parties and dropped names with breathtaking speed and ease; so many influential names were mentioned that it was strongly feared the Government would be brought down. Following the Fraud Squad investigation – the officers were working up to eighteen hours per day – a public tribunal under the direction of Mr. Justice Lynskey was held at Church House, Westminster.

During the thirty-four-day hearing, it was established beyond doubt that Stanley was a rather greasy and very persuasive con-man. Practically all the names of the great and the good that Stanley had mentioned were exonerated, save two. John Belcher from the Board of Trade and George Gibson, a former director of the Bank of England, were held to have accepted small gifts and hospitality from Stanley, as inducements to secure their influence; both were disgraced.

But not Stanley. Giving the police the slip, he turned up later in Tel Aviv and there he died in May 1969. For his work in the case (carried out when he was simultaneously assisting in Capstick's murder investigation) Millen received his thirteenth commissioner's commendation on 15 February 1949.

Millen had passed his examination for first class detective sergeant as a qualifier, not as a competitor, which ordinarily would have meant several years' wait before promotion came his way. But within four months of passing the exam, he had leap-frogged his way to the next rank – almost certainly with a kind word or two from Capstick, because with promotion came a posting to the Flying Squad.

*

A tremendous battle against crime was being fought by the Flying Squad under the leadership of Detective Superintendent Bill 'The Cherub' Chapman, and that would be Millen's home for the next two-

and-a-half-years. Did Millen make a significant contribution to this offensive or was he perhaps a fish out of water? On the balance of probabilities, I rather think the latter. Millen had fifteen years' service under his belt at the time of his posting to the Flying Squad, yet he later admitted that this was one of the first times he had used an informant and the first time he had arrested a pickpocket. This was a rather surprising admission, when one remembers that men like Greeno and Sharpe had built their reputations on arresting pickpockets (or dips) long before they came to the Flying Squad. The importance of arresting dips was obvious to detectives – it was because they often made the best informants; this was something that was sadly deficient, in Millen's department.

But there is no denying that he was a great investigator and a painstaking one, too; Millen was awarded commissioner's commendations for ability in a case of larceny, effecting the arrest of a troublesome criminal, and after he was commended for ability in a case of larceny by the Petty Sessions and later by the Southend-on-Sea Quarter Sessions, he was again commended by the commissioner.

On 1 August 1951 Millen was back at C1 Department, doing what he did best: tackling large, complex investigations in a meticulous manner. One of the first was the case of Ernest Walter Silverman, the brother of the MP, Sydney Silverman. Ernest was a fraudsman pure and simple and he had spent twenty-eight years in prison to prove it. At his appearance at the Old Bailey in March 1952, he pleaded guilty to six charges of false pretences and asked for eight other offences to be taken into consideration. His sentence of ten years' preventative detention was his last; six years later he died in Parkhurst Prison. One of his more accurate statements was that he had served the equivalent of three life sentences in prison, without murdering anyone but himself.

Leslie Green, however, *was* a murderer. On 16 July 1952 he bludgeoned Mrs. Alice Maud Mary Wiltshaw to death with a poker in her sumptuous fourteen-room mansion in Barlaston, Staffordshire. Seizing jewellery, a gold cigarette case and cash, together worth over £3,000, Green also helped himself to the old raincoat belonging to

Mrs. Wiltshaw's husband, to cover up his victim's blood which had splattered his own clothing. The raincoat had three cigarette burns in it.

Millen was sent with Detective Superintendent Reg Spooner to investigate the case and their enquiries quickly focused on Green, who had been employed as a gardener and chauffeur by the Wilstshaws and who had been dismissed two months previously and was now nowhere to be found. A pair of bloodstained gloves, one of which had a tear on the left thumb, had been found in the garden of the mansion. Just beyond the garden was a path, which led across the fields to Barlaston Railway Station. It was discovered that Green had a girlfriend in Leeds, and judging by the time of death, Green would have had enough time to walk along the path, catch a train at Barlaston which connected with another train to take him to Leeds. Millen felt that at some stage, Green would have to have discarded the bloodstained raincoat.

He sought the help of the British Transport Police who explored the track between Stafford and Holyhead, searched every left luggage office en route and checked all the tickets. It paid off. The raincoat, complete with bloodstains and cigarette burns was discovered in the rack of a compartment on the Stafford to Holyhead express. The porter who found it, on the same night as the murder, had booked it in to a lost property office. Now Millen took possession of the raincoat, together with a ticket, purchased at Barlaston on the day of the murder and surrendered at Leeds.

When Millen caught up with him, Green made a statement in excess of thirty pages, in which he admitted nothing. Millen simply let him go on and on. Eventually, the statement was proved to be a complete lie. Items of the stolen jewellery were recovered at a friend's address, shoes found in Green's possession were found to match footprints found at the murder scene and the tear on the bloodstained glove was found to correspond exactly with a recent scar on Green's thumb. With an abundance of circumstantial evidence, Green was found guilty and hanged at Winson Green Prison two days before Christmas, 1952. For his contribution to the enquiry, which was described as 'valuable assistance', Millen was commended by the Trial Judge at Stafford Assizes, the Director of Public Prosecutions and for the eighteenth time, the commissioner.

And there was a further commendation, as well. As Millen went into the witness box at Stone Magistrates' Court, to provide testimony for Green's committal to the Assizes, Green turned to Reg Spooner and said, "If Ernie Millen gives evidence which hangs me, I'll come back and haunt him."

Ever laconic, Spooner murmured, "You'll have to get in the fucking queue."

Reg Spooner figured in Millen's next case, which took them to Laugharne in Camarthenshire. Seventy-eight-year-old Miss Elizabeth Thomas had been bludgeoned and stabbed to death, and the prime suspect for the offence was George Roberts. There were, however, certain difficulties surrounding Roberts' proposed interview. Not only was he deaf and dumb, he could not read or write, nor was he conversant with sign language. The investigators secured the services of a couple who ran a special school in Llanelli. Roberts would be asked a question; the wife would translate it into sign language and her husband then converted the question into 'illiterate Welsh sign language'. It is rather difficult to assess how helpful this was, but in any event Roberts responded by answering with nods or shakes of the head, grunts, hand movements or drawings. Over a period of five days, during which Roberts gave every indication that he was enjoying the whole business, this whole laborious interview went on, using the simplest of questions. Spooner finally felt that he had sufficient evidence with which to charge Roberts; at Cardiff Assizes on 24 March 1953, Mr. Justice Devlin directed the jury to acquit Roberts after the prosecution, following a series of legal arguments, decided to offer no evidence. Unusually, following an acquittal, Millen was awarded a commissioner's commendation for 'valuable assistance in a murder investigation'.

He attended the junior course at Ryton-on-Dunsmore Police College from 6 July until 11 December 1953 and early the following year made his final and exceptionally brief return to division – in this case, a home posting to 'R' Division, probably so that his file could state that he had acquired divisional experience – before being promoted to detective inspector on 10 May 1954 and posted to the Fraud Squad.

*

Millen must have felt that he had died and gone to heaven; he enjoyed investigating fraud and had been seconded to the Fraud Squad before but this was the posting of his dreams, which would last for over three years. His mentor Nat Thorp had just retired and Thorp's successor, Detective Chief Superintendent Bob Stevens handed him a case which was not especially difficult by Fraud Squad standards but would turn out to be an unusual one.

A local firm of manufacturers wanted to lease ten acres of ground from Stockport Corporation to use as a sports ground. An alderman, sitting at a meeting of the Council to discuss the matter, was bound under the Local Government Act 1933 to disclose that he and his wife had 750 shares in the company; but he did not.

When Southport Magistrates dismissed the summonses that Millen had brought, he was furious. He returned to London and reported the matter to the Director of Public Prosecutions, who also thought that a proper prosecution had been brought. Lord Chief Justice Goddard agreed and informed the Justices that they should sit again and this time they should convict. Perhaps, rather grudgingly, they did, fining the alderman £25 with 25 guineas costs; Millen received another commendation.

William Henry Allen was convicted under the name of Anthony John Hawkes – not his real one but then he so seldom used his baptismal name. Even when the game was up, like so many con-men he persisted in lying for lying's sake. The offence that he carried out was no more than a sophisticated long-firm fraud: he obtained goods on credit from textile firms and then sold them off at knock-down prices. By the time justice caught up with him, he was charged with obtaining goods to the value of £12,300. He was supposed to plead guilty at the Old Bailey on 10 May 1951. Because he was known to be a master of disguise as well as possessing a string of aliases, it would have been prudent to have remanded Allen in custody, but this was not done – instead, he jumped both bail and the English Channel.

Using a passport bearing the alias Arthur Eric Waters, it was not too long before he was up to his tricks in France. Eventually, he was caught and sentenced to eight months' imprisonment. Five years after his original arrest, Millen was waiting for him as he stepped off the boat from Calais. At the Old Bailey he admitted thirty-nine cases of fraud and was sentenced to six years' imprisonment.

Millen's next investigation as a Fraud Squad detective inspector was one that seriously taxed his own capabilities. John William Robinson had run a stockbrokers' company in Halifax; within four years, the company crashed and at Halifax Bankruptcy Court, Robinson admitted a deficiency of almost £129,000. Matters that were brought to light during the course of the bankruptcy proceedings were so blatant that the official receiver insisted on a criminal investigation. The company's ledgers and accounts were seized, but when Millen looked at them in December 1955 he realised that his already substantial knowledge of fraud and accounting did not encompass the dealings of stockbrokers. He therefore returned to London, approached a firm of stockbrokers and subjected himself to a week-long crash course in the mysteries of their work; then he was ready to return to Halifax to commence his investigations.

Robinson's dishonesty had included his defrauding an aunt and also his own father, as well as many other investors, and it took Millen months of work before Robinson pleaded guilty to charges of fraudulent conversion. These charges, plus the offences which Robinson would ask the court to take into consideration, amounted to £83,000, and the huge schedule which Millen had prepared stretched from one side of the courtroom at Leeds Assizes to the other. Robinson was sentenced to six years' imprisonment. Millen, who had been commended at Halifax Magistrates' Court, was also commended by the Trial Judge, the Director of Public Prosecutions and the commissioner, who awarded Millen his twenty-third commendation.

A disgruntled former Brighton police officer had made allegations of corruption about certain members of his Force, but these had been investigated and the allegations dismissed. However, he persisted in his complaint which eventually found its way to the desk of the DPP. Millen was sent for and he discovered that the key to the whole business rested in the hands of one Frank Rose, a local businessman. Rose had started what on the face of it was a charitable concern, employing disabled ex-servicemen to make furniture, and he sent a number of salesmen throughout the country to acquire orders for the goods. Having obtained the order money, which went straight into his private account, Rose ensured that the goods were either never sent or, if they were, were of exceptionally poor quality. Corruption now entered into what was a common or garden fraud. If dissatisfied customers complained to Brighton Police, they would often find themselves fobbed off and their allegations dismissed: or, if the customer looked like becoming a nuisance, a corrupt police officer would suggest to Rose that it might be prudent to return the money.

After he had put Rose's charitable company into liquidation, Millen obtained bankruptcy orders and now had access to the accounts. Meanwhile, a local detective inspector and detective sergeant were becoming very interested in Millen's investigations. But then something happened to pull Millen away from Brighton and back to London – another allegation of police corruption.

The Assistant Commissioner (Crime) Sir Richard Jackson CBE had sent for Millen to investigate a case where diamonds were being stolen at a regular and alarming rate from a safe deposit company in Hatton Garden. The thefts had all been reported at the local police station, Gray's Inn Road but nothing had been done about them. Worse still, an examination of the crime book revealed that no record had ever been made of the thefts; it all pointed to a massive cover-up and collusion by corrupt police officers.

It was nothing of the kind. The losers of the diamonds had simply reported them as being 'missing' – as a result, the loss had been entered by the station's uniform officers in the 'Property Lost' book, which was kept in the front office of the police station and as such was not routinely inspected by the CID staff. But missing the diamonds certainly were.

"Ernie Millen had a close contact in Hatton Garden," Bob Robinson told me, nearly fifty years after the event. "It was said that if something happened in the Garden one day, Millen would be sure to know who was responsible the next." Well, Millen certainly needed help on this one and he got it. A custodian at the safe deposit company was crooked and he and two jewellers had been helping themselves. Conscripting Tommy Butler and some other Flying Squad officers on to the team, Millen waited until all the suspects were in Hatton Garden before giving the signal to stop all the traffic and make the arrests. All of the prisoners were sentenced to thirty months' imprisonment and on 9 April 1957, Millen and Butler were both commended by the commissioner. On the same day, Millen received another commendation for ability and persistence in a difficult case of false pretences and uttering forged documents, a case which he had commenced investigating three years previously. It marked his twenty-fifth and final commissioner's commendation.

Back now to Brighton. Millen amassed sufficient evidence to see and question Rose about his activities; he did so and found Rose to be fairly unconcerned. Possibly he thought that the protection money he had been paying would keep him safe. Millen applied for and was granted summonses alleging carrying on a company for fraudulent purposes, failing to keep proper books of account, fraudulent conversion and obtaining money by false pretences.

The local detective inspector asked Millen if he could serve the summons himself; since local police officers always made the arrests in provincial investigations, not too much suspicion should have been aroused regarding the service of a summons. But having done so, the inspector reported back to Millen that he could find no trace of Rose having any previous convictions. Millen thought this highly unlikely, but since, with the service of a summons, no fingerprints were taken to compare with any on record, he decided that further investigation was merited. He searched all of the Criminal Records Offices throughout the United Kingdom and his persistence paid off; he discovered that Rose had six previous convictions, three of which were for fraud. When Millen confronted Rose with the list of convictions on the steps of Lewes Assizes, Rose was dumbfounded and asked if Millen had obtained the list from Brighton, which was where they had been held all the time. Rose pleaded guilty and was sentenced to three years' imprisonment – not at all what he had expected. He felt thoroughly let down; and from his prison cell, he began to talk.

Millen was promoted to detective chief inspector on 6 May 1957 and three months later was posted to the Flying Squad, on paper, at least. In fact, he was part of a massive investigation, under the direction of Detective Superintendent Ian Forbes-Leith, which was a knock-on part of the Rose enquiry.

Alan Roy Bennett was the proprietor of the Astor Club in Brighton, which due to the frequent fights which broke out there was known locally as 'The Bucket of Blood'. When the club had first opened in 1955, only modest business was forthcoming, but a local businessman brought along a police officer who indicated that for £20 per week Bennett could run the club as he liked. And he did – no matter what happened at the club (and a lot did) no police action was taken. If a disgruntled resident did complain, the crooked police officer would hear of it and suggest that the club stayed closed on the night of the raid.

But as is common with venal police officers, they nipped Bennett once too often and he went to the Yard to lodge a complaint. In consequence, the Forbes-Leith enquiry was launched and Millen had ten Flying Squad officers, including the Terrible Twins, Tommy Butler and Peter Vibart to assist him. They interviewed scores of witnesses, owners of every kind of licensed premises that merited inspection by the police and prisoners serving sentences all over England: vulnerable witnesses were put into hotels and safe houses and guarded night and day. This precaution appeared to be necessary – a bookmaker gave evidence and the following day, his club went up in flames. Allegations of corruption, accepting bribes, destroying evidence and perverting the course of justice poured in, and all were scrupulously investigated.

In October 1957 a detective inspector, a detective sergeant, the chief constable and later, a bookmaker were arrested. At the Old

Bailey, on 27 February 1958, the chief constable was acquitted by the jury. The two other police officers were each sentenced to five years' imprisonment and the bookmaker to three years. The investigation and the trial had taken up a good deal of time and Millen had little of it left on the Flying Squad. On 8 December 1958 he was promoted to detective superintendent and posted back, after a four year absence, to C1 Department.

There at the Murder Squad, he went to Wolverhampton to investigate the murder of Nurse Martha Giles. Her skull had been smashed in but neither robbery nor sexual molestation was the motive behind what appeared to be a senseless attack. In fact, the blows to the skull had *not* caused Nurse Giles' death – the autopsy revealed that she had died as the result of being stabbed in the chest with what could well have been a surgical scalpel. Whoever had been responsible must have had an acute knowledge of anatomy to have pierced the heart; the bludgeoning of her head with a stone had been a blind.

Millen's investigation brought him to the door of a doctor who worked at the same hospital as Nurse Giles. Having questioned him and having collected incriminating forensic evidence, Millen charged the doctor with murder, although at his trial at Staffordshire Assizes, he was acquitted.

In February 1959 a man named Samuel Clifford Vosper stood trial at the Old Bailey on charges of conspiracy to steal, procuring others to steal and receiving stolen goods valued at £21,000. Since 1943, forty-seven-year-old Vosper had worked as a police informant, but he grew greedy. When Vosper gave information regarding the activities of criminals, there were other matters which he neglected to inform the Yard about, and in so doing he became a very rich man. His downfall came when he set up a theft and employed two thieves to carry it out; over a period of time, the thieves were caught and during the course of their admissions, they implicated Vosper. Perhaps he thought that revealing his past activities with the police to the court would protect him from conviction but if so, he was wrong. Not only did he expose himself as a grass, he was also sentenced to six years' imprisonment.

Vosper wanted revenge. He sent a series of letters to the Yard in an attempt to blacken the characters of the officers with whom he had dealings which he claimed were corrupt, and it was Millen's unenviable task to investigate these allegations. Over a nine-month period, Millen interviewed over fifty police officers alone and he eventually submitted a detailed report to the commissioner. Five senior detectives who had been accused by Vosper of impropriety were cleared of any wrongdoing. One detective superintendent was accused of four offences under the discipline code and appeared before a disciplinary board. He was cleared of three of the offences; the final offence was one of hiring a car with Vosper's help, and in respect of this matter, he was found guilty. For what may be regarded as a trivial offence, the officer, who had in excess of thirty years' service and who had been commended on many occasions, was demoted to the rank of chief inspector.

On 4 January 1960, Millen was posted to the Research and Planning Department and six weeks later he was promoted to detective chief superintendent. His brief was to advise on how the CID could be reorganised and improved. One suggestion that was implemented was to form C11, the Criminal Intelligence Department: at the same time, the Stolen Car Squad which had been part of the Flying Squad since the early 1950s was now given its own department, C10. Much of the rest of Millen's time was spent lecturing on crime prevention.

In fact, with his promotion on 16 February 1960 he had been earmarked for No.3 District Headquarters but this clearly did not suit him, geographically or intellectually; he stayed where he was and waited for better things. On 19 June 1961, it came – head of the Flying Squad.

*

Millen was described as being 'gruff and bluff' – a very strong Squad Guv'nor who would back his men to the hilt, providing, of course, that they were right! His demands would be trumpeted down the corridors of the Yard without the need of a telephone or an intercom, and when he spoke, he 'barked'. John Simmonds, who was posted to the Flying Squad as a detective constable just after Millen's appointment, recalls that a standing joke from seasoned Squad personnel to newcomers was, "Hooter spoke to me, this morning." The goggle-eyed youngster would invariably reply, "What did he say?" and the reply, amidst gales of laughter was, "'Get out of the fucking way!'"

Perhaps Millen's bark was worse than his bite. The late Terry O'Connell, (later to reach the rank of commander and be awarded the Queen's Police Medal), then a detective sergeant (second class) on the Squad recalled, almost fifty years later, "Ernie Millen was a schemer, in a nice sort of way, and would have made a good politician. He seemed to know all that was going on; he knew all the dodges that officers were likely to pull. He had the job at heart, he was caring and saw to it that good officers were rewarded."

Millen certainly knew what was going on, plus the dodges being pulled, and being a new broom, he decided to do a little cleaning up. A number of questionable practices were happening on the Squad during the 1960s, one of which was the use of 'participating informants' – a perfectly sound piece of police work, if carried out properly. Millen, however thought that this practice was occurring on a far too regular basis and decreed that he would not tolerate any more cases where a member of a gang of robbers miraculously 'escaped' despite the fact that there were sufficient numbers of police officers present to quell a full-scale riot. Another practice that Millen clamped down on, was where down-and-outs – commonly referred to as 'Mugs' – were arrested for serious offences which were way beyond their capabilities, the inference being that the real perpetrators of the crime had offered them up as sacrificial lambs. In Millen's words, "It is the 1960s and this has got to stop."

But other changes were much more to the Squad's liking. The vehicle strength of the Squad was increased to thirty-two and this included three new taxis and four vans. The Rovers and Jaguars were held in high esteem by drivers and crews alike. Millen increased the manpower to almost 100 officers, and the returns for 1961 jumped correspondingly. Arrests rose to 1,410 and property to the value of £484,931 was recovered, an increase of £170,000 on the previous year. In 1962, the number of arrests was up to 1,684, property recovered amounted to £738,094 and the commissioner, at Millen's prompting increased the Squad manpower by another 25%. The following year, it would be needed.

*

On 8 August 1963, as the Glasgow to London mail train was approaching Sears Crossing, north of Cheddington, Buckinghamshire at three o'clock in the morning, a red signal caused the driver, Jack Mills to bring the train to a halt. Within a very short space of time, during what would become known as 'The Great Train Robbery', the guards were relieved of £2,631,684, by approximately fifteen determined and well-briefed criminals.

Brigadier Cheyney, the Chief Constable of Buckinghamshire, immediately realised that an investigation purely by his own men with their limited knowledge and resources was out of the question, and called in the Yard. The robbers vacated their hide-out at Leatherslade Farm, which was discovered four days after the robbery, and the forensic experts moved in. The loss adjusters, Hart & Co. offered rewards of up to £225,000 for information leading to the arrest and conviction of the gang and the recovery of the money. It was inevitable that the Flying Squad would be called in.

In his rather pompous autobiography, *Specialist in Crime*, in which he often, and irritatingly, refers to himself in the third person, Millen states that it was he who obtained information from a serving prisoner which brought about the discovery of the identities of the great train robbers. Quite frankly, I do not believe it. I think it possible that he may have received some sketchy, fragmented information, but that is all.

Tommy Butler was pulled off his duties at No. 1 District Headquarters and put in charge of the Flying Squad team to catch the robbers. Nobody better could have been chosen. It was he who discovered the identities of the robbers from his informants, and their fingerprints matched those found at the gang's hideout. But Millen now took the incredible decision to publish the names and photographs and the photographs of some of the suspects' wives, in the national press. Butler and his deputy, Detective Inspector Frank Williams were vehemently opposed to such a course of action. They felt that by using their own contacts and informants they would be able to find the robbers themselves; and in addition, argued Butler, this course of action could drive the robbers into hiding, perhaps out of the country where it could take years to trace them; a prophesy that unfortunately turned out to be correct.

Although Butler was leading the hunt, and despite he and Millen being the same rank, Millen won the day, having the backing of the CID Commander, George Hatherill. But when, on 1 October 1963 Millen took over as deputy commander, following the death of Reg Spooner and Butler took over the reins as the head of the Flying Squad, Butler made it quite clear that things would be done *his* way. So why did Millen take this catastrophic decision to inform the press? Impatience? Not very likely. As a methodical detective, he was used to taking his time to ensure that everything was right. In fact, Butler criticised Millen on the Hatton Garden job for taking too long to arrest the suspects, and Butler himself was a patient investigator. Did Millen think that in taking this course of action to arrest all the suspects, he would have been completely credited with the success of the Great Train Robbery investigation? Probably. Was it done to ensure there was a fascinating chapter when he came to write his autobiography? Did he feel that here he was, the detective chief superintendent of Scotland Yard's elite squad, with twenty-nine years service and a sure-fire way to find himself included in the Honours List? Was it an ego trip – or was it just plain cussedness? I asked 'Nipper' Read for his opinion and his reply was this: "As you will know, the names came in the frame very early in the investigation and became common knowledge. I think Millen decided that because of the enormity of the job and the publicity it was generating, that he wanted it seen that the Yard was taking some positive action. He must have decided therefore that it was important to release the pictures in order to indicate at this early stage the identity of the participants had been established and their apprehension was being actively pursued." From someone who was never a friend of Millen's, it is a remarkably generous explanation.

But assuming that Read's explanation is correct, nevertheless it was a bad decision and the wrong one. Millen should have heeded Butler and this is not said with the gift of hindsight. Butler was a Squadman through and through, well used to dealing with violent robbers and running informants; and Millen was not. I do not seek to denigrate Millen; that he was a brilliant detective, I do not dispute. But there is a world of difference between on the one hand soberly perusing columns of disputed figures, taking months, years sometimes, before serving a summons on a suspect and on the other chasing dangerous, armed robbers. As a man who had previously served on the Flying Squad, Millen should have known that.

*

Millen was appointed to head a working party to help streamline the CID. Beat Crimes were henceforth to be dealt with by uniformed officers, and because of the good results obtained from the television programme, *Police 5*, this was extended; the following year, a similar programme on BBC Radio, entitled *Scotland Yard Calling* was broadcast every evening at 6.35. The CID were given a manpower increase of 186, bringing their numbers to 1,774 and the Prisoners' Property Office and store was transferred from the Yard to Chalk Farm, North London. C1 Drugs Squad was augmented and investigated over 1,000 cases (as opposed to 150 the previous year), and the Obscene Publications Squad dealt with over 300 cases. One year to the day after his appointment, Millen was promoted to commander (crime) and as such, was in charge of all the CID officers in the Metropolitan Police.

*

On 1 April 1968 Millen was posted to 'C' Department's Admin and Division duties – he had already applied to the Home Office for an extension of service, which was granted in a letter dated 21 January 1968 – and he allowed the successes of the Richardson and Kray investigations to rub off on him. His rank was regraded on 1 June 1969 to that of deputy assistant commissioner and it was at that rank that he retired, twenty-three days later.

Millen had served in the Metropolitan Police for thirty-four years, eleven months and two days. He had been awarded the CBE in the

1968 New Years Honours list, his conduct was 'exemplary' and with an annual pension of £2,854 7s 0d he returned home to Ena at their house at Tile Kiln Lane, Bexley, Kent. He was put in charge of security for Giltspur Investments, who controlled hotels and gaming clubs and he died on 15 April 1988 at the age of seventy-six.

Despite my few negative comments, Millen was undeniably a great investigator and a great Guv'nor, but his reputation had a lot of help, especially from the Flying Squad. Perhaps he realised it as well. "I always think of the Flying Squad as being rather like a duck on a mill pond," he once said, at one of the annual Flying Squad dinner and dances, "serenely gliding along on the surface, with its legs paddling furiously along underneath."

The sentiment was much appreciated by the assembled guests!

CHAPTER 8

Tommy Butler – Mr. Flying Squad

By January 1958 the Flying Squad fleet had received a much needed updating. True, the civilian staff responsible for acquiring the cars had to be told for the second time to ensure that the registration numbers of the vehicles should not run consecutively, but the real bugbear was the four black Wolseleys, which were still on the Flying Squad strength. The worst of them had 100,680 miles recorded on the clock and during the previous seven months had been to the workshops on no fewer than sixteen occasions. The other three were hardly any better.

On 25 January 1958, a furious acting detective chief inspector thrust a Form 728 into a typewriter and acidly informed his senior officers:

> The cars are, to say the least conspicuous, and it is not unduly stretching veracity to say they constitute a hindrance to officers endeavouring to effect the arrest of any criminal possessing even a modicum of intelligence or experience.

The author of this stinging report was Tommy Butler. In the years that followed, he would become known as 'The Grey Fox' – and also, as its detective chief superintendent, 'Mr. Flying Squad.' In addition, he would form one half of 'The Terrible Twins'.

*

Thomas Marius Joseph Butler was born on 21 July 1912 at Shepherds Bush. He lived with his widowed mother at 41 Washington Road, Barnes and received an elementary education. After working as a warehouseman, he joined the Metropolitan Police on 22 October 1934 and was posted to the East End as Police Constable 965'K'. He found the Canning Town section house as unappealing as was being separated from his mother and he successfully campaigned for a transfer to 'F' Division so that he could live with her. Now Police Constable 349'F', Butler continued his probation and sitting his final examination, he did well, obtaining marks of over 85%. He became an aid to CID, notched up successes and received two commissioner's commendations for sagacity in a case of larceny, and zeal in a case of attempted larceny.

In May 1938, he was appointed detective constable and posted to London's West End Central police station. There, he passed his first class educational examination, signed a declaration for a long-term engagement, passed the examination for detective sergeant (second class) and was awarded one commissioner's commendation for initiative and persistence in a case of demanding money by menaces, two more for ability and promptness in cases of shopbreaking and a DAC's commendation for ability in a case of larceny.

Butler arrived at the Flying Squad in September 1941. This appointment would last for five years and it would be the first of four such postings. They would total seventeen years, and as well as serving in the rank of detective constable, Butler would serve on the Squad in the ranks of detective inspector, detective chief inspector, detective superintendent and finally as its head, detective chief superintendent.

He had done well to become a member of the Flying Squad with less than seven years service and was already making a name for himself. Just five feet nine-and-a-quarter inches tall, slim, with a hairline that was already starting to recede, dark eyebrows and a 'Mr. Punch' nose, Butler was a non-smoking, virtual teetotaller who was obsessive in playing his cards close to his chest and fanatical in his hunt for criminals. They, in turn, were scared stiff by the dark, intense, little man. Butler was in good company. Only a year before, Peter Beveridge had taken over the reins as the Squad's new chief, and the five detective inspectors who were under his command were Jack 'Charley Artful' Capstick, who would later head the Ghost Squad, the two-fisted Ted Greeno, Alf Dance, who during his twenty-three years on the Squad rose from detective constable to detective inspector (first class), plus John Ball – who, within five years, would be promoted to detective superintendent – and John Black, a very astute investigator.

Butler had an enormously successful tour on the Squad, quickly making his mark with a commissioner's commendation for his promptitude, perseverance and ability in a case of receiving. The Second World War was a period when commendations were handed out grudgingly, not that this seems to have stopped Butler from receiving them. Within four months of his first commendation, he had been awarded another, for ability and persistence in a difficult case of offences under the Food Orders and the Defence Regulations and one month later, one more for acumen and discretion in a case of larceny and receiving. The following year he was awarded a commendation for ability and perseverance in a case of receiving – convictions for receivers of stolen property were highly prized during the austere war years.

Four months later, he was commended for vigilance and initiative in a case of warehousebreaking and four months after that, for ability and prudence in a case of forgery. Three weeks later he received a commendation for perseverance and industry in a case of receiving.

Early in 1945 he was commended for his persistence and ability in a case of conspiracy and larceny and five months later again for diligence in a case of housebreaking. Within three months he was commended for skill in a case of receiving and in February 1946 won a commendation for good work in a case of storebreaking and receiving. One month later he collected another commendation for skill in a case of larceny and conspiracy to receive stolen goods and five months after that he finally bowed out of his Squad debut with a commendation for zeal, in a case of receiving.

Butler was promoted to detective sergeant (second class) and posted to 'G' Division on 15 July 1946. He had acquired a tremendous reputation, having served a very tough apprenticeship. Butler's first posting on 'G' Division was City Road; he did not stay long, due to a succession of run-ins with Detective Inspector Bert 'Iron Man' Sparks. Probably because he worked such long hours,

Butler would turn up for duty in the CID office at ten in the morning, instead of the traditional nine o'clock. This infuriated Sparks, who was a strong disciplinarian, and after several warnings went unheeded, Butler found himself transferred to Islington police station.

But as always, Butler worked hard and was awarded two commissioner's commendations, one for ability in a case of warehousebreaking and another for persistence in a case of robbery, as well as a DAC's commendation for initiative and ability in an arrest for larceny, for which he was also commended by the Magistrate at Old Street Court.

Within three years, Butler was promoted to detective sergeant (first class) and given a posting to 'D' Division where he would stay for the next six years, as well as being promoted to detective inspector. During this posting, Ian Forbes, later to become a deputy assistant commissioner, remembered Butler as being, 'his best friend in the service.' Forbes described him as being outstanding, unflappable and supremely capable in everything he touched, and few would have disagreed. 'Nipper' Read, who at that time of Butler's career was a detective constable at Paddington Green police station, recalls being in the CID office when a call came in regarding a robbery. He and Butler rushed to the scene and arrested two men, and Butler was responsible for putting the case together which resulted in the two prisoners being committed to stand their trial at the Old Bailey. All of the evidence was contained in Tommy Butler's pocketbook; Read had not one word of evidence in his. There would have been no objection to Read referring to Butler's notes, except that Butler had neglected to show him the book prior to the trial commencing, and the events surrounding the arrest had happened some time before and were now rather hazy in Read's memory.

So with the prisoners pleading not guilty to the charge, Butler went into the witness box, gave his evidence in chief and was then cross-examined. This took him up to the lunchtime adjournment by which time he had completed his evidence; upon the resumption of the trial, Read was in next, without a clue as to what he was going to say. Unable to discuss the case with Butler, Read spent a miserable lunch hour before returning to court. However, during the adjournment, the prisoners discussed the case and decided that Butler's evidence was so compelling that upon the resumption of the trial their barrister asked the Clerk of the Court to put the charge to his clients again, whereupon they both pleaded guilty and were sentenced.

Read expelled a deep sigh of relief; Butler behaved as though he had known that this would be the outcome all along. Fred Lambert told me of a similar encounter with Butler, which had occurred at Islington, several years before; I feel many other officers could tell similar tales.

Nevertheless, 'Nipper' Read thought that Butler was "a great investigator". When an officer put a report that was less than perfect in front of Butler, he would caustically remark, "What a lot of bollocks": but then he would assist the author to put it right, sentence by sentence. Only very occasionally would Butler have a drink with the rest of the office; usually, he spent the evenings in his office, typing. Read told me he thought that Butler might have been typing his memoirs, although no such papers were ever found. The other explanation, Read suggested was that Butler had examined the reports of his subordinates and found them wanting, and rather than let them go in front of the Detective Inspector, John McIvor, there to receive a ruthless 'red-penciling', Butler re-typed them himself. This could well have been the case. John Simmonds (later to become detective chief superintendent of the Yard's Serious Crime Squad) remembers a contemporary of Butler's telling him that when he was at Islington, Butler would go through officers' 'In' and 'Pending' trays at night and type outstanding reports for them. Having seen some of Butler's reports, I can confirm that the presentation, grammar and punctuation would have done a professional typist credit.

Butler was promoted to detective inspector on 1 July 1954 and a few days later, whilst still being retained on 'D' Division, was shifted sideways to Albany Street Police Station, where the detective superintendent was Herbert 'Suits' Hannam, a strict martinet when it came to correspondence so presumably he had no problems with

Butler on that score. Ron Goodall had just been appointed detective constable and speaking to me about Butler, he remarked, "Being the new boy, I was taken under his wing – and what a great tutor he was – very knowledgeable, patient and extremely hard working."

And now that he had reached 'Guv'nor' rank, Butler was starting to demonstrate that he would not tolerate sloppy and lazy practices. There were a number of older detective constables and detective sergeants at Albany Street who fell far below the standards practised and demanded by Butler, and he regarded them as 'deadwood'. He decided to 'ginger them up' according to David Pritchard who, at that time, as Police Constable 197'D', was on a week's attachment to the CID office. This is what happened.

"When a report came in from the local hospital that an elderly lady had been admitted with injuries consistent with a fall downstairs," recalls Pritchard, "a D/S was dispatched to investigate and took me along for experience. We saw the old lady and noted her injuries consisted of a broken right arm and extensive bruising."

It appeared that the victim had lived in the same flat for forty years and that the landlady, described by Pritchard as being, "a large, fat, arrogant black woman," had been subjecting her to constant abuse in an effort to make her vacate her home. That morning, as the elderly lady had started descending the stairs from her flat, she had heard the landlady bellowing abuse at her and then had felt a sharp push to her back, causing her to fall down the stairs. The resultant injuries had caused her admittance to hospital.

Astonishingly – and quite appallingly – the detective sergeant advised her that this was a civil matter and that her best course of action was to apply for a summons. Worse still, on the way back to Albany Street, the officer told Pritchard that, "he had a lot of similar 'rubbish' complaints and he was going to write this off as 'No Crime'."

Whilst he was doing just that, Butler came out of his office and asked Pritchard what had happened. Upon hearing the whole story, Butler lost his temper, castigated the incompetent sergeant and, taking Pritchard with him, went straight to the hospital where he saw the victim. Pritchard recalls that, "Tommy was very kind and gentle with her and promised she would have no further trouble." Probably Butler could imagine his own widowed mother in similar circumstances; but when he saw the landlady, the cunning Butler was calm and polite and merely asked if she had been experiencing any trouble with her elderly tenant. Deceived by Butler's attitude and thinking that he was on her side, the unpleasant landlady stated that the victim had sworn at and attempted to strike her, so she had merely given her a push. It was … a mistake.

No sooner were the words out of her mouth than the landlady was seized by Butler and Pritchard, dragged forcibly down the stairs and charged with causing actual bodily harm. Butler presented the case with considerable relish at Marylebone Magistrates' Court, and saw the repellent landlady receive six months' imprisonment. The reluctant sergeant, meanwhile, was ordered to carry out all of the paperwork associated with the case, endured a deeply embarrassing interview in Butler's office, from where he emerged with a very red face and in a state of shock, and was soon thereafter transferred to 'the sticks'. As Pritchard laconically remarked, "The arrest rate increased considerably during DI Butler's term at Albany Street." But within a year, Butler had gone, back to the Flying Squad and was put in charge of 5 Squad.

By coincidence, on the day that Butler had left the Squad in 1946, his vacancy was filled by a newcomer. Jasper Peter Vibart had spent seven years with the Royal Horse Artillery and joined the Metropolitan Police in 1936, aged twenty-two. After a couple of uneventful years at Twickenham, the toughly-built ex-soldier was posted to the East End of London and after he was awarded a commissioner's commendation for the arrest of eleven housebreakers, his career really took off. As an aid to CID, he distinguished himself by arresting 198 criminals in a twelve-month period and in 1946 he arrived at the Flying Squad. During Butler's absence, Vibart arrested scores of criminals – especially receivers – and then one year before Butler's return, he was promoted to detective sergeant (first class). When Butler did return to the Squad, he and Vibart teamed up. Although two individuals never looked less alike, but probably because they were inseparable, they became known as 'The Terrible Twins'.

Butler and Vibart energetically went to work; as Butler was commended for ability and determination in arresting a persistent and troublesome safe-blower, so was Vibart – as he was when Butler was commended for ability and perseverance in a case of robbery, for determination in arresting two violent criminals, for ability in arresting a persistent criminal and ability in a case of robbery with violence.

Butler worked excessively long hours all his service and expected every member of his staff to do the same. The late Ernie Bond OBE, QPM remembered, as a detective sergeant, passing Butler's office at two o'clock in the morning and seeing him still busily typing away. "What, another early night?" was Butler's frosty comment. When John Swain QPM (later to become detective chief superintendent of the Flying Squad) first went to the Flying Squad as a detective sergeant, Butler explained that early duty was 9am to 5pm, although he would be expected to book off at 10pm. Late turn, said Butler, was 2pm to 10pm, and on those days, Swain could have a lie-in. "You don't have to get here until 9am," said Butler. Thinking the remark was a humorous one, Swain laughed. Butler exploded. "If you think that's a joke," he roared, "just try coming in a few minutes late!"

This was a busy time for Butler. On 2 May 1956, the amalgamation between gang leaders Jack Spot and Billy Hill took a turn for the worse. As Spot and his wife were returning to their home in Hyde Park Mansions, Spot was attacked by a number of men and savagely slashed, requiring the insertion of seventy-eight stitches, plus a blood transfusion. Butler and Vibart went to Ireland and arrested two of the men responsible, Bert 'Battles' Rossi and Billy Blythe. In an effort to be helpful, their solicitor, Patrick Marrinan said (as solicitors do) to his clients, "They are all outside and are going to nick you again. If I were you, I should make a dive for it." At the subsequent trial, Marrinan alleged perjury against Butler, not that it did him or his clients any good. Rossi and Blythe received four and five years' imprisonment, respectively, and following an investigation by Butler, Marrinan was disbarred by the bar counsel for 'conduct unbefitting a barrister and a gentleman'. Butler undoubtedly felt vindicated; so, I imagine, did Vibart who had had twenty stitches inserted in his face, following a razor attack by Blythe, some twelve years previously.

Alfie Hinds, sentenced to twelve years' preventitive detention for safe-blowing, escaped to Ireland from Nottingham Prison in October 1955; Butler brought him back. In 1957, two cunning jewellers and a crooked custodian, working for a safe deposit company, were responsible for the theft of diamonds from Hatton Garden. The street was closed off, traffic came to a halt and Butler and his men arrested the team, who employed the most expensive barristers to defend them. Instead, they received thirty months' imprisonment each, and Butler notched up another commendation. The same year, Butler and Vibart assisted in the investigation of police corruption in Brighton. At the trial at the Old Bailey that followed, he was commended by the Trial Judge, the Director of Public Prosecutions and, for Butler, the thirty-fifth, and Vibart, the thirty-seventh time by the commissioner. Awarded his Long Service and Good Conduct Medal, Butler was promoted to detective chief inspector and in June 1958 posted to Hammersmith. One week later, Vibart was promoted to detective inspector and posted to Lavender Hill. Within five months, Butler and Vibart were seconded to the British Police Unit, Cyprus, to join the hunt for Colonel Grivas, and a year after that, on 2 November 1959, Butler was promoted to detective superintendent and was posted back to the Flying Squad, which was under the command of Butler's old adversary, Bert 'Iron Man' Sparks.

Meanwhile, Vibart had been highly commended by the commissioner for tackling an armed criminal, was awarded £15 from the Bow Street Reward Fund and received the Queen's Commendation for Brave Conduct. A year later, he was again highly commended by the commissioner for arresting a man who had shot dead a police officer.

*

Under Butler's leadership, the Squad thrived. In his first year of office, arrests exceeded 1,500 and property valued at £312,716 was recovered, both figures representing the highest on record. And in 1961, more than 1,400 arrests were carried out and property to the value of £484,931 was recovered by the Squad – this latter figure being £170,000 more than the previous year's record figure.

During that year, John Simmonds was appointed to the Squad, and on his first morning he was walking along the corridor of the Yard when a small, insignificant looking man asked, "You all right, mate?" Simmonds thanked him and asked the way to the Flying Squad clerk's office. Pointing in the general direction, the man replied, "Yeah, it's down there, on the right." After the formalities, the clerk, Detective Constable Bob Dunham, took Simmonds to the detective superintendent's office and introduced him to 'Mr. Butler'. "Yeah, we met in the corridor!" drily remarked the small man. But, added Simmonds to me, "Throughout my contact with Tom Butler over the subsequent years, he was never either small or insignificant."

Simmonds served four years on the Squad as a detective constable, and when he was posted to 'J' Division upon his promotion to detective sergeant (second class), Butler called him into his office and told him that as soon as he was promoted to detective sergeant (first class), he would have him back on the Squad. So Simmonds duly sat and passed the examination for that rank; and at that time, there was a dearth of first class sergeants, so whilst he was still on probation as a second class sergeant, he attended a promotion board for the next rank. One of the board members was Detective Chief Superintendent Fred Gerrard, whom Simmonds had never met before. He was flabbergasted when Gerrard launched into a blistering attack on his Flying Squad background; why, Simmonds had no idea. One of Gerrard's comments was, "All you have done on the Squad is to see satisfied losers!" It was clear to him that other board members were feeling uncomfortable about Gerrard's vituperative outburst, and Simmonds left the room, having failed the board and, fully aware that he had an enemy right at the top. Simmonds mentioned the incident to no one, but within a couple of days, he received a telephone call. It was Tommy Butler. "Just remember," he said to Simmonds, "Freddy Gerrard was never good enough to be on the Squad and never will be!" Simmonds was amazed. "Only a member of the board could have told Tommy Butler what had gone on," he told me. "It certainly liftcd me to think that he could be bothered to telephone me with such a message of support. I am not so sure that many others would have done the same". Gerrard's comments suggest that he may have been turned down for the Flying Squad at some stage of his career; whether this is true or not, Gerrard's remarks to a junior officer on a promotion board were indefensible. But it was ever thus!

Another of the officers under Butler's command was one Harold Gordon Challenor who, as a member of the wartime 2 SAS, had been parachuted behind enemy lines, carried out demolition work, been captured, escaped and awarded the Military Medal. Joining the Metropolitan Police in 1951, he notched up a creditable 105 arrests as an aid to CID, and appointed as detective constable and posted to the Flying Squad, he took to Squad work as a duck takes to water.

It was probably due to Challenor's insistence on referring to everybody, regardless of rank or status as, "me old darling" that prompted Butler to write, with masterly understatement on one of Challenor's annual qualification reports: 'He continues to apply himself strenuously to the job in hand. Is capable and willing but is inclined to noisy tactlessness.'

Challenor had certain behavioural traits which set him apart from even the most unorthodox of Squad men. It was certainly considered laudable to have escaped through enemy-occupied Italy disguised as a woman, but many would have thought that as a Metropolitan Police officer, this cross-dressing practice might well be discontinued when meeting an informant, no matter how cogent the reasoning behind it. So when Butler wrote in Challenor's next appraisal,

'He is capable and fearless in his dealings with criminals. Has improved in general bearing ...'.

it is possible that he was referring to Challenor's arrest of a vicious armed robber by hitting him across the throat with a straight-arm Commando chop. Nevertheless, I imagine that Butler breathed a sigh of relief when Challenor was promoted to detective sergeant (second class) and posted to West End Central in July 1962. Unbeknown to either of them, both would have rather pressing problems to address within a year: Butler with the great train robbery, and Challenor with the provenance of disputed segments of a housebrick.

In 1962 the Squad carried out over 1,600 arrests and stolen property to the value of £738,094 was recovered. Butler had spent four years with the Squad and now he was promoted to detective chief superintendent and posted to No. 1 Area, District Headquarters. It was his shortest posting ever. Three weeks later, the great train robbery occurred and Butler was back on the Flying Squad – so, inescapably, was Vibart.

At that time, Ernie Millen was the head of the Flying Squad and he had his own way of doing things, one of which met with Butler's immediate opposition. Scores of fingerprints had been discovered at the gang's hideout; Butler, who had got on to his informants to find out who was associating with whom, requested the Home Secretary to authorise a number of telephone interceptions. The resultant names were passed to fingerprint branch – "Try these first," said Butler – and an impressive number of identifications were made. But Millen decided to publish the names and photographs of the suspects in the newspapers, and when Butler and his deputy, Detective Inspector Frank Williams protested, saying the suspects would simply disappear, Millen overruled them. Of course, Butler was right. Some of the suspects named in the newspapers *did* disappear and took years to catch. A few weeks later Millen was promoted, and Butler took over as head of the Flying Squad.

Jack Slipper was one of the team selected by Butler to catch the great train robbers, and in the end, they did; in the six weeks following the robbery, 419 searches were carried out and nineteen out of the twenty-one prisoners for the robbery were caught by the Flying Squad. Slipper found Butler to be a shrewd, deep-thinking, old-style policeman, very serious and very thorough, without an impulsive side to his nature. Like many of his era, he had little faith in technological and scientific advances. Butler's way of working was, 'arrest them, lock them up and interrogate them.' His working days, including Saturdays and Sundays, were as long as ever.

Sometimes – not often – he would join his team for a glass of *Tio Pepe* in the snug at the Red Lion in Derby Gate, next to the Yard, before getting a lift home from whoever was left on duty.

It was still the same old Tommy Butler, playing his cards close to his chest, with information being a one-way street. This was highlighted when he told his arresting team that one of the suspects' fingerprints had been found at the hideout. So they had; what Butler had not said was that they had been found on a Monopoly board, and in court, the prisoner's barrister successfully argued that his client could have put his fingerprints on that item at any time and place, and he was acquitted. But Butler was still as relentless as ever in his quest to arrest all of the team; his annual leave was spent in the south of France after he heard that some of the gang had fled there, and he cut a solitary figure as he strolled up and down the beach on the Côte D'Azur, questioning the English holidaymakers and showing them photographs of the wanted men.

Following the thirty-year sentences that were imposed on many of the gang, (and at which the investigating team took no pleasure, since the length of the sentences had thoroughly surprised them) Butler and his men were having a quiet drink in the office, when the door opened and in walked the Commissioner, Sir Joseph Simpson KBE. He accepted Butler's offer of a drink and requested a gin and water. Detective Sergeant Lou van Dyke told me that as he poured the drink Butler took this Heaven-sent opportunity to inform the commissioner of the reason for this modest celebration, with a view to getting his men on the bottom rung of a commissioner's commendation. "Never mind that, Butler," interrupted Sir Joseph. "What are your men doing about this spate of fur robberies, that's what I would like to know!"

It is a matter of record that the simultaneous dropping of the detectives' jaws occurred precisely at the same moment as Lou van Dyke dropped the commissioner's glass!

But with the sentencing out of the way, the train job was far from over. First Charlie Wilson escaped from Winson Green Prison; then, the following year, Ronnie Biggs escaped from Wandsworth Prison. Butler roared his displeasure; they might have escaped purely to spite him. The search for them, plus Bruce Reynolds, Ronald 'Buster' Edwards and Jimmy White who had never been caught, went on. By now on age limit, Butler pleaded for extensions to his service so that he could catch them.

Not that the Train Gang were his only concern. On 7 March 1966 there was an affray at 'Mr. Smith's Club' in south London where a local gangster named Dickie Hart was murdered, and Butler took up the investigation. Two days after that murder, Ronnie Kray shot George Cornell dead in *The Blind Beggar*. Butler arrested him and his brother Reg and put them up on an identification parade, spending months in the East End, trying to put together a case, all without success. Butler had tried previously to arrest the twins; in a report which he had submitted six years previously, he stated:

> Their reputation is already such, that persons threatened almost frantically deny visitations by anybody connected with the Kray twins. Not one victim can be persuaded to give evidence against anyone connected with their organization. The fact that Ronald Kray is certainly mentally unstable (to put it at the very least) is of immense importance to the others. And it adds considerably to the victim's undeniable urge to comply with demands made upon him, and to his atrocious memory when questioned by police at any later stage.

His inability to convict the Twins was one of Butler's few failures; in the Richardson torture case, he dealt with the retrial of Eddie Richardson and his conspiracy to pervert the course of justice with his brother, Charlie.

Jimmy White was arrested for the Train Job and 'Buster' Edwards gave himself up. On a mountain road outside Rigaud, Quebec, a man named Ronald Alloway helped push a car which appeared to have broken down and was seized. Alloway, whose real name was Charlie Wilson said, "Oh no, it's you Mr. Butler." It was. Butler had received some top-rate information that took him to Heathrow Airport in January 1968, with his aid, Detective Sergeant Ted Fuller. Not even Fuller's wife knew where he had gone. Fuller thought he knew where he was headed but he was wrong. Butler had put the rumour about that they were travelling to Italy and had his Squad driver drop them off at Heathrow's Terminal Two. As soon as the Squad car was out of sight, he and a bemused Fuller made their way to Terminal Three and thence to Canada.

Ten months later, Butler raided a house in Torquay, Devon. "Hello, Bruce," he said. "It's been a long time." Bruce Reynolds sighed. "*C'est la vie*," he replied. The arrest had come about after Butler had sent Bob Robinson to Torquay, having received information that Reynolds was somewhere in the area. "I was given four names that Reynolds had used in the past," Robinson told me, "but on no account was I to tell the local police that I was from the Flying Squad. Instead, I told them I was a Fraud Squad officer investigating a trade directory fraud and I went along to the local estate agents with my four names. I soon found the house where Reynolds was staying and I phoned Tommy."

John Simmonds who had by now returned to the Squad as a detective sergeant (first class), takes up the tale. "When Bob Robinson located Bruce Reynolds, Tom came into the Squad office at about 10.30pm. I was acting DI on the night provincial team." (Teams were kept ready for 'early, late and night provs', to assist provincial forces who telephoned the Flying Squad to request an arrest or a search within the Metropolitan Police District.) "He called me into his office and said, 'I'm taking all your team and leaving you here with the telephonist. You will not allow anyone – *under any circumstances* – to know that I have been here or that your team is not with you in London. No matter what happens, you will have to deal with it on your own.' The team and three drivers were called together. Tom told them he was going to take them out, they were to follow his car but maintain total radio silence and not answer any calls to them. One of the drivers asked if they would need to fill up their cars and Tom said, 'No, we're not going that far.' Outside of Central London, he pulled into an all-night petrol station and told the drivers to fill right up but still did not divulge the destination! I fielded several calls that night for assistance from outside forces, passing them on to local 'Q' Cars and when the dawn patrol arrived for the 7am handover, I told them we had been quiet so I had let all my team off early! The news of Reynolds' arrest broke during the day and the next morning, the conversation with the dawn patrol on handover was more colourful!"

Back now to Bob Robinson. "Down he came, nicked Reynolds and typically, forgot I was there so eventually, I had to come back by train." Not one word of the operation had leaked out, much to Robinson's relief - "imagine what Tommy's reaction would have been!"

On 4 April 1968 the civil rights activist, Dr. Martin Luther King Jr. was sitting on the balcony of the Lorraine Motel in Memphis, Tennessee when he was killed by a single shot. Found in a nearby boarding house were a rifle (which was confirmed as the murder weapon) and a set of binoculars; both bore the fingerprints of one James Earl Ray. Fleeing the country, Ray went first to Canada, then to Portugal and finally England, where he was arrested.

On 8 June 1968, David Pritchard, then a detective sergeant, was dealing with a prisoner in the charge room at Cannon Row police station, when in swept Tommy Butler and his entourage, one of whom was handcuffed to Ray, a large, well-dressed American. Butler and Pritchard chatted for a few moments, and then Pritchard, who had finished the formalities with his own prisoner, asked Butler if he could assist with the newly arrived prisoner; if, for instance he should take his fingerprints. Butler grinned and replied, *"This* prisoner, I have to fingerprint myself!"" His aid, Detective Sergeant Ted Fuller, had a chuckle over that one – "a very crafty move!" was his rejoinder. If anyone was going to give evidence in the USA that Ray's fingerprints matched those found on the offending rifle, it was going to be Tommy Butler – and nobody else! But in the event, neither Butler nor anybody else gave evidence, because Ray pleaded guilty to the murder.

John Simmonds' second tour on the Flying Squad lasted almost two years and during this time, his wife became seriously ill with septicemia following the birth of their second son: at one stage, she was not expected to live. Tommy Butler immediately gave him unconditional compassionate leave. At the worst of these nerve-racking times, Simmonds was due to give evidence in a case of robbery at the Old Bailey. As well as having a chronically sick wife and looking after their older son, Simmonds was also giving their six-week-old baby four-hourly feeds. Butler arranged for a car to take him to the Old Bailey as soon as he had completed the morning feed, leaving Woman Detective Constable Merle Taylor (who later married John Du Rose) in charge. Upon arrival at the Bailey, Simmonds was ushered straight into the witness box, the prosecuting counsel mentioning to the Trial Judge, 'This is the officer I've spoken about': and with his evidence disposed of, Simmonds was whisked back home, in time for the next feed. It was an example of how Butler looked after his men; the two robbers, incidentally, received five years each.

Some time later, there was a certain amount of discord in the Squad office in respect of the drivers' duties. The main thrust of the argument from the drivers' spokesman concerned Butler's harsh regime and his lack of understanding of his men's welfare. Simmonds took the driver to one side and explained Butler's concern in his own recent case, whereupon the rather bolshie driver replied that it was no more than Butler should have done. Simmonds' response to the driver would, no doubt, nowadays have elicited a demand for stress counselling!

Butler had been appointed MBE in the 1967 New Year's Honours lists and he remained in office until his retirement at the end of the following year. After that, he lasted just over a year. The cancer which had been making its insidious way through his body finally caught up with him. Bob Robinson visited him in hospital and showed him a photograph which Ronnie Biggs had used to support his false passport application in the name of Terance Furminger. The man who had been so fanatical about catching the last of the Great Train Robbers gave the photograph no more than a cursory glance before sighing and turning his head away. Tommy Butler died, aged fifty-seven, in April 1970.

His great friend Peter Vibart followed him into retirement in January 1969, having attained the rank of detective superintendent. His career had been just as distinguished as Butler's; he received a total of sixty-five commendations and was awarded the Queen's

Police Medal. He died six years after his comrade.

A selfish man in many ways, Butler nevertheless earned the admiration of his men. He had a long-term girlfriend, Dorothy, who was a 'Clippy' for London Transport and they were devoted to each other. On the few occasions that he permitted himself to relax, Butler watched Western films. His favourite was *Shane* although he knew the directors and stars of hundreds of others.

Butler and Vibart were workaholics, both of them putting in anything between sixteen and twenty hours a day. As an aid, Vibart was so committed to catching criminals that during the war he would stay in the section house, rather than go home to Twickenham; as a Squad guv'nor, Butler would get a lift home in one of the night-duty Squad cars. But he would never permit a Squad driver to drop him outside his mother's address; even if it was raining, he would always walk the last hundred yards home, in order not to wake her.

'The Terrible Twins' reputation was best summed up by the great train robber, Roy James. Upon hearing who was leading the hunt for the gang, James said, simply, "We're nicked."

They were.

CHAPTER 9

Ian Forbes – The Tarland Ploughman

Aberdeenshire, in the north-east portion of Scotland covers over 6,300 square kilometres and is bound on its north and east coasts by the North Sea. So enchanted was Queen Victoria with that part of Scotland that in September 1848 she was prompted to record: 'All seemed to breathe freedom and peace, and to make one forget the world and its sad turmoils.' The area is famed for its granite, its cattle, its farmlands – and its pipe bands.

Just east of the Grampian Mountains is the town of Tarland. On a sunny day in 1958 the Braemar Band had been well-received by the townspeople – their rendition of *The March of the Cameron Men* had been especially applauded – and now the band was taking a break and a much-needed glass in the hospitality tent. Tony Bruce sometimes played the bagpipes in the band, although on that day he was playing the drum. He was chatting to one of his colleagues when a man entered the tent. Bruce had never seen him before but he was immediately struck by the visitor's charismatic presence. It was not his height; the man, who was in his mid-forties, was just half an inch over five feet eight. But he was strongly built and he looked tough, too; Bruce noted a scar on the side of his rather pudgy face – a souvenir received from a German sniper near the Reichwalde Forest, some thirteen years previously.

There was certainly something about the man that made the company take notice of him; he already knew some of them, and from the laughing and joking that was going on there was no doubt that he was well liked and respected. The visitor announced that he would like to buy everybody in the band a drink and the offer was greeted with great enthusiasm.

"Who is he?" Bruce asked a fellow band member. "Him? Why, that's Ian Forbes," replied his companion, and as he noted the lack of comprehension on Bruce's face, he added by way of explanation, "He's one of the Big Five."

Bruce wondered what exactly being one of a Big Five actually was, although his colleague had possibly let his enthusiasm run slightly away with him. 'The Big Five' was the journalists' name for the four area detective chief superintendents, plus their counterpart at the Yard who controlled all of the CID officers in the Metropolitan Police: at that time, Ian Forbes was merely a detective sergeant (first class) on the Yard's Flying Squad.

But after Forbes had, with almost unheard of generosity, bought the band a second round of drinks, Bruce struck up a conversation with him. At that time, Bruce held the very responsible position of gamekeeper, but as he and Forbes spoke more and more about the world of the Metropolitan Police, Bruce's inclination to continue his present employment grew less and less; it would lead Bruce to commence a career that would last thirty-eight years in London's Police Force. Although he and Forbes would never work together, this chance meeting would forge a friendship between the two men which would last until Forbes' death, nearly forty years later.

As the conversation came to a close, Bruce asked his benefactor what connection he had with the town of Tarland. Forbes grinned, swallowed the remainder of his Glenfiddich – the only Malt he ever drank – and clapped Bruce on the back. "Laddie," he laughed, "I'm the Tarland Ploughman!"

Few police officers at the Yard could claim to have ploughed farmland, using a pair of giant Clydesdales, as their former trade or calling. But Forbes, who would rise to the rank of deputy assistant commissioner, had – and this is how it all came about.

*

Ian Forbes (he pronounced his name 'For – bes' in the traditional Scottish style) was born on 30 March 1914 at Lumphanan, Aberdeenshire and he was one of a family of seven children. His was a family of farmers – their farm had been the last in the 1870s to plough using a team of oxen – and although there was a suggestion of further education (he had received an elementary education at the Scottish Day School, obtaining a Higher School Certificate) the family budget simply would not stretch to it and Ian Forbes left school at the age of fourteen and went to work on the farm.

Forbes looked for interests outside the world of agriculture; he joined the Territorial Battalion of the 5th/7th Gordon Highlanders on 1 October 1932 and remained with them until 30 September 1937. Between times, he applied to join the Metropolitan Police; he was turned down. Five more years passed before 'The Tarland Ploughman' applied again; this time, he was accepted and was one of seventeen candidates who joined the Metropolitan Police on 13 February 1939. After the rolling pastures of Aberdeenshire, his introduction to the East End of London, with his posting to 'G' Division, was unlike anything he had encountered before.

Forbes got straight on with the job at Commercial Street police station as Police Constable 469'G', and in policing one of the toughest areas of the Metropolitan Police District, he received enormous help and encouragement from the other constables and sergeants; everybody looked after everybody else.

He made an impressive number of crime arrests as a constable on the beat; within two years he applied to become an aid to CID and now he covered the area surrounding City Road and Islington, as well as Commercial Street. Like many other officers before and after him, Forbes fell in love with the area and its inhabitants; he would return to 'G' Division time and time again, both on postings and during his time on the Flying Squad. In 1941, he married Lillian, the daughter of an East End police officer. It was a marriage of great happiness which lasted over fifty-five years. They were devoted to each other and as Tony Bruce would later say, "they were like a double act. When Ian was off-duty, Lillian would inevitably be with him and if he forgot a name – not very often! – she would remind him of it." A son was born later that year and then tragedy struck; a daughter was born in 1946 but died the following year. Another son was born in 1948.

In 1943 Forbes had just been awarded his first commissioner's commendation for his action in a case of shopbreaking and receiving, when he was called up for service with the war-time armed forces. On 4 November he joined the regular battalion of his old territorial unit, the Gordon Highlanders and served with them until he went overseas, when he was transferred to the 2nd Battalion of the Seaforth Highlanders.

Landing on Arromanches Beach in 1944, his unit fought its way through France, Holland and Germany. The encounter with the German sniper curtailed any plans for a field commission, and after administration work in Germany at the end of the war, Corporal 14669371 Forbes was happy to be demobilised on 13 January 1946 and be returned to 'G' Division.

His skills as an embryo detective needed little honing; on 4 November 1946 he was appointed detective constable and posted to Gray's Inn Road police station in 'E' Division. He was awarded a second commissioner's commendation for what was described as 'valuable assistance and ability in a case of murder' – in fact, Forbes had used tact and kindness when arresting a frightened, deaf man, who had murdered a part-time prostitute.

Now, he really learnt his trade as a detective; in the four-and-a-half years that he spent at Gray's Inn Road he helped investigate several murders and also dealt with the waves of Scotsmen, especially Glaswegians, who arrived at Kings Cross and Euston Stations, ready for any kind of violent crime in the capital; plus the legitimate and illegitimate trading in gold, precious metals and gems in nearby Hatton Garden.

Forbes had passed his examination for second class detective sergeant within one month of becoming a detective constable, but when he was promoted in 1951, it was to the dreaded Criminal Records Office (CRO) that he was sent. Working detectives viewed this posting with horror; it was considered (with some justification) to represent two years of unadulterated misery. It is not entirely clear how he achieved it – Forbes was certainly a resourceful man – but within two months of being posted to CRO, he was transferred to 'D' Division – Paddington police station.

At the time of his transfer on 4 June 1951 there were some magnificent police officers serving on 'D' Division. The detective superintendent was John Pretsell Jamieson, a fellow Scot, with a tremendous reputation as an investigator. Another Scot, John McIvor was divisional detective inspector at Paddington; he would go on to become commandant of the Detective Training School in the 1970s. Tommy Butler was there as a first class detective sergeant; before long, promotion to detective inspector would take him back to the Flying Squad - and again and again – culminating in his successful investigation of the Great Train Robbery. Leonard 'Nipper' Read, who would go on the smash the Kray Twins was also there as a detective constable and it was a happy, hard-working office. Forbes was certainly hard at work; in 1952 he collected a commissioner's commendation for ability in a case of conspiracy to defraud. A year later, another for ability in a case of warehousebreaking and two days after that, another for effecting the arrest of three persistent criminals. When, the following year, he was awarded another commissioner's commendation for his ability in a case of larceny and fraudulent conversion, being brought to notice time and time again paid off and on 1 February 1955 he was transferred to the Flying Squad.

The head of the Squad at that time was the highly respected Reginald William Lockerbie Spooner, the chain-smoking, former wartime major in Military Intelligence. Detective Sergeant Ted Fuller had followed Forbes on to the Squad from Paddington and now they worked together for the rest of Forbes' four-year posting there. Fred Lambert, who served on the Flying Squad for eleven years in four ascending ranks and retired as a detective chief superintendent, recalls that Forbes and Fuller were known as "'Fimph & Fumph, the gin ponces' but they were a very well informed and hard working pair. They were not on our team," he added, "but if ever we thought we might need assistance, we always called on them."

And six months after Forbes' posting, Tommy Butler, now a detective inspector also followed him on to the Squad; both of them would be commended by the commissioner on 9 April 1957 for their work in a case of conspiracy to steal.

Other commendations were awarded to Forbes before and after that one: on 22 July 1955 for 'initiative and determination' in a difficult case of conspiracy and four days later, another for 'ability and determination' in a case of larceny and false pretences. Later that year, both he and Fuller were commended for their 'ability and persistence' in arresting two troublesome criminals; these were a pair of toffs who had carried out a series of very successful and high-value distraction shopliftings. But violent robberies were on the increase and of the three other commissioner's commendations that he would be awarded during his time on the Flying Squad, two of them were for the arrest of violent criminals for robbery with violence.

Towards the end of his first tour on the Flying Squad, on 5 January 1959, Forbes reported to the Police College at Ryton-on-Dunsmore and two-and-a-half months after the conclusion of the course on 12 June 1959, he was promoted to detective inspector.

He had served his five year posting on the Flying Squad in three ranks – second class detective sergeant, first class detective sergeant and now, detective inspector – and nine months later, he utilised his experience from the Squad and the knowledge gleaned at the Police College to become an instructor at the Detective Training School at Hendon.

John Simmonds was on his CID course and Forbes was one of his instructors. On Wednesday evenings it was the practice to have a drink in the clubhouse at Hendon and Simmonds recalls the occasion when one of his contemporaries, noted for his obsequiousness, spotted Forbes, who had just entered the club. "Mr. Forbes," he cried, across the bar, "can I get you a drink?" A hush descended across the room, at this blatant attempt at toad-eating. "Aye, laddie," replied Forbes, "I'll have a wee drop of Scotch." "Anything to go with it, Mr. Forbes?" simpered the crawler. "Aye, laddie," answered Forbes, a wry smile on his lips. "Another wee drop of Scotch!" The bar erupted with laughter at the way Forbes had put the class sycophant in his place!

But the second tale that Simmonds remembers was an example of Forbes' compassion to a subordinate. On the same course was an overseas officer who was well liked but not academically sound, and his future depended on his success at Hendon. During the final (and all-important) examination during which Forbes was the invigilator, he strolled around the classroom, glancing at the various candidates work. As he arrived at the overseas student's desk, he looked at what he had written in response to one of the questions. Gently picking up his paper, he pushed the student's chair towards the candidate next to him (who was obviously a lot brighter) and murmured, "Read what he's written!"

"Ian would give a detailed lecture on his subject and cover all the aspects of the law," Simmonds told me, almost forty-four years later, "but he would balance it with sound advice from his years of being a practical detective; which not all the instructors were able to do." Doug Bowles agrees with those sentiments, remembering Forbes' excellent lecture on pickpockets.

Eighteen months later, Forbes returned to the Flying Squad and with lorry hi-jackings on the increase, receivers' run-ins were turned over on an almost daily basis. Armed robbery was also becoming more prevalent and on 7 March 1962 Forbes received his fifteenth and final commissioner's commendation for 'ability and determination' in the conviction of four persistent criminals for robbery.

It was around this time that Billy Milne first met Ian Forbes. Commercial Street police station provided a safe haven against the driving rain of a winter's evening and Milne, then an aid to CID was grateful for the arrests that had brought him into the warmth of the CID office. His back to the door, Milne suddenly heard the sound of a voice with a real Doric brogue, not so different from the voices he recalled from his home town of Banff. Turning, Milne saw Forbes – "stocky, weather-beaten complexion, smiling, sparkling eyes, short, dark hair. He was wearing an old mackintosh, a battered dark brown trilby, suited and stout shoes. With this description and the manner of his dress, to me he epitomized an Aberdeenshire farmer. His walk was the slow and measured tread of the farmer, 'gan' across a ploed park' – 'a farm chiel fae back hame."

Milne remembers that Forbes' Squad team was very active that night – they had prisoners in from south and east London – and also, that Forbes was very forthright with those prisoners. He left them in no doubt what was going to happen to them: "when he spoke, his eyelids would almost close and his head would slightly tilt back – and then it was done, take it or leave it."

One of the reasons for Forbes' many successes, Milne told me, was the use of informants. Forbes gained their trust because he never went back on his word. Similarly, he was just as straight with his team members; he was loyal and supportive towards them and he expected dependability in return. If anybody crossed him or displayed 'any dodgy tendency' then that person was off the team; the same applied equally to shirkers.

After eighteen months of Squad service, Forbes was promoted to detective chief inspector and posted back to 'G' Division, where he stayed for just over a year. Then something curious happened. On 6 July 1964, he was posted back to the Flying Squad. A month later, on 4 August 1964, he was posted to C1 Department. Two weeks after that, on 17 August 1964, he was promoted to detective superintendent and posted back to 'G' Division. Some of the shortest postings ever. But he busied himself with the arrest of David Barnard, a highly dangerous young man who was convicted of assault with intent to rob and possessing a firearm with intent to endanger life, in which he was assisted by some of the 'G' Division aids. The aids who struck terror into the hearts of the thieves and tearaways of the area would feature prominently in his next case, which would bring the name of Ian Forbes to everybody's attention.

*

The specialty of Walter 'Angel Face' Probyn was a hatred of police; on one occasion as a juvenile, he had stabbed a police officer with a knife, and on another he had attacked a police officer with the jagged edge of a sardine can before attempting to use a chopper on him.

During one of his innumerable escapes from prison and other places of confinement, he had used a gun to resist arrest, was overpowered and duly sentenced to thirty months' imprisonment. Probyn married Beryl, a long-term girlfriend, in 1963 and the following week he was arrested for shopbreaking and larceny: on 30 July he was sentenced to five years' imprisonment. Just over a year later, he escaped from Dartmoor Prison.

It appeared that Beryl had been cohabiting with a certain Alfie 'Punchie' Hines during Probyn's enforced absence and she and Hines had quarrelled. During the seven weeks that Probyn was on the run, Hines had been lured out of a pub by a woman with dark hair, wearing dark glasses, whereupon he was shot in the legs by an unknown assailant. He refused to assist Forbes in any way with his investigation into the matter.

Forbes then received a tip-off that Probyn and his wife had been seen on 'G' Division's ground; the informant did mention that Forbes might find it difficult to identify Beryl, since her fair hair had been dyed black and she now continually wore dark glasses.

Forbes learnt that Probyn had arranged to meet someone during the evening of 16 October 1964, outside the Post Office situated in Burdett Road, Limehouse at the junction with Dod Street. The area was staked out by a Flying Squad team and also a large number of 'G' Division aids. Probyn and Beryl duly arrived in a hired car, which they parked around the corner in Piggott Street. They got out and walked towards the Post Office and then Probyn, with his criminal's instinct for self-preservation, realised that something was well and truly up. He and his wife made a break for it, and when they were chased across a flat roof Probyn turned and fired the first of nine shots from a .22 Star target pistol at the pursuing officers.

How nobody was killed was nothing short of a miracle. It was clear from the direction of travel that the Probyns were making for their car; after being hit with a broom and being brought down by a rugby tackle, Probyn struggled to his feet and kept going, firing as he went.

By now, police cars had hemmed in Probyn's car; Beryl, who had been exhorting her husband to shoot at their pursuers, had been arrested but Probyn still managed to get into the car. Police Constable Terry Brown grabbed hold of a broom, smashed the windscreen with it and jabbed it at Probyn: but firing a shot at Forbes, Probyn dived through the broken window and landed on the pavement on all fours. Police Constable Kenny Bowerman hit him with his truncheon; Probyn retaliated by pistol-whipping him so savagely that Bowerman's head, as he later told me, "Swelled up like a football." Two other police officers tackled him but still he fought his way loose, fired another shot and ran off. He was chased and finally overpowered in the back garden of a nearby house; sadly, he suffered the loss of two teeth, a broken arm and several broken ribs during the course of his arrest and did not make an appearance at Thames Magistrates' Court until five days later.

Both Probyn and his wife pleaded not guilty to a whole range of charges at the Old Bailey, stating that they thought that the police officers were "Punchy Hines and his lot". Unfortunately, the jury disbelieved them; worse still, the Trial Judge was the very crusty and pro-police Mr. Justice Melford Stevenson who, on 20 February 1965, sentenced Probyn to a total of twelve years' imprisonment for shooting with intent to cause grievous bodily harm, inflicting grievous bodily harm and firearms offences, this sentence to run consecutive to the five-year sentence imposed before his escape. Beryl Probyn had told the court, "I just shouted to my husband to get himself away," but her credibility took a dent, after it was revealed that inside her handbag were 174 rounds of ammunition, and for aiding and abetting her husband, she was sentenced to five years' imprisonment.

Four of the police officers were awarded the George Medal. Three others were awarded the British Empire Medal for Gallantry – one of them, Detective Sergeant Pat Gibbens was awarded a bar to the award four years later for tackling an armed gang in Barking – and others were commended by the Commissioner.

In the New Year's Honours list for 1966, Forbes was awarded the Queen's Police Medal for distinguished service. He had solved the eight murders that had been committed during his stay on 'G' Division. Billy Milne recalls receiving a telephone call from Forbes one Christmas Eve, at three o'clock in the morning. "Billy, it's Ian. Get to 'GI' (Islington police station) as quick as you can and start getting the lads in. We've got a murder; I'll be there as soon as I can." There were three shootings that Christmas and although none of the suspects were 'names on a plate' (or more prosaically, immediately identifiable), Forbes arrested them all. He did this by the judicious use of informants and by selecting the most suitable officers for the various enquiries from all over the Division. No-one was permitted to try to tell Forbes how to run his Division. The senior officers at the Yard wanted results and Forbes got them, but he would brook no interference and anyone who tried to interfere with him or, worse still, 'his lads', would get the sharp edge of his tongue.

Forbes was indefatigable. After a few Glenfiddichs in *The Eagle*, the pub just around the corner from City Road police station, Milne would see him in the CID office, jacket off, sleeves rolled up, two-finger typing a report for the typist to tidy up the following morning. Then he would be driven home to his house in Wembley, where Lily would always have the offer of soup for the driver who would often stay until he drove Forbes back to the office at eight o'clock, sharp.

On 7 March 1966, Forbes was posted to C1 Murder Squad at the Yard. His first investigation took him to County Durham to investigate the death of a woman who, it appeared, had been highly unpleasant to her husband. In convicting him of murder, the jury added a recommendation for mercy. It had been an unpleasant case all round; the man convicted was a fellow police officer.

Next, the murder of a bus conductress sent Forbes to Tynemouth; a great deal of patient work, especially by the local officers, resulted in the arrest of Thomas Alan Duffy. Forbes felt that he was one killer who should never be released.

He was called to Ealing police station to investigate what was initially thought to be a case of murder, where the victim had sustained terrible injuries through a shotgun blast and was not expected to live. Gerry O'Donoghue, then an aid to CID, remembers every telephone ringing in the CID office, officers racing about grabbing handfuls of statement forms, with a detective sergeant trying to control and organize the enquiry. The uniform inspector was at the house where the offence had been committed; he was in possession of the offending shotgun, three suspects and the baying press, and he wanted to know what to do with all of them. Another uniformed officer was at the hospital and he wanted assistance with the forensic aspect of the victim's bloodstained clothing as well as statements from the ambulance crew and the doctors.

Into this scene of orchestrated chaos, stepped Ian Forbes. Everybody was talking to him at once. He simply held up his hands for quiet, and spoke with "a quiet, reassuring Scottish accent," recalls O'Donoghue. "The voice, combined with his genial, smiling appearance immediately calmed things down and introduced much needed confidence to the team."

"Steady, laddies," said Forbes. "The first thing I need … is a nice, wee cup of tea." When O'Donoghue returned with the requested cuppa, "Ian was directing operations like a ship's captain, with a steady hand at the helm." Forbes then calmly and methodically gathered the evidence, carried out his investigations and ensured that the three suspects, all of whom were claiming that they had pulled the trigger, were locked up. They and the press were demanding to speak to Forbes; he ignored the lot of them and sent his staff home, telling them that he wanted them 'nice and fresh' to start hard work the following day at nine-thirty, sharp.

It turned out not to be a murder; not that that mattered to Forbes. Two of the suspects – the perpetrator's parents – decided in the cold light of day that neither of them had pulled the trigger. Their son, who had, later pleaded guilty to attempted murder and was sentenced to eight years' imprisonment. Gerry O'Donoghue described the investigation as "faultless" and added, "Everyone on Ian's team learned an invaluable lesson from him on keeping calm and planning ahead."

The following March, what had initially been believed to be nothing more than a car accident in Reading was then thought to be a murder; that was the suspicion of an alert young police constable, aptly named Sherlock. Forbes thought so too, took charge of the investigation and assembled a team of detectives from Nos. 5 and 6 Regional Crime Squad. A plot to murder Mrs. June Cook, estranged from her husband Ray, who was having an affair with a girl named Kim Newell, twenty-one years his junior, was uncovered when another man named Eric Jones was arrested for the offence; he later pleaded guilty and gave evidence against the others. At the trial, Newell, Cook and Jones were all sentenced to life imprisonment and the judge commended the investigating team, especially PC Sherlock. Because of Kim Newell's beauty, the case received a great deal of publicity.

It would be as nothing compared with one of Forbes' last murder investigations.

*

Child murders always have and always will be deeply emotive. In January 1966, two little girls aged five and six were found murdered in Staffordshire; one at least had been sexually assaulted and both bodies were found in a ditch, one lying on top of the other. The Yard was called in and Detective Superintendent Cyril Gold, a veteran investigator with a string of successful murder investigations to his credit was appointed investigating officer. Gold worked non-stop for five months on the case and got precisely nowhere.

Twenty months later, there was another murder in the same area; this time, the victim was a seven-year-old-girl named Christine Darby. Her body was discovered on Cannock Chase – described by one of the local officers as being, 'the greatest open-air brothel in the Midlands' – and as Forbes looked down at the pathetic little body, who had obviously suffered sexual molestation, perhaps he thought of his own daughter who had died twenty years before; or perhaps not. But what he did feel was rage that a person could do this to a child, and with that rage was a feeling of utter resolution that he would find the person responsible.

Christine had been seen getting into a grey car – possibly an Austin A55 or A60 – and Forbes had every owner of those types of car traced, with a view to eliminating them, including those who had moved abroad. Over 80,000 people were questioned. House-to-house checks were made at 185,000 addresses. An artist had produced a coloured picture taken from descriptions the police had received, and apart from being published in *Police Gazette*, it was circulated to every notice board at every police station in England, Scotland and Wales.

A year went by, with Forbes working every single day, fourteen hours per day. Like Gold, he had got nowhere. After taking a much needed break, he returned to Staffordshire to continue the investigation. And then, this happened.

Two months after Forbes' return, a man tried to tempt a ten-year-old girl into his car, the evening before Guy Fawkes Night, on the promise of there being fireworks in the car. The girl refused, the man grabbed hold of her but she managed to pull herself away. The man then jumped into the car – it was a green and white Ford Corsair – and quickly drove off. Fortunately, his actions had been observed by an adult who noted the registration number of the car.

The registered owner of the car was a man named Raymond Leslie Morris. Four years previously, he had been questioned about an attack on a little girl, but his wife had given him an alibi. Two years later, he was questioned about the murder of the two little girls which had been investigated by Detective Superintendent Gold; again he was released. Then ten months before the murder of Christine Darby he had been arrested for indecently assaulting two girls, aged ten and eleven and taking photographs of them. Morris was interviewed, but denied the allegations and the matter was submitted for legal advice; no action was taken.

He had twice been interviewed about Christine's murder; Raymond Morris' own brother had told police that his brother had an abnormal sexual appetite and could well have been responsible for the murder of the little girls. In fact, Raymond Morris bore a strong resemblance to the artist's picture which had been circulated all over the United Kingdom: but Morris' wife once again gave her husband an alibi and he was released.

Morris was questioned about the attempted abduction and predictably he denied it. But this time, his wife gave him no alibi. The evidence was building up and the net was closing in on Morris. Enquiries revealed that Morris had owned a grey Austin A55 – and it was discovered that prior to marrying for the second time he had made indecent approaches towards two girls aged eleven and twelve, who were relatives of his first wife.

Forbes arrested Morris, and now his wife admitted that the alibi she had provided for him in respect of the Christine Darby killing was untrue. Morris was identified as being at Cannock Chase at the time of the killing, and amongst the mass of photographs of young girls found in his flat was one of him, taken with a delayed action shutter, indecently assaulting his wife's five-year-old cousin.

Because of the lack of evidence, Morris was never charged with the murders of the other children; then again, neither was anybody else. But Forbes was given a tremendous commendation from the judge, Mr. Justice Ashworth, after Morris was convicted of the murder of Christine Darby and sentenced to life imprisonment.

*

When it was discovered that 1964 represented the worst crime figures of the twentieth century for London, something fairly dramatic had to be done to fight back. It was. The Regional Crime Squads were formed and they covered nine areas, not purely in London but all over the United Kingdom: at Manchester, Durham, Wakefield, Birmingham, Hatfield, Brighton, Bristol and Cardiff. The London Branch – No. 9 Squad – originally had five offices dotted around the perimeter of the Metropolitan Police District and these were staffed with experienced Metropolitan detectives, plus provincial officers from the adjacent constabularies. The Crime Squads were tasked with combating country house burglaries, lorry hi-jackings and indeed, any type of serious cross-border crime. In addition (and this was kept purely to the Crime Squads in the constabulary areas) they were used in large-scale enquiries, such as murders. In 1966 the five London offices were extended to six offices in outer London and four in inner London. The following year, the latter four offices came under the control of the Flying Squad.

On 1 January 1969 Forbes was promoted detective chief superintendent and became co-ordinator of No. 9 Regional Crime Squad. Half-way through the year, his rank was regraded to that of commander, and it was at that time that he also assumed command of C9 Department, the Metropolitan and Provincial Crime Branch, which was tasked to assist provincial forces investigating specific crimes with a London connection.

It was a good year for No. 9 Regional Crime Squad. In fact, "the best year ever," according to the commissioner in his annual report, with 850 arrests and property valued at almost three-quarters of a million pounds recovered. "These results," enthused the commissioner, "more than justify the original concept of the various Regional Crime Squads." On 1 January 1970 Forbes replaced John Bliss after successfully applying for his job of National Co-ordinator of the Regional Crime Squad and was promoted deputy assistant commissioner; three rank jumps within a year – not bad going!

As National Co-ordinator, Forbes worked from the Yard. His first year in office saw No. 9 Regional Crime Squad make 915 arrests and recover property valued in excess of £800,000. In 1971 the co-operation between the Regional Crime Squad offices had been outstanding, resulting in investigations into and arrests for murder, as well as dealing with an international gang counterfeiting American Express cheques, armed robberies, the theft and re-sale of caravans and organised theft from trains: in London alone, 772 arrests had been made, resulting in the recovery of property valued at £883,000.

Stolen property worth more than £1 million was recovered during 1972 and 827 arrests (including over 25% more arrests for robbery than in 1971) were made by No. 9 Regional Crime Squad. "It is clear," said the commissioner, in his Annual Report for that year, "that the squad has got its priorities right in concentrating on the professional violent criminal. The squad has continued to develop its liaison with other branches, notably the Criminal Intelligence Branch, and with provincial forces, and the extent of the co-operation that it has received from other Regional Crime Squads has been noteworthy." That this had been achieved was due to Forbes' leadership.

Forbes had already applied successfully to the Secretary of State for an extension to his service but now was a good time to go. The posting as National Co-ordinator had crowned his career with success. He was enormously popular with the rank-and-file police officers because he would never forget a name, or so it seemed. Like many successful detectives of his era, he kept a small notebook with the names and details of police officers whom he had met, often years before, and a quick glance at the book when he was in their company again would quickly refresh his memory. In fact, Forbes went further than his small book; he took care to find out about the details of officers whom he had never even met before. John Jones, later to become a detective superintendent, remembered when he was an aid to CID at Ruislip Police Station, having just been transferred from Birkenhead. He was alone in the CID office, when Forbes entered the office with his wife, Lily. They had never met before, but Forbes greeted him with the words, "You must be John Jones. How're you enjoying the Met?" This was astonishing enough, but Jones was utterly flabbergasted, when he continued, "and your wife Doreen, and your baby son; Mark's his name, I believe?"

"Gobsmacked, is the word," Jones told me. "Following this, he got down to 'doing the books' whilst giving me a fiver to get a bottle of malt which I shared with him and his wife. What a guv'nor!"

And that just about sums up Ian Forbes. A kind man. A generous man, although not a wasteful one. Mike Hoare MBE recalls him screwing the top on an almost empty whisky bottle, leaving it upside down overnight on a window ledge and then the following day rewarding his thriftiness with a nip from the bottle top – as Hoare remarked, "A real Scotsman!"

Brian Baister QPM, MA, later to become a deputy chief constable of Cheshire Constabulary, remembers driving through Staffordshire in 1968, as a detective constable on the Fraud Squad, when his car had to be repaired. The local constabulary arranged accommodation for him at the Country Club in Cannock, where Ian Forbes was staying whilst investigating the Christine Darby murder. Upon hearing that a fellow Met officer was there, Forbes took Baister to a drinks party with the Chief Constable, Arthur Rees, followed by dinner and then the lowering of a bottle of Glenfiddich. After breakfast, early the following morning, Forbes took the trouble to show him around the incident room. "Throughout our time together,"

Baister told me, "I was properly 'gobsmacked' that this legend should extend such time and courtesies to a young DC whom he had never met before. It was a man-management experience that was to stay with me for the rest of my service."

Peter Legge was already aware of Forbes' reputation for remembering names but in the early 1970s, he was going to find out just how justified it was. Legge was at a Regional Crime Squad retirement function, when he saw Forbes; it was only the second time they had met, the first occasion being several months before when he had attended a board for detective sergeant (first class). Forbes had been a member of Legge's board, which he had failed. "During the course of the farewell do, he came up to me and immediately addressed me by my name," recalls Legge, "and went on to talk about my appearance before the earlier promotion board and commented on the answers I had given to some of the questions that had been asked. I must say that I was gobsmacked and of course terribly impressed that this important man not only remembered my name but was able to discuss a selection board appearance many months before." So three individual officers admitted to being 'gobsmacked' as a result of their encounters with Forbes; it is easy to see why.

John Walsh was performing an admin job for Ferguson Walker, then the CID commander of No. 2 Area in February 1968, and when Walker accepted Walsh's invitation to wet his baby son's head, Walker's close friend, Ian Forbes came along, as well.

As the evening progressed, both men (each of whom was wearing a regulation fawn raincoat and brown trilby) had been discussing crime reduction over a bottle of scotch and were by now speaking in very quiet, measured tones. Forbes had started his slight rocking motion, already described by Billy Milne, whilst Walker, moving in precise synchronization, had started to rock sideways. Eventually, Forbes said, "You know the trouble with you, Fergie?" "Na," replied Walker, after a moment's deliberation. There was another pause, followed by a sip from his glass, before Forbes replied, "Ye drink too much!"

"Needless to say, they continued chatting, sipping and swaying for some considerable time," recalls Walsh, "and I am sure that much serious crime was solved during the proceedings!"

Although Forbes could not know it, the storm clouds were gathering; later that year, Ken Drury, the commander of the Flying Squad would be hopelessly compromised in a corruption enquiry, and the whistle was about to blow on the Flying Squad, the Obscene Publications Squad and later, the Central Drugs Squad.

So Forbes retired on 9 April 1972, having served thirty-three years and fifty-seven days. Aged fifty-eight, he moved to Wolverhampton and became head of security for the Tarmac Company. He was always pleased to see his old colleagues and often attended reunions; his appearance at the one for the 'G' Division's aid squad was especially well received. He adored his family and his grandchildren; he always said that a working man needed a good wife behind him to give stability in life and household, and in Lily he certainly had that.

In researching Forbes' career, I never once found anybody prepared to say a bad or even an unkind word about him. I find it strange that Ian Forbes never received any further public recognition for his work in the form of another decoration from the Queen, to complement his QPM; he surely merited one.

*

Forbes died on 13 August 1996, aged eighty-two; his health had been failing for some time. His funeral was well attended and Lily, who followed him to the grave five years later, asked Billy Milne to be one of the six pallbearers, four of whom had formerly been aids from 'G' Division. It was to those aids that he left one cherished memory. During the 1960s when they were in their heyday, the Kray twins lived and operated on neighbouring 'H' Division. "I hope they set foot on my patch," said Forbes, grimly.

Perhaps the twins heard the Tarland Ploughman's words. They were not the most intelligent of persons but then again, neither were they stupid. They never did.

CHAPTER 10

Bert Wickstead – The Gangbuster

When Reginald and Ronald Kray were each convicted of murder and sentenced to life imprisonment ("which I would recommend should not be less than thirty years," said the trial Judge, Mr. Justice Melford Stevenson) at the Old Bailey on 5 March 1969, it left a gap in London's underworld – particularly in the East End. It was not long before there were moves afoot to fill that void. The brothers Dixon tried and failed. Then it was the turn of the Tibbs family; they were also defeated. The man who was responsible for frustrating the activities of both families then looked around for other challenging targets; he found it with the Maltese Syndicate, who were controlling vice, prostitution and racketeering in the West End of London. They, too, were split up, arrested and imprisoned.

These tremendous inroads into organised crime were the result of the leadership of one man. Although under five feet ten inches tall, he was built like a tank and like that piece of machinery he barged through life, through the underworld and often, along the corridors of New Scotland Yard. He was blunt, his opinions were unshakeable, his rudeness was legendary and he got results; his name was Bert Wickstead.

*

Albert Sidney Wickstead was born on 26 April 1923 in Plaistow, a tough suburb of east London. The son of a foreman on the London Midland & Scottish Railway, Wickstead was the leader of the local gang who, possibly due to the impetuosity of his remarks, received well-merited clouts round the ear from the local copper, on a fairly regular basis. Like many boys of his age, he dreamed of becoming a professional footballer, but after twice breaking a leg these aspirations were permanently shelved. Wickstead received an elementary education at Burke Senior School, left when he was fourteen and at the age of seventeen and a half enlisted in the Royal Corps of Signals and saw war time service in India and the Far East. On 13 December 1947, Sergeant 5835081 Wickstead was demobilised. He was put on reserve until 10 September 1952 but he never returned to the colours. Wickstead was unaware of it, but he would have his own private war to fight.

He drifted from one job to another and toyed with the idea of re-joining the army. He was working as a clerk when he got into conversation with an uncle who was a detective sergeant at Chiswick police station, who suggested that his nephew might care to join the police. With his less than perfect eyesight, Wickstead had to struggle to get through the medical, but that was all; he passed his entrance exam with 421 marks out of a possible 650. At Training School he registered 100% in the passing-out exam, at the nine months intermediate exam he passed with 86% and in his final probationer's exam again he registered over 85% marks.

On 28 June 1948 Wickstead was posted to 'S' Division, went to work as a probationer police constable at Hampstead and expressed an early desire to join the CID. But Hampstead was not the busiest of areas for a keen young aspirant for the Department to 'make his bones' and it took him almost six years to be appointed to the CID. Fortuitously, he was awarded his first commissioner's commendation for 'ability in a case of larceny and receiving' at just about the time he went on a selection board for detective constable, which was a considerable help in getting through the board. He was posted to 'X' Division and within a couple of weeks he was sent to Eire on an extradition case. Whilst he was there. he developed quinsy and was hospitalised for several weeks. Whether or not his senior officers were annoyed at a very junior member of the Department presenting them with a bill for several thousand pounds'-worth of treatment or whether there was some other reason (his uncle, Jack Wickstead was also serving on the division) the fact remains that Wickstead's stay on 'X' Division lasted just six weeks before he was posted to 'N'

Division, where he would stay for the next four and a half years. Caledonian Road police station is now no longer operational but in the 1950s it was a focal point in a very tough area which was a hot-bed of villains and villainy.

Wickstead spotted a local criminal who was wanted for officebreaking, whilst he was travelling on the Tube. His arrest brought Wickstead his second commissioner's commendation and a third followed when he exercised 'alertness and initiative' in a case of housebreaking.

He spent a year at the Yard, attached to C1 Branch; it was a dreary posting and his successor in the post, David Pritchard, recalls that it was said that Wickstead never completed any enquiry he was given. He returned to Division on 21 September 1959, when he was promoted to detective sergeant (second class) and posted to 'G' Division's Commercial Street, which was almost certainly a merciful release. Less enjoyable was a painful boil adorning one of his buttocks, in consequence of which he was unable to take a dynamic part in the investigation of 'The Pen Club Murder', where, on 7 February 1960, Selwyn Keith Cooney, one of Billy Hill's associates, was shot to death. Instead, he was assigned to run the murder office and in learning much about the investigation of murder under the auspices of John Bliss, who would later be responsible for setting up the Regional Crime Squads, he was awarded a fourth commissioner's commendation. It was his first excursion into the world of high-level crime – some of the characters who featured to a lesser or greater degree in the case (who included the Krays) went on to become highly successful in the world of crime in the years that followed. Witnesses in the trial suffered from amnesia, others were threatened and then disappeared, attempts were made to nobble the jury and the three defendants were acquitted of the murder. Jimmy Nash, who witnesses swore had fired the fatal shot, was found guilty of inflicting grievous bodily harm and sentenced to five years' imprisonment; Joey Pyle and John Read each received eighteen months for assault. Wickstead was as incredulous at the result as anybody else.

After a short, nine-months stay on 'G' Division, Bert Wickstead was posted back to 'N' Division on 7 June 1960, and worked at Kentish Town and again, Caledonian Road. Whilst he was there, he collected a commissioner's commendation for 'alertness and perseverance' in a case of conspiracy to steal a loaded lorry: then on 11 February 1963 he was posted to Barnet on 'S' Division and two weeks later promoted to detective sergeant (first class). By his own admission, Wickstead loathed it there, saying there was nothing for him to do; and it was a considerable distance from his home, as well. Was it a punishment posting? By the fact that he was not promoted until two weeks after his posting, it could have been, but in any event, Wickstead protested so much that he lasted just five months, before he was posted back to 'G' Division.

"It's a funny thing," said one of Wickstead's contemporaries to me, at the time of his reign as a gangbuster, "but I remember old Bert as a DC and a second-class and he was as lazy as arseholes. Then he went to 'G' as a first class and that's when his career really took off." He might well have had a point. Between the ranks of detective constable and detective sergeant (first class), Wickstead had been commended by the commissioner five times; good, but not how one would envisage a potential gangbuster. My slanderous informant's assertions were to a certain extent substantiated, because it was Wickstead's practice to disappear on the Saturday afternoons when he was on duty, possibly to check the fortunes of West Ham United, leaving a couple of junior detectives to look after the office. Towards the end of the afternoon he would ring up the office and tell them to book him off-duty at five o'clock.

On one such afternoon, he had left the office in the care of Geoff Parratt and Gerry Wiltshire, then both aids to CID and all went well, until the arrival of an unexpected visitor. Asked the whereabouts of Wickstead, Parratt uneasily replied that he had 'just popped out.' Hardly had this travesty of the truth left Parratt's lips when the telephone rang, but before either of the aids could answer it, the receiver was picked up by the visitor. "DS Wickstead, 'ere," said a familiar voice. "Book us off at five o'clock."

"Book you off at five o'clock, Sergeant Wickstead?" said the visitor. "Certainly. And by the way, this is Detective Chief Superintendent Gerrard, speaking. Would you kindly present yourself in my office at City Road at nine o'clock on Monday morning?"

Fred Gerrard, who as Detective Chief Superintendent for the area was renowned for being a strict disciplinarian, especially when it came to matters of booking on and off duty, duly spoke to Wickstead on the Monday morning; what he said was not recorded and Wickstead would have gone to the block before he revealed the details of his admonishment but upon his return to the office he savagely castigated Messrs Parratt and Wiltshire for their sluggishness in answering the telephone. Yet all parties survived; Parratt and Wiltshire both rose to the rank of detective superintendent and Wickstead was about to have his hands full to such an extent that there would be no Saturday afternoons off for some considerable time. It was now that Wickstead's career to began to rocket.

*

A gang of young tearaways had stopped being a nuisance and graduated to being thoroughly dangerous when they acquired firearms. Apart from being a threat to the local neighbourhood, the ringleader had fired a shot at one of the crew of the local 'Q' Car, and Wickstead and six 'G' Division aids, with only the ringleader's nickname to go on, spent weeks searching for the gang. With the arrest of the gang leader, the names of the others followed, and at the Old Bailey, seven members of the gang were sent to prison. Wickstead was commended, first by the Trial Judge, Sir Carl Aarvold OBE, TD, then by the Director of Public Prosecutions and finally, for 'courage and ability' by the commissioner. But more importantly, the publicity that was generated by the case was unlike anything he had experienced before – the *Evening News* dubbed Wickstead and his team, 'The Magnificent Seven' – and he decided that he liked it.

It helped his promotion, too. Just two years after his advancement to first class sergeant, Wickstead was now promoted to detective inspector, and although he remained on 'G' Division, he was moved from Dalston to Stoke Newington. Then, as now, Stoke Newington was famed for its murder rate – sometimes five cases would be running from the same office – and Wickstead was thrown in at the deep end. He investigated a succession of murders and, to his intense annoyance, he was commended for none of them; probably because murder was so commonplace in that area. Matters changed when Wickstead arrested nine youths for senselessly attacking and stabbing orthodox Jews at their synagogues: apart from a commissioner's commendation for his 'persistence and ability' in the case, he received another welcome blast of publicity.

Wickstead was on a roll. He arrested ten people, some of whom were affiliated to the extreme right-wing National Socialist Party, who had sprayed offensive, anti-Semitic slogans on the walls of synagogues before setting fire to them; thirteen such places of worship were damaged. He was commended by Mr. Justice Phillimore at the Old Bailey and also by the commissioner: two years later he received another commissioner's commendation after the fanatical leader of the arsonists was jailed for eighteen months at the Old Bailey. This time the resultant publicity went through the roof, providing Wickstead with the proof, if ever it were needed, of the fame which accompanies the exploits of a small, select group of dedicated detectives.

Again, after the very short period of two years in the rank of detective inspector, he was promoted to detective chief inspector and posted to East Ham police station. Wickstead was never tolerant of corruption; he investigated the activities of two venal police officers and saw them kicked out of the Metropolitan Police and straight into a prison cell, both for a considerable period. Mick Gray, who later became a Flying Squad driver, remembers driving 'Kilo one-one' 'Q' Car and at the end of a successful tour, receiving a hand-written note from Wickstead, congratulating him on his efforts; it was not unusual for Wickstead to jump into the car and go out on patrol with the rest of the crew.

After just eighteen months in the rank of detective chief inspector, Wickstead was promoted again; it should have been to the rank of detective superintendent, but because the rank had been regraded he became detective chief superintendent of 'J' Division, which covered an enormous area.

Within a year of his arrival, a robbery occurred on 9 February at Barclays Bank, in the Ilford High Road – with £237,736 missing, it was England's biggest post-war bank robbery. With the assistance of an inside man and two security guards, the gang rather effortlessly seized and escaped with the money. It was the type of offence which normally would have been dealt with by the Flying Squad, but Wickstead had a profound dislike for the Squad, formed his own team and conducted the enquiry personally.

One by one, the prisoners for the bank robbery were brought in. It was rumoured that Wickstead had been part of the war -time SAS (in fact, he was not but the myth persisted) and one prisoner had to be actually carried sobbing up the stairs at Ilford Police Station, when he discovered that Wickstead was going to interview him. Wickstead enjoyed scouring the newspapers for details of his exploits: the prisoners were ferried to court in vans, accompanied fore and aft with marked police cars, their blue lights flashing and their two-tones wailing: when Wickstead strode into court, in an immaculately cut grey suit, a fashionable paisley foulard tie and an ostentatiously flopping silk breast-pocket handkerchief, everybody knew that they were in the presence of 'The Guv'nor'. The defence barristers might have saved their breath, because they did their clients no good whatsoever. "Why do you think my client would abscond, if he were to be granted bail?" asked one of them, at a remand hearing at Barking Magistrates' Court. "'Cos I know 'im," replied Wickstead, which was quite enough for the Magistrates, who nodded sagely and remanded the unfortunate prisoner in custody.

Graham Howard, who later served on the Serious Crime Squad, (and also achieved the rank of detective superintendent on the Regional Crime Squad) remembers that during the case at the Old Bailey, a witness was called for the defence. Into court came a large, long-haired and flashily-dressed man, who described his occupation as being an accountant. Never did a more unlikely-looking (or indeed unlikely sounding) accountant exist, and half-way through his evidence, a very puzzled trial Judge courteously interrupted him: "I beg your pardon, but would you be so kind as to tell the court precisely what *sort* of an accountant you are?"

There came a concentrated roar of laughter from the packed courtroom, as the witness explained that he was, in fact, a turf accountant!

The security guards and the inside man were convicted of conspiracy and jailed. Eventually, even though £3,000 was all that was recovered of the stolen money, Ronnie Dark and Micky Green were each sentenced to eighteen years' imprisonment for their parts in the raid. Arthur Saunders received fifteen years. He had served two years of his sentence when Bertie Smalls (who had participated in the Ilford robbery) started his new career as Supergrass, admitted his part and named all of the other participants in the raid; however, he was able to state categorically that Saunders was not one of the gang and the latter was released from prison.

John Woodhouse was a very new aid to CID in 1970 and within weeks of being appointed, he was swept up as part of Wickstead's team. Woodhouse described Wickstead as being, "terrifying", the more so when after one weeks service on the squad, Wickstead called him into his office. Trembling, Woodhouse was treated to a Wickstead tongue-lashing for failing to put in for enough expenses. It was something that Wickstead persisted in doing – looking after the troops. If you were on his team, you were one of his boys – this included his team's wives, who received flowers from Wickstead when they were ill – and therefore to be looked after. Later, at a Yard meeting, during the time that Wickstead headed the Serious Crime Squad, he was one of a number of detective chief superintendents seated around the deputy assistant commissioner's table. The matter of budgetary restrictions was raised and, doubtless hoping to gain some kudos, one of the senior officers made the snide remark, "Well, we all know Mr. Wickstead's views on that, with his men putting in expenses of £20 per week."

"Yes!" shouted Wickstead, jumping to his feet and crashing his fist down on the table, "and it's all wrong!" The other chief superintendents only had time to gape momentarily before Wickstead, still at full volume, continued, "because with the sort of work they're doing, they ought to get *ten times* as fucking much!"

Terrifying or not, Woodhouse found Wickstead enormously charismatic: when Wickstead entered a room, he said, it was like being in the presence of a superstar – all eyes were focused on him and conversation ceased.

John Woodhouse had one other memory of Wickstead. The 'J' Division annual CID Dinner and Dance was held at Manor Hall, Chigwell – every CID officer, without exception, was expected to attend – and Woodhouse was told that, as the youngest aid, it was incumbent on him to make a speech. So he did, and considered he was doing quite well, when suddenly Wickstead made a remark. Without even thinking, Woodhouse said, "Do you mind? I'm talking!" and a sudden, horrified silence descended on the hall. The seconds ticked by and then slowly Wickstead smiled and the whole of the assembled 'J' Division CID breathed normally again. Of course, several of the workforce gloomily predicted that come the following morning, Woodhouse would "find himself wearing a top hat", and a grey-faced Woodhouse conceded that this might well be true. In fact, nothing of the kind happened; Wickstead knew an officer who could keep his head in trying circumstances when he saw one. He posted Woodhouse on to the next available 'Q' car which turned out to be one its most successful tours.

*

When Leonard 'Nipper' Read, the man who had brought down the Krays, put forward the proposal to form the Serious Crime Squad, many people naturally thought it would be headed by him. But Read attended the senior command course at Bramshill College, and after he was promoted to detective chief superintendent, he was posted to run 'Y' Division and was therefore unavailable.

Wickstead appeared the obvious choice. Tough and honest, there was no doubt he would do the Metropolitan Police a power of good, as head of the Squad. He appeared in the press as 'The Old Grey Fox' although in reality he probably promulgated the nickname himself. Like Read, he eschewed the Yard as a place of toil, thinking there were too many corrupt officers there, and initially took over Read's old suite at Tintagel House, on the south side of the Thames, opposite the Houses of Parliament. He also inherited Detective Sergeant Bill Waite, a tough veteran of the Regional Crime Squad who had also worked on the Richardson torture case and the Kray enquiry.

The Dixon Brothers were natural candidates to slip into the shoes so recently vacated by the Kray twins. They had a considerable reputation as hard men; George, at six feet tall and heavily built was a hard puncher who exuded menace and a man of few words. Although he had originally got on well with the Krays, he had somehow incurred the displeasure of Ronnie Kray (it did not take much), so much so that when he was seated in the Green Dragon club, Ronnie walked up to him, put a Luger to his head and pulled the trigger. The pistol failed to go off and Kray later sent Dixon the offending bullet, complete with an indentation of the firing pin on the casing, in case he wanted to have it put on his watch chain.

The younger brother, Alan, was not quite as big as George and had a livid scar on his face, which ran down to his chin. He appeared easy-going and to an extent he was, but he was also just as violent as his sibling. Both men were part of a gang, under the control of Phillip Jacobs and Leon Carlton, who had been running protection rackets and handing out punishment beatings. Wickstead's case against them came from prosecution witnesses whose characters were often just as bad as those that they gave evidence against; there was no other way round it, as 'Nipper' Read had discovered when he went after the Krays. Wickstead's critics would say that the people he approached would be issued an ultimatum – "come over to my side or end up in the dock."

On 25 August 1971, the morning of the raids to arrest all of the gang, Wickstead, who had very few officers indeed on his team, was provided with ninety officers, both uniform and CID, taken from all different departments, to make the arrests. Upon their arrival, many of the gang stated that they knew that they were going to be arrested; moreover the *Evening Standard* knew all about it as well, because their headlines had already been prepared. In fact, everybody was arrested, with the exception of Jacobs, who was picked up later. But Wickstead was furious and blamed the leakage on the members of the arrest teams who had been drawn from the Flying Squad, a department for whom Wickstead had held an uncompromised loathing for some considerable time. Allegedly, he had scrawled, 'NOT C8' (the departmental code for the Flying Squad) in red ink on his Divisional Record Sheet, in order that he would not be transferred there in error.

At the Old Bailey on 4 July 1972 Jacobs, Carlton and George Dixon were each sentenced to twelve years' imprisonment, with brother Alan receiving nine years. If anybody in London had not heard the name of Bert Wickstead before, they did now. The commendation from the trial Judge, Mr. Justice O'Connor was echoed by the commissioner and the newspapers rocked with stories of how bribery and threats had been unsuccessfully applied to the name that had been coined for Wickstead and his team by the East End underworld – 'The Untouchables'. This and the other nickname, 'The Gangbusters', was the product of imaginative newspapermen – helpfully aided and abetted by Wickstead, naturally!

*

The Serious Crime Squad was now substantially enlarged, with a number of officers being drawn from the Flying Squad; contrary to Wickstead's misgivings about that department, they were highly regarded by him and they stayed for a considerable period. Wickstead's second in command was Detective Chief Inspector Ken Tolbart, whom he first met when he was serving at Ilford. They were like chalk and cheese: Wickstead roaring through life like a bull in a china shop, riding roughshod over porcelain and personnel alike; Tolbart quiet, charming, eminently approachable. As a mark of the esteem that the squad members held him in, they referred to him as 'Uncle Ken': such was their adoration of the man whom Wickstead admitted, "could charm the birds out of the trees."

As well as building up a first-rate team of officers, Wickstead consolidated his stable by securing the services of Senior Prosecuting Counsel, Michael Corkery QC, who had prosecuted in the Dixon case. Now he would head the prosecution in several more of the Serious Crime Squad cases. Friendly relations were established with the Director of Public Pprosecutions' office so that everybody was part of a team – not a ridiculous 'us and them' situation as would later exist so often with the lacklustre Crown Prosecution Service. Officers from the Leytonstone office of the Special Patrol Group were used for the arrests and searches, and both they and the Serious Crime Squad held each other in very high esteem. Wickstead had the ear of the hierarchy, as well; Sir Robert Mark, as deputy commissioner had swept through the ranks of the CID like an angel with a flaming sword, determined to break their power but in Wickstead, he knew a good thing when he saw one and left him alone. But not everyone respected what Wickstead was doing. Wally Virgo, the venal commander of C.1 Department paid him a visit, placed an envelope containing £500 on his desk and told him that a similar sum would be on his desk every week, providing that Wickstead avoided the West End during the course of his enquiries. Wickstead threw him out – and thereafter, ensured that all of his reports were forwarded direct to the office of the Deputy Assistant Commissioner 'C' (Operations), thereby effectively leap-frogging the office of the commander. In fact, Wickstead had plenty to keep himself busy in the East End of London. However, Virgo had a singularly pressing reason to keep a straight police officer out of major West End investigations, as will be seen.

*

It was touch and go whether the Tibbs family or their enemies, the Nichols brothers would be Wickstead's next targets. There had been a long running feud between the two factions with an escalating number of assaults, shootings, stabbings and bombings. When Wickstead came to decide who represented the greatest danger to the public, it was the Tibbs (who it seems had taken exception to being referred to as "dirty, pikey bastards") for whom the coin came down tails.

The squad set to work with a will. The mainstay of the Tibbs family was the father, Jimmy senior. The sons – John, Robert and Jimmy the younger, were all hard men, the latter being a very promising middleweight boxer. All of the family lived in East Ham; unfortunately, so did Wickstead and his family. He and especially his wife, Jean – an earlier war-time marriage had ended in divorce – and their two sons were vulnerable, and following a stream of threats made to the whole family, round-the-clock protection was provided. This, of course, was no way to live and the family moved out to a secret address in Loughton, Essex.

During the ensuing trial at the Old Bailey, each of the barristers acting for the seven defendants, who were charged with conspiracy to inflict grievous bodily harm, had agreed not to ask Wickstead any questions, knowing that to do so could well cause their clients to suffer untold damage. Instead, with Wickstead having completed his evidence in chief, each stood up in turn and said, "I have no questions but I do not accept any of your evidence." Wickstead, of course, was trying to comment on this but the barristers were not permitting him to say one word in contradiction. He was furious but there was nothing he could do about it. Nothing, that is, until the last barrister who fortuitously was the youngest and least experienced, got to his feet. "I have no questions but I do not accept any of your evidence," he said. And then, he added, "And do you agree that the worst you can say about my client is that he was present, but took no part in the assault?"

Wickstead's face lit up and he replied, "Actually, the worst I can say about your client, is this …" and he then proceeded to inform the court of all the worst aspects of the defendant in question and in the space of the following fifteen minutes managed to include every other defendant in the dock, involving all of them in the major conspiracy.

The barristers protested to the Judge, Mr. Justice Lawson, who remarked that counsel had asked him what was the worst he could say about his client and Wickstead had merely answered the question. The day ended with the other barristers rounding on the luckless youngster, who kept apologizing, to the delight of the Serious Crime Squad personnel!

In January 1973 seven members of the Tibbs gang received a total of fifty-eight years' imprisonment, with Jimmy Tibbs senior receiving fifteen years and Jimmy Tibbs the younger ("who left home for a training run one morning," a squad member told me, "and failed to return,") getting ten years. Once again, the Trial Judge went overboard in his commendation for Wickstead and his team, which was echoed with congratulations from the Home Secretary and the commissioner.

Pausing only to assist the late DAC Ernie Bond in a sensitive enquiry into the activities of a Peer – Lord Lambton – and a call-girl (Norma Levy), Wickstead now launched his next investigation into vice in the West End of London, run by, amongst others, the Maltese Syndicate. It was the enquiry that Virgo had been dreading.

*

Bernie Silver was the only member of the gang who was not Maltese; but all of them were concerned in running prostitutes and brothels and operating strip clubs. Witnesses to their crimes were intimidated, beaten up or blown up. The squad also looked at the activities of another well-known Soho personality, Jimmy Humphries, and on 23 October 1972, Peter 'Pookie' Garfath, who Humphries believed had re-started an affair with his ex-stripper wife, Rusty, was cornered by four men in the lavatory of a Marylebone club and was stabbed and slashed. Humphries subsequently acquired a false passport in the name of Leigh and fled to Holland. The following June, Humphries was followed to a hotel in Volendam by two of Wickstead's men and six months later was extradited to stand trial for his part in the Garfath attack; he was sentenced to eight years' imprisonment.

In the meantime, in order to house his expanded squad, Wickstead moved his headquarters to the old married quarters at Limehouse Police Station where the enquiries continued into the activities of the Soho gangsters. By October 1973, Wickstead was set to execute warrants and make arrests, only to discover that all of the principal defendants had vanished. Worse, it had been discovered that there was a crooked police officer on the team. He had, in fact, been caught out by his own colleagues, who now approached Wickstead with their suspicions. There was no direct evidence to link the officer with corrupt practices but Wickstead had him immediately transferred; now, perhaps, he would realise that officers other than those attached to the Flying Squad could be venal.

Wickstead grumpily put the word about that his plans had been thwarted and went through the pretence of withdrawing the warrants.

He actually did nothing of the kind; in fact, he swore out several more to supplement the first batch. Sure enough, the ruse worked and word filtered back to the gangsters, who drifted back to London two months later. Wickstead was ready for them. On 30 December 1973 Wickstead was on a high. Firstly, he had heard that he was to be awarded the Queen's Police Medal, in the New Year's Honours list, for distinguished service; next, he received word that Bernie Silver and his girl friend had returned to London. They had been spotted by two of his officers, who had arrested them. Some hasty telephone calls were made to the other squad members and the Special Patrol Group and then Wickstead swooped on the Scheherazade Club, which was known to be frequented by many of the gang members and their associates. Wickstead leapt up on to the stage and seized the microphone. "My name is Detective Chief Superintendent Albert Wickstead!" he roared. There came a ragged cheer from the customers, which faded as Wickstead added, "and you're all nicked!"

"What d'you think of the cabaret?" asked one of the clientele of his companion. "Not much," was the laconic reply.

All of the club's customers were lodged in police stations in and around the Limehouse area, to be interviewed as and when time permitted. Three days later, a sergeant at one of these stations kept trying to speak to Wickstead on the telephone and eventually his persistence paid off. "Guv'nor," said the sergeant, in response to the familiar growl at the other end of the telephone, "what do you want me to do with these two RAF officers we've got in the cells?" "What RAF officers?" grunted Wickstead. "The ones from the club," explained the Sergeant. "I mean, they were all right for the first couple of days but now they're getting a bit grumpy!"

Wickstead was completely unfazed; the two officers were later seen, told they were lucky not to be charged and kicked out.

With the exception of Frank Mifsud, all of the gang members were rounded up, and on 18 September 1974 eleven defendants stood trial at the Old Bailey. More threats were issued, not only to the prosecution witnesses in the case but also Wickstead, his wife and sons.

On 18 December, Silver and others were convicted of conspiracy to live on immoral earnings: he was sentenced to six years' imprisonment and fined £30,000, six of his associates also went to prison.

Wickstead had been infuriated during the trial when three senior police officers (two of whom had retired) were called by the defence and had given evidence on Silver's behalf. And if Wickstead had been annoyed, the temper of the new Commissioner, Sir Robert Mark, completely boiled over. Just as intolerant as Wickstead about corruption, he now launched an enquiry that would have far-reaching consequences for a great many people. In this he was considerably assisted by a diary belonging to Jimmy Humphries which had been seized from a wall safe by two Serious Crime Squad officers. It detailed his corrupt dealings with fifteen police officers during 1971 and 1972. Not only that, but Humphries decided to co-operate fully in the investigation; he made a statement at Wandsworth Prison, where he was serving his eight-year sentence, which implicated thirty-eight officers.

There followed a series of arrests, and by several high-profile trials at the Old Bailey. It was Virgo's worst nightmare. A number of police officers were sent to prison for lengthy periods – Virgo received twelve years – and although his conviction was eventually quashed, he was a broken man and died shortly afterwards. The enquiry led to a complete reorganisation of the CID.

Meanwhile, Frank Mifsud was brought back to England from Switzerland where he had been hiding and in August 1976 he stood trial for murder and suborning a witness to commit perjury during a case at the Old Bailey in 1967. Cleared of the first charge, he was sentenced to five years' imprisonment and fined £50,000 on the second; later this conviction would be quashed on appeal, but like Virgo, he was a broken man.

During the trial, John Lewis (who would later retire as a detective chief superintendent) remembers that a former detective inspector, who was able to verify a matter which had occurred years before, had been called to give evidence. Since retiring from the Metropolitan Police, he had busied himself in the scrap-metal business and now, in his seventies, he was very prosperous and immaculately attired, complete with trilby and Crombie overcoat. He was also in a hurry to give his evidence so that he could be released from the court to attend a meeting, but the reason for the delay was that the prosecuting barrister was addressing the Judge. Wickstead came out of court and apologized to the old gentleman. "I'm very sorry you're being kept waiting," he said, "but counsel is addressing the Judge on a matter of integrity, honesty and ethics." "Ah!" replied the veteran, nodding knowingly. "That must be something they introduced after I retired!"

But by now Wickstead had moved on; on 6 January 1975, he was transferred to 'J' Division and four months later promoted to the rank of commander and posted to No. 3 Area Inspectorate. To all intents and purposes, the Old Grey Fox was well and truly desk-bound; except, of course, he was not.

Information had been received by the Yard's hierarchy that Albert Taylor (who was commonly known as 'Charles', having filched his long-dead brother's identity) and who was being investigated in respect of a Dollar Premium fraud, was being protected by CID officers who were not only allegedly corrupt but also very senior. Assistant Commissioner (Crime) Gilbert Kelland deputed Wickstead to investigate the matter.

The former Deputy Assistant Commissioner, Michael Taylor QPM was at that time a detective superintendent attached to A.10, the Police Complaints Branch and he was detached from his normal duties, to be seconded onto Wickstead's team. Taylor liked and admired Wickstead, and told me, "He was one of just three men I knew, whom the troops would follow blindly."

Michael Taylor arrested his namesake, Charles, in Kensington and took him to premises in Mortlake where gold half-sovereigns were being counterfeited. He also arrested a number of Taylor's associates, who were charged and committed to the Old Bailey to stand their trial. Meanwhile, Charles Taylor started talking about the allegedly corrupt police officers and an internal investigation was launched by the Chief Constable of Kent. But then Charles Taylor suddenly died whilst his trial was underway; and not unnaturally, his co-defendants ensured that he took the blame. Michael Taylor gave evidence in the witness box of No. 1 Court at the Old Bailey for seven days, taking some blistering cross-examination from the defence – each defendant had a senior and junior barrister – and was accused in no uncertain terms of police malpractice.

After Taylor had completed his evidence, Wickstead was called to clear up some ambiguities which were so minor that none of the defence counsel bothered to cross-examine him – none, save one. This very junior counsel thought it might be an enjoyable experience to belittle the Gangbuster. It was a fatal mistake.

Pompously rising to his feet, the barrister said, "Now, Commander Wickstead – "and then, as though the thought had suddenly occurred to him, "or may I call you 'The Old Grey Fox'?"

Wickstead's face was stony. "I'd rather you didn't," he replied.

The barrister's eyebrows lifted and his face registered mock-surprise. "But surely, that is how the popular press refers to you?"

Wickstead nodded. "They do."

"And I feel sure you revel in that description?"

"I don't."

This exchange went on for several minutes; something that had absolutely nothing whatsoever to do with the case being tried and everything to do with humbling Wickstead.

"So let us be clear about this, Commander Wickstead," intoned the barrister, as he looked, smirking, around the courtroom. "You are referred to by the popular press as 'The Old Grey Fox' and you tell us you don't like it. Why not, pray?"

Being the experienced copper that he was, Wickstead waited a full two seconds, before replying quietly, "Because I'm not old."

As the whole of the dignified No. 1 Court rocked with laughter, whatever other questions the barrister might have had for Wickstead went right out of the window as, red-faced, he sat down with a bump, having learnt a lesson the hard way: don't ask a witness a question, unless you're already sure of the answer!

There wasn't much else for Wickstead to laugh at. With his main defendant (and witness) dead, the trial more or less collapsed, and several very senior officers at the Yard were either moved or permitted to resign.

*

Wickstead's last case would be the most controversial of his career.

Robert John Maynard (also known as 'Fat Bob') and Reginald John Dudley were friends who both hailed from North London. Maynard had a number of small-time convictions whereas Dudley, who described his occupation as jeweller, had a far more serious criminal past: he had been sentenced to six years' imprisonment for slashing his wife's face.

Billy Moseley was also a friend of Maynard's and when he was released from prison on 18 September 1974 he was perturbed to discover the friendly relationship between his old friend and Dudley, whom Moseley suspected was a police informant. Moseley had had an affair with a woman named Elaine 'Frankie' Fright whilst her husband, Ronnie (who found out about the relationship) had served a seven-year sentence for robbery; Moseley now desired to restart the relationship. A meeting was arranged for the matter to be resolved between Ronnie Fright and Moseley on 26 September 1974, and Moseley was never seen alive again. Five parts of his body, excluding his head and hands, were found floating in the Thames at Rainham, Essex between 5 and 15 October 1974.

Micky Cornwall was a career armed robber who completed an eight-year sentence on 18 October 1974. He had been friendly with Moseley, was very upset to discover that his friend had been murdered and began making enquires as to who might be responsible. The following year, in August, Cornwall, who had been staying with friends, left hurriedly, and a quarter of an hour later, two men, later identified as Maynard and Dudley turned up at the house. Cornwall was last sighted on 22 August; just over two weeks later his body was discovered in a shallow grave in Hatfield, Hertfordshire. He had been shot through the head.

The Hertfordshire police investigated Cornwall's murder and kept hearing the name 'Moseley' mentioned. Now, the Metropolitan Police enquiry team had discovered that the torso was indeed that of

Billy Moseley, the whole matter began to smell of a linked, double gangland murder: this was all Wickstead needed to launch a Serious Crime Squad-style enquiry. True, Cornwall's body had been found in another constabulary, marginally just a few miles outside the boundaries of Wickstead's area, but Moseley's body had been recovered just inside it. A joint operation was formed with Detective Chief Superintendent Ron Harvey and his men from Hertfordshire CID, an incident room was opened at Loughton Police Station and the combined units went to work.

Basically, the police felt that because of Moseley's involvement with 'Frankie' Fright, his belief that Dudley was a police informant, and the fact that he had previously been involved in a fight with Dudley, Moseley had been killed; and when Cornwall had discovered that his friend had been murdered, he made it known that he thought Maynard and Dudley were responsible and consequently had been murdered in turn.

On 22 January 1976 eighteen people were arrested and over a period of four days they were interviewed and eleven were released. Maynard and Dudley were charged, as was Dudley's daughter, Kathleen Bailey (with whom Cornwall had had a brief liaison), Maynard's brother Ernie, Charles Edwin Clarke and George Spencer (who were both friends of Dudley's) and Ronnie Fright. The trial opened at the Old Bailey on 11 November 1976 with Michael Corkery QC once again prosecuting.

It was an extraordinary trial, which lasted 136 days and was duly entered into *The Guinness Book of Records* as being the longest murder trial on record, with its cost coming to half a million pounds. In addition, there was no forensic evidence. Anthony Wild, an armed robber gave evidence that whilst they were on remand in prison, Dudley and Maynard had gloried in the murder of both men. In fact, much of the basis for the prosecution was a series of incriminating statements allegedly made by the accused, which they had declined to sign and which they now vociferously denied making.

On 17 June 1977, Maynard and Dudley were both convicted of murder and sentenced to life imprisonment, with the trial Judge, Mr. Justice Swanwick recommending a minimum of fifteen years.

Charlie Clarke was sentenced to four years' imprisonment for conspiracy to inflict grievous bodily harm, and Kathleen Bailey's sentence in respect of the same charge was suspended. Ernie Maynard was acquitted on the directions of the judge, and Ronnie Fright and George Spencer were acquitted by the jury.

Moseley's head was discovered in a public lavatory in Islington six weeks after the sentencing; wrapped around the head was a copy of the *Evening News* dated 16 June 1977 – in other words, the day before the sentences were imposed, the inference being that who was responsible for the murder, it could not have been Maynard or Dudley, since they were in custody at the time.

A campaign to free the three imprisoned men – Maynard, Dudley and Clarke – was launched, but an appeal against conviction was thrown out by the Court of Appeal on 2 April 1979. The controversy trundled on; Anthony Wild claimed he had lied in court, Dudley was paroled in 1997, Maynard was released on bail in November 2000 and a fresh appeal, heard on 16 July 2002 resulted in all of the convictions being quashed.

*

Wickstead was not around to see it. He retired on New Year's Eve, 1977. He was fifty-four years of age and with the days which were still owed to him he had completed thirty years service. He was made a Freeman of the City of London, became security adviser to the News Group newspapers, retired to his family home in Loughton and followed the fortunes of West Ham United. He wrote his memoirs in a rather dire book, entitled *Gangbuster*, in which he made no reference whatsoever to any of his more controversial cases; the Ilford Bank Robbery case, the Charles Taylor enquiry or the Maynard and Dudley investigation received no mention at all. He suffered from emphysema, was seldom seen at police retirement functions and indeed, had little to do with many of his former colleagues. He died, aged seventy-seven in March 2001.

*

Wickstead's career was dogged with controversy and he was frequently accused of embellishing the evidence to suit the crime. But it must be remembered that these allegations were inevitably made against many detectives, from squads other than the Serious Crime Squad, who were going up against high-profile criminals – and the criminals whom Wickstead dealt with were more high-profile, than most. Wickstead was certainly one of the Yard's great detectives and his genius lay in getting a strong, determined bunch of loyal men and women around him and then going full-tilt for the target. "I look for three main qualities in my officers," he said. "Honesty, integrity and professional capability." When a report had to be submitted, Wickstead would walk, chain-smoking, around the typist, sheaves of paper, covered in his scrawl in his hand, dictating the report to her, as her fingers flashed across the typewriter's keys. At the conclusion, he would say, "Right, give us it 'ere – I'll sign it," and, without reading the report, he would. Was this arrogance, that he thought himself so infallible he could not have left anything out, or complete confidence in the typist's ability? Perhaps a bit of both; but the fact remains that his reports were excellent, both in content and presentation.

Whoever called him the Gangbuster, whether it was the underworld, the media or Bert Wickstead himself, it really matters not. The point is, it was a fitting nickname for an extraordinary man, because he did just that.

Bibliography

ADAMSON, Iain, *The Great Detective* (Frederick Muller, 1966)

BALL, John, CHESTER, Lewis & PERROTT, Roy, *Cops and Robbers* (Andre Deutsch, 1978)

BEVERIDGE, Peter, *Inside the CID* (Evans Bros., 1957)

BURT, Leonard, *Commander Burt of Scotland Yard* (Heinemann, 1959)

BOOTH, Nicholas, *ZigZag* (Portrait Books, 2007)

CATER, Frank (with TULLETT, Tom), *The Sharp End* (Bodley Head, 1988)

CHALLENOR, Harold & DRAPER, Alfred, *Tanky Challenor - SAS and The Met* (Leo Cooper, 1990)

CHERRILL, Fred, *Cherrill of the Yard* (George G. Harrap, 1954)

COOPER, Henry, with GILLER, Norman, *Henry Cooper's Most Memorable Fights* (Stanley Paul, 1985)

COX, Barry, SHIRLEY, John & SHORT, Martin, *The Fall of Scotland Yard* (Penguin Books, 1977)

DARBYSHIRE, Neil & HILLIARD, Brian, *The Flying Squad* (Headline Books, 1993)

DONNELLY, Mark, *Britain in the Second World War* (Routledge, 1999)

DURNFORD-SLATER, John, *Commando* (William Kimber, 1953)

DU ROSE, John, *Murder was my Business* (WH Allen, 1971)

EDWARDS, Robert, *Henry Cooper* (BBC Worldwide, 2002)

EVANS, Jimmy & SHORT, Martin, *The Survivor* (Mainstream Publishing, 2001)

FABIAN, Robert, *Fabian of the Yard* (Naldrett Press, 1950)

FABIAN, Robert, *London After Dark* (Naldrett Press, 1954)

FIDO, Martin & SKINNER, Keith, *The Official Encyclopedia of Scotland Yard* (Virgin Books, 1999)

FORBES, Ian, *Squadman* (WH Allen, 1973)

FRASER, Frank (with MORTON, James), *Mad Frankie* (Little, Brown, 1994)

FROST, George, *Flying Squad* (Rockliff, 1948)

GOSLING, John, *The Ghost Squad* (WH Allen, 1959)

GREENO, Edward, *War on the Underworld* (John Long, 1960)

HIGGINS, R.H., *In the Name of the Law* (John Long, 1958)

HILL, Billy, *Boss of Britain's Underworld* (Naldrett Press, 1955)

HINDS, Alfred, *Contempt of Court* (Bodley Head, 1966)

HONEYCOMBE, Gordon, *The Complete Murders of the Black Museum* (Leopard Books, 1995)

HOSKINS, Percy, *No Hiding Place* (Daily Express Publications, undated)

HOUGH, Richard, *Winston & Clementine - The Triumph of the Churchills* (Bantam Press, 1990.)

INWOOD, Stephen, *A History of London* (MacMillan, 1998)

JACKSON, Sir Richard, *Occupied with Crime* (George G. Harrap, 1967)

KIRBY, Dick, *The Squad - A History of the men and vehicles of the Flying Squad at New Scotland Yard, 1919 - 1983* (Unpublished manuscript, Metropolitan Police History Museum, London, 1993)

KIRBY, Dick, *Rough Justice – Memoirs of a Flying Squad Detective* (Merlin Unwin Books, 2001)

KIRBY, Dick, *The Real Sweeney* (Constable & Robinson, 2005)

KIRBY, Dick, *You're Nicked!* (Constable & Robinson, 2007)

KIRBY, Dick, *Villains* (Constable & Robinson, 2008)

KRAY, Reg, *Villains we Have Known* (Arrow Books, 1996)

LANE, Brian, *The Murder Guide* (Robinson Publishing, 1991)

LEE, Christopher, *This Sceptred Isle* (BBC Worldwide Books, 1999)

LUCAS, Norman and SCARLETT, Bernard, *The Flying Squad* (Arthur Barker, 1968)

LUCAS, Norman, *Britain's Gangland* (WH Allen, 1969)

MACINTYRE, Ben, *Agent Zigzag* (Bloomsbury Publishing, 2007)

MARK, Sir Robert, *In the Office of Constable* (Collins, 1978)

McCALL, Karen (ed), *London Branch NARPO Millennium Magazine* (Orphans Press, Leominster, 1999).

McKNIGHT, Gerald, *The Murder Squad* (WH Allen, 1967)

MILLEN, Ernie, *Specialist in Crime* (Harrap, 1972)

MORTON, James, *Gangland - London's Underworld* (Little, Brown, 1992)

MORTON, James, *Bent Coppers* (Little, Brown, 1993)

MORTON, James, *East End Gangland* (Little, Brown, 2000)

MORTON, James & PARKER, Gerry, *Gangland Bosses* (Time Warner Books, 2005)

MURPHY, Robert, *Smash & Grab* (Faber & Faber, 1993)

NARBOROUGH, Fred, *Murder on my Mind* (Allan Wingate, 1959)

PEARSON, John, *The Profession of Violence* (Weidenfeld & Nicolson, 1972)

RAWLINGS, William, *A Case for the Yard* (John Long, 1961)

READ, Leonard (with MORTON, James), *Nipper* (MacDonald, 1991)

REYNOLDS, Bruce, *Autobiography of a Thief* (Bantam, 1995)

ROSE, Andrew, *Stinie – Murder on the Common* (Bodley Head, 1985)

SAMUEL, Raphael, *East End Underworld* (Routledge & Kegan Paul, 1981)

SAVAGE, Percy, *Savage of the Yard* (Hutchinson, 1934)

SCOTT, Sir Harold, *Scotland Yard* (Andre Deutsch, 1954)

SHARPE, F.D., *Sharpe of the Flying Squad* (John Long, 1938)

SIMPSON, Keith, *Forty Years of Murder* (Harrap, 1978)

SLIPPER, Jack, *Slipper of the Yard* (Sidgwick & Jackson, 1981)

SPARKS, Herbert, *The Iron Man* (John Long, 1964.)

SWAIN, John, *Being Informed* (Janus Publishing, 1995)

THOMAS, Donald, *An Underworld at War* (John Murray, 2003)

THOMAS, Donald, *Villains' Paradise* (John Murray, 2005)

THORP, Arthur, *Calling Scotland Yard* (Allan Wingate, 1954)

TULLETT, Tom, *Strictly Murder* (Bodley Head, 1979)

WENSLEY, F.P., *Detective Days* (Cassell & Co., 1931)

WICKSTEAD, Bert, *Gangbuster* (Futura, 1985)

WILLIAMS, Frank, *No Fixed Address - The Great Train Robbers on the Run* (WH Allen, 1973)

WOFFINDEN, Bob, *Miscarriages of Justice* (Hodder & Stoughton, 1987)

WYLES, Lilian, *A Woman at Scotland Yard* (Faber & Faber, 1952)

YOUNG, Filson (ed), *The Trial of Bywaters and Thompson* (William Hodge, 1923)

Index